I dedicate this book to my sister, Zelda Montoya,
whose genealogy work, three decades ago,
provided the foundation for this story.

———

ISBN: 1-890437-18-2
Library of Congress Catalog Card Number: 98-87156

Western Reflections, Inc.
P.O. Box 710, Ouray, Colorado 81427

ACKNOWLEDGMENTS

This book would not have been possible without the generous assistance of library, museum, newspaper and courthouse employees throughout western Colorado. They are truly special people who, without exception, were courteous and eager to aid my search.

Zelda Montoya, Orien Etcheverry, Norman(Bud) Herwick, Esther Hoffman, Winifred Fletcher, Olive Duplice, Donna VanAlden, Lillian Deming, Marilynne Cox and Cecil Cox graciously volunteered family information and pictures. They patiently answered my many questions, while I probed their recollections of events which happened so long ago.

My daughter, Debra Roberts acted as unofficial editor and general cheering section throughout the entire writing process. She encouraged me on days when the words wouldn't come and rejoiced with me during the more productive times. Bud, Hazel, Zelda, May, Vivian, Riecke, Mary and Grace also contributed valuable time and effort to the first edits

I am truly indebted to Peter Jaffe, of the Double J Ranch at Burns, Colorado. Mr. Jaffe not only allowed me access through his beautiful ranch, he acted as personal tour guide to the old log dugout which is presumed to have housed the Herwick family in 1891. The picture of that primitive dwelling can be found in this book.

PREFACE

When I first conceived of writing a biography about my grandmother, Ida Oyler Herwick, I had only a few scraps of family lore passed down from one generation to the next. The job of chronicling over forty years of this woman's amazing life seemed insurmountable. I frequently felt myself to be merely an observer as I watched the story unfold, much as her daily life must have also revealed itself. There were times when I felt a connection to some unseen force which directed me on the right path. There were also frustrating times when I felt thwarted in my search for the truth, almost as if something or someone did not want me to report on a particular event. Heirloom quilts are made from the fabric of each family, one piece blending with another in beautiful symmetry. Occasionally the quilter has to introduce new material into the design in order to create a harmony. It was thus with this story. I spent countless hours in libraries and courthouses to find tidbits of information about the Herwick family. Frequently an article would pop off of the page to verify my theory, and it would lead me on a serendipitous journey to the next story. Just as often I would hit a dead end, and then I had to introduce material which was probable and plausible, if not provable. Is all the information contained herein the gospel truth? No. Could it have happened that way? Yes. I have gone to great lengths to ensure the historical accuracy of the material. The events actually happened, but how they unfolded in the lives of the Herwick family was left to my interpretation.

I hope the reader will join me in celebrating not only the life of this sturdy pioneer lady but all the women who helped to settle Western Colorado. May we never forget their contributions.

part one

1873-1881

ᐁ *Tekamah, Nebraska flourished as a small town from 1855 to 1861 when the Civil War brought a temporary halt to immigration. The Soldiers Homestead Law and the building of the Union Pacific Railroad through Omaha revitalized the small town in the early 1870s. Banks, churches and school houses were all constructed in 1873, which was known as a "boom year." A Methodist church was built by the Rev. W. G. Olinger, using his own funds. The Nebraska Methodist Board later reimbursed him for the structure, which was originally called Unity Chapel. Rev. Olinger served as pastor for several years.*

ᐁ *During the 1870s Missouri River steamboats and the rapidly expanding Union Pacific Railroad were in stiff competition with each other. By 1887 the death of the steamboat trade was virtually assured by the arrival of the first train into Fort Benton, Montana.*

ᐁ *Horace Tabor of Leadville fame was elected Lieutenant Governor of Colorado in 1873.*

MAY, 1873   TEKAMAH, NEBRASKA

The wind blowing up the high bluff tugged at her braids. Ida longed to uncoil the heavy burden and let the breeze ripple through the chestnut-colored strands of hair, but Ma would be mad if she did that, saying that there was plenty to do without "fiddlin' around" with her looks.

The whistle of the paddlewheeler echoed up the muddy waters of the Missouri. She loved watching the upstream traffic from her observation point on the bluff, imagining that she was one of the lucky people aboard the smoke-belching craft, going to all sorts of adventures up river.

"I'd have a beautiful satin dress to wear like some of the ladies I see on the deck. I think it'd be a rose color, which Pa says makes my eyes even darker. And, I'd be goin' right to the end of the steamboat route at Fort Benton, Montana." Ida shivered from the excitement of just thinking about this imaginary adventure. "Someday I'm gonna see those wonderful sights myself," she sighed.

Her mother's strident voice cut into the abstract moment. "Idie, get in this house and take care of the baby. I've got my hands full with gettin' supper on."

Ida reluctantly turned from her reverie to the sound of that shrill, tired voice which became more tense each year with each child. She had watched what this country did to women, beating them down before they were into their third decade, if they were lucky enough to live that long. Babies came every two years without fail. Ma said it was a woman's duty to bear children and take care of her man, but Ida angrily decided that she would not be caught in that trap. She wasn't sure what was happening in her parents' bed at night, but suspected the strange, groaning noises weren't much different than what happened when the bull was brought over each year. It made her blush to think of it and angry at her mother for allowing such things to happen to her body.

Walking into the kitchen, Ida looked at Ma's bulging stomach, the fifth pregnancy in thirteen years, not counting the several miscarriages. Ma's stringy hair, loosened from its bun, hung limply around her face, a sad example of her present physical and emotional condition. She was having a difficult time with this baby. She had been sick for much of the eight months and was so swollen that she could hardly get her feet into shoes. Thank heaven for the warm weather that allowed her to go barefoot. In a dim, distant past, almost twelve and a half years ago, Ida remembered soft arms cuddling her and a loving voice singing lullabies. The memory of that woman bore small resemblance to the woman in front of her now.

Ida grabbed for her little brother, Grant, who was clinging to Ma's skirt. A warm rush of love went through her as she snuggled the squirming two-year-old in her arms. As the oldest child, Ida had been a surrogate mother for her brothers and sisters for as long as she could remember. Besides Grant, Ida helped "mother" Emer and Ella. Her other sister, Missouri, died of the fever last year, and Ida struggled to hold back tears every time she remembered her dear little face.

"Ella, play with Grant while I help Ma with supper. Pa and Emer will be comin' in soon," said Ida, putting the baby on the floor.

A tall, rangy man of few words, William Oyler showed the signs of hard work and endless scratching for a living. Ida supposed that he had been quite handsome at one time, but now his back was stooped, and his hands looked like the knots on the old gnarled trees along the shore. The only unchanged part of his face was the dark, penetrating eyes which seemed to stare right into your soul. She couldn't recall Pa ever laughing out loud, but an occasional smile competed with the thick, bushy beard that covered the entire lower half of his face.

A thin girl of average height, Ida was feeling the surge of coming womanhood. She knew that her serious nature made her seem far older than others her age. This was her last year in school and that was fine with her. She'd completed six grades, and that was more schooling than most girls had. Besides, she was tired of all the giggling girls. They were so childish!

She would rather stay home and help Ma with the chores, or maybe hire out as housekeeping help to one of the neighbors. If she hungered for reading, there was always the big family Bible which had been brought west from Virginia. Most of her free time was not spent reading but sitting on the bluff dreaming about the glittering world inside the paddlewheelers that challenged the Missouri River.

Looking across the supper table, Ida realized that her mother was merely picking at the plate of stew.

"What's wrong Ma? You're hardly touchin' your supper."

"Oh, this youngun's pushin' so hard against my innards, I can't eat much."

Ida knew it was more than that. Ma was sick. Ida would be glad when the baby was born so Ma could get back to feeling normal again. She hoped this would be the last one. Ida was glad that Mrs. Owen lived so close to them and would be available when the time came.

The midwife was renowned in their community, unlike the boozy-breathed Dr. Brown who was called only as a last resort in childbirth. Women cringed at the thought of being attended by him, and it was more than a coincidence that many babies and their mothers attended by him did not survive the child-birth ordeal. Mrs. Owen had gone south to see her sister in Omaha last week with promises of being back long before Ma went into labor, but Ida knew everyone would feel more comfortable when the midwife returned.

*R*oused from a sound sleep, later in the night, Ida heard signs of movement and voices downstairs. Climbing down the steep loft stairs, she peered into her parents' bedroom. Ma, lying on the bed, looked as pale as the dingy sheets surrounding her. Pa was dressed and pulling on his boots. His worried look told her that Ma's time had come. Beckoning Ida out of the room, he whispered that he was going into town to see if he could rouse the drunken doctor. He started to give her instructions, and Ida waved him away, replying that she remembered when Grant was born, and she would get things ready.

Going back into the bedroom, Ida could see that Ma was still resting in between pains, so she quietly stoked up the fire and started water boiling. She tried to still her mind long enough to remember what supplies had been used two years ago.

Going to a battered old trunk, she found some garments which had been washed and worn so many times the cloth was almost transparent. As she caressed the material, she briefly wondered if she might have worn these when she was born.

A cry from the bedroom interrupted her anxious thoughts. Going to the door, she could see that Ma was in much greater pain. Her fingers were twisted in the bedclothes, pulling and straining in tempo with the rhythm of her womb. Ida helplessly moved to the bed and looked down at her mother. Mary Hewitt Oyler had been a beautiful woman at one time, but the past fourteen years had done much to erase all but the faintest of her beauty. The once vibrant red hair was now liberally sprinkled with strands of silver. Her lovely blue eyes were faded to almost gray. The sun and prairie winds had sandpapered her peaches and cream complexion until it more resembled soft leather. And her once plump body had become lean and angular. Ida clenched her fists and shuddered with the thought that Ma might die.

She leaned over and smoothed her mother's hair just as she heard the sound of horses coming into the yard. Her father burst through the door, followed by a bleary-eyed physician who reeked of whiskey. The doctor swayed as he entered the bedroom, telling Ida to leave and muttering that children shouldn't be allowed in childbirth rooms. She thought how silly that was, but she was glad to leave. She couldn't bear to look at Ma's tortured face. Climbing to the loft bedrooms, she made sure the children were still sleeping soundly, then she lay down on her bed and wrapped herself in the old patchwork quilt she had slept in since she was a baby.

"What will happen if Ma doesn't get well? How will we get along without her?" Ida shivered as she felt tears running down her face. She opened her eyes to see her father bending over her bed. His rough hands gently wiped away the tears, and he self-consciously patted her hand. They sat in silence for some time, each lost in their own thoughts and fears. At last he rose and climbed back down the steps to be close at hand in case the doctor needed him.

Ida dozed, and awoke to the first gray light of dawn and the hushed activity in the rooms below. Peering down the stairwell, she could see her father sitting in his arm chair holding a cloth covered bundle. The baby–it must be the baby! Quietly, so she didn't disturb the others, Ida crept down the stairs to her father's side. Opening the blanket she saw a tiny pinched face with a halo of dark hair. Its little mouth was puckered and was making sucking sounds. In answer to her questioning gaze Pa said, " Idie, this is your little sister." She stood mesmerized by the sight of the tiny infant until the doctor came wearily tottering from her mother's room.

"She's had a hard time, Will. She's pretty badly torn up. I doubt that she'll be able to have more children."

Pa handed the small bundle to Ida and went to a kitchen shelf. Taking an old biscuit tin down, he pulled out two dollars.

"I'm sorry, Doc. This is all the cash I have right now, but I maybe could give more this fall after the crop's in."

Waving his hands in dismissal, the doctor opened the door. "You'll be needin' some help," he muttered. "I'll try to send someone out."

The doctor found a young woman to help take care of Ma. She was fairly dim-witted and slow, and she had no nursing experience, but her presence gave the family a sense of security. Ma was so still at times that she hardly seemed alive. Her skin was ghostly pale except for the bright fever spots on her cheeks. She could be urged to take a few drops of water now and then, but refused all food, including the steaming chicken broth the woman tried to coax into her mouth. The babe lay at Ma's breast nuzzling the nipple and trying to find nourishment from the hot, dry teat. Periodically, the infant emitted a high-pitched cry, which seemed to be getting weaker.

"We gonna lose bof, iffen we don't get some food in 'em," the young woman said.

Pa seemed to have lost all sense of authority. He sat beside Ma, silently holding her hand or rocking the baby. Ida instinctively knew that she had to take charge. She managed to keep little Grant busy in spite of his fretful whining for Ma. He had been weaned six months ago when Ma was sure she was in the family way, but he still missed the comfort of nursing. Ida had found him several times lying next to Ma on the bed, patting her flat spare breast and sucking his thumb.

By the evening of the second day, Ida sensed that Ma and the unnamed baby would soon be gone if something wasn't done. She quietly went to the barn and bridled the old mule. Jumping on bareback, she kicked the animal into a fast trot and headed straight to Mrs. Owen's house.

"Let her be back," she prayed as she jogged along. "Please help me God. Please help my Ma and sister."

The May daylight was fading as she pulled into the Owen's yard. Frantic barking heralded her arrival and the lamplight outlined a figure in the doorway.

"Land's sake child. What are you doing here?" called Mrs. Owen." I just got off the stage not two hours ago, and I've been thinking 'bout your Mama all the way home. I was going to visit you folks tomorrow."

"Please Mrs. Owen. You've got to come see Ma right away. She birthed the baby two days past and she's not doin' well. The baby cries all the time 'cause she's not getting anything to eat. Please, please, can you come with me?"

Mrs. Owen looked into the dark brown eyes and realized that this woman-child knew her mother was in danger. Yelling to her husband to get the team hitched up, she bustled around gathering up midwife supplies and other assorted things she thought might be needed. Calling instructions to her family, she climbed over the wagon wheel and flicked the reins over the broad backs of the team.

"Let's go fellas," she said to the horses." We've got a sick lady to take care of."

But the childbirth fever raged in spite of all the remedies the midwife tried. On the evening of the third day, Mary Oyler slipped beyond all the burdens, pain, and sorrow of her hard life, leaving behind a young family unprepared for her death. Mrs. Owen had arrived too late to save the baby who followed her mother a few hours later.

"God gives and God takes according to His will, not ours," Mrs. Owen mused.

That was small comfort for a father and children who had lost their maternal anchor as well as a new young sister.

A hot June wind whipped the drying clothes upon the line as Ida finished scrubbing another tub of soiled garments and threw them into the rinse water. Her back and arms ached unmercifully from lifting the heavy wet garments, and she still had three more tubs to do. Wiping her hands and straightening her slight frame, she collapsed upon a bench, tears of frustration rolling down her young cheeks. The past month had been an ordeal for her. Pa was beside himself with grief, moping around day after day doing just the bare essentials. Seven-year-old Emer appeared to have adjusted to Ma's death reasonably well, although she had heard his muffled sobs at night. However, little Grant and Ella had been more vocal about their mother's absence. Grant shadowed Ida's every step, and she had taken him to bed with her so he wouldn't cry himself to sleep. Although she was not apt to admit it, the presence of that warm, little body next to her also gave her the comfort she longed for.

Ella had wrapped herself around any woman coming to pay respects and bring food for the grieving family. One lady in particular, Nellie Rising, had taken a fancy to the child, and asked William Oyler if she might take the little girl to her home for awhile. She argued that he and Ida had their hands full with the boys and the farm. William reluctantly agreed, on the condition that his daughter be promptly brought back if she got homesick for her family. It had been a month, and Ella was still with her foster parents, who were showering her with attention. They had approached William about adopting Ella and taking her back to their home state of Michigan, and he had finally given his reluctant approval seeing how attached the little girl had become to her foster parents.

Ida wasn't sure how she felt about Ella being adopted. After all, she had been a surrogate mother to the child since she was born and she would miss the tiny arms around her neck. But she also felt a tinge of envy at the thought of her little sister's abundance of loving attention and her lack of it. Oh well, there was no use crying over spilled milk. That wouldn't get the rest of the wash done.

∾ The Omaha & North-Western Railroad was pushing its way to Tekamah in 1875. It reached the town in the fall of 1876, and continued on to the north.

∾ Two Leadville mining men started to quietly buy up or refile on claims abandoned after the 1860s California Gulch gold rush. They built a twelve mile ditch from the upper Arkansas River to supply water for hydraulic mining. Investigating the black sand, they discovered it was lead carbonate loaded with silver. The Leadville boom was on again following their first ore shipment.

DECEMBER, 1875 BURT COUNTY, NEBRASKA
Ida stared longingly at the beautiful rose-colored fabric displayed in the bin at the general store. Her silent reverence was broken by the storekeeper's voice. "Here you go, Ida, here's your jar of molasses. Looks like you're fixing to bake a special treat for Christmas."

"Yes, Mr. Taylor, I thought I'd try to make one of Ma's harvest apple cakes. We've got plenty of apples this year, and I thought Pa and the boys would enjoy it."

The grocer intercepted her longing glance at the bright material. "It's only forty cents a yard. I think Mrs. Taylor would help you sew up a fine dress for yourself."

Ida shook her head. "I'm afraid not Mr. Taylor. This hasn't been a real good year, and Pa has better places to spend his hard-earned money. But I hope he'll be in before Christmas to look at some of your goods for Emer and Grant. It would be nice to have a little something for them under the Christmas tree."

Both turned to the door which had opened, letting in a blast of cold air. A giant of a man walked through with a self-assured swagger that announced to the world his confidence. He had the most electrifying blue eyes Ida had ever seen. As she looked up into his eyes she felt trapped in his gaze. Amused, he smiled down at her. "Why, aren't you a pretty little thing!"

Ida wished the floor would open up and swallow her. She could not find her voice. She stood rooted to the spot until Mr. Taylor broke the mutual reverie. "Well, well, Si Herwick, what can I do for you today?"

Turning to the storekeeper, the man replied, "My boss sent me in to pick up some supplies for the construction camp."

While the two men were talking, Ida's feet propelled her out the door in a rush. She felt like a silly little schoolgirl, and that made her angry. "What is the matter with me? I can't believe that I made such a fool of myself. That man and Mr. Taylor must think I've taken leave of my senses." Mumbling to herself, she trudged up the snow-packed path to their house, but the memory of those blue eyes lurked in her mind.

The warmth of the kitchen stove bathed her face as she opened the door to their small cabin. The soup, simmering on the back of the range, gave off a welcome aroma along with the fresh bread she had baked just this morning. Pa and the boys were gathered within the warm limits of the heat. Pa was mending one of the old harnesses that should have been replaced a long time ago. The boys were playing some game on the floor. Emer quietly watched over his little brother. Four-year-old Grant was growing into a normal little boy, noisy and boisterous, but he still clung to Ida at times.

"He doesn't remember Ma anymore," she sadly thought. "Come to think of it, I really can't remember her face very clearly." It seemed many years since she had taken over the care of this family. She was a mature little woman with so many responsibilities compared to other girls her age.

The next few weeks seemed to fly by with their few inexpensive plans for the holiday season. Pa and Emer had gone out to the hills and brought back a pretty little pine tree. They couldn't afford the candles to light it, but Ida and the boys strung popcorn and brought out the few ornaments that Ma had brought with her when she was married. Ida decided that it was good enough, and little Grant's boyish eyes thought it was beautiful.

The hams had been curing in the smokehouse for a month, and Ida looked forward to Christmas dinner with the wonderful smells of baked ham permeating the entire cabin. She was so tired of their everyday diet of rabbit and birds. She planned what she would prepare for the rest of the meal. Sweet potatoes, corn pudding, some hoarded sweet pickles and a jar of apple butter that would taste good with freshly baked bread. The harvest apple cake, with its dark molasses richness had turned out perfect, and it would make a fitting end to their holiday meal.

Christmas Day arrived, crisp, clear and very cold. Emer's eyes lit up at the sight of the jack knife wrapped in a piece of soft, tanned leather. He immediately brought out the whetstone and started sharpening the shiny blade to a razor edge. Grant climbed sleepily from his little bed in the adjoining room, rubbing his eyes. He was soon playing with his new red top on the braided rug by the stove, while Ida started to prepare their morning meal.

Pa came up behind her and cleared his throat. "Idie, I think there's another package under the tree. Why don't you come see what's in it."

Finding it hard to keep tears from her eyes, Ida sat down to receive the little packet wrapped in tissue paper from the store. Inside was a lovely, soft woolen scarf in a colorful plaid design of blues, reds, and greens. "Oh Pa," she exclaimed, "it's beautiful! Thank you so much." She hugged his neck while he stood clumsily patting her back. "You're a good girl, Idie. I wish it could be more."

The human concern caused her tears to start. Pa was a decent man, but he was short on showing affection. The feel of his hands on her back made her realize how seldom she felt a loving touch, aside from little Grant, and he was usually asking for affection rather than giving it. For the briefest moment, Ida could relish the feeling of not being the strong caretaker. She could feel the same feelings as any other 14-year-old girl on Christmas morning. But then Pa self-consciously pulled his hands away, and she knew that her brief moment of dependence was over.

Even Pa and the boys were going to church services with her. She checked to be sure Emer had washed his neck and behind his ears, and she brought out a clean change of clothes for Grant. Just before leaving, she wrapped her new scarf around the collar of Ma's old brown worsted coat. Looking in the small mirror, she decided that the scarf lent a festive air to her otherwise drab apparel. She had not had any new clothes since Ma died, leaving a few dresses and the coat for Ida to grow into. Money was too precious to spend on material for new clothes when there was an available supply of old.

Newly formed frost laid heavy over the bottom land with a diamond-like sparkle. The snow crunched under their feet as they made their way to the little Methodist church. Other families were also arriving on foot by wagons, sleighs or buggies. The air was heavy with wood smoke from all the roaring fires. Occasionally a spicy smell would escape from a nearby house. Sounds of people greeting people lent a holiday atmosphere to the scene.

The church organist was pumping furiously on the old wheezing organ from which strains of favorite Christmas carols came. The Oylers crowded into one of the wooden pews and smiled at their neighbors left and right. Turning slightly to see other friends, Ida's eyes roved over the congregation. A shock went through the very soles of her feet and raced through her body. It was him, and he was looking right at her! Those bright blue eyes were trained on her with amusement and admiration. He smiled widely and gave her a broad wink. She jerked her head around to the front of the church and shivered with fear and delight. Little Grant felt her tremble and looked up inquiringly. She gave his hand a preoccupied pat just as the minister walked to the pulpit and asked for a moment of prayer.

The remainder of the Christmas service was a hazy experience for Ida. "What is happening to me?" she wondered. "Why does this man make me feel so giddy?"

She knew she was a handsome girl, although certainly no beauty. Her high cheekbones and dark brown eyes were her best features. She thought her mouth was much too thin and her nose much too long. In her rare moments of introspection she acknowledged boys had been giving her sur-reptitious glances for the past six months. She was much too busy taking care of her family to spend time thinking about them. But this person wasn't a boy, he was a man! No man had ever looked at her the way this fellow did, and she shivered from the recollection of his gaze.

As the congregation filed out of the church, Ida could see him standing apart with other workers from the road construction company. Usually a rowdy bunch, the group was properly subdued for the religious holiday. Pa dropped behind to visit with some of his friends, leaving Ida and the boys to continue on a direct path to where the workers were talking. Emer also spotted some of his school chums and hurried away to show off his brand new knife. As she and Grant advanced, the tall man broke from the group and made his determined way to her side.

"Pardon me miss, don't you think it's time we were properly introduced?"

Her little brother, with the typical brashness of a four-year-old looked up at this giant and said, "Hello, Mister. My name is Grant Oyler and this is my sister, Idie. What's your name?"

Placing the tiny hand in his huge paw, the man replied, "Josiah Lafayette Herwick, son, and I'm mighty pleased to make your acquaintance. I'm also very pleased to meet you, Miss Oyler." His eyes sparkled with fun. "Do you ever speak?"

Ida regained her composure and coolly acknowledged his self-introduction. "How do you do, Mr. Herwick, and Merry Christmas to you. Now if you'll excuse me, I must go home and start preparing our Christmas dinner."

Grabbing Grant's hand, Ida pulled him along the snow-covered path as the child tried to look back at this giant of a man. "Jeepers, Idie, he's really big!"

"Yes he is, Grant, but he's none of our concern. Those construction workers are here today and gone tomorrow. I doubt we'll ever see him again But somewhere inside herself she was saying, "Oh, pray God that we do!" Shivering in spite of herself, Ida couldn't help thinking of those blue eyes and strong mouth. She felt so small along side him. "Why, he must be at least a foot taller than me!" She almost skipped down the snowy path to her home.

The week between Christmas and the new year was filled with community activities. People made an effort to get to their neighbor's for long overdue visits, and children attended skating and sleighing parties. Ida usually felt out of place with people her age and made excuses to stay home. But this year she felt a tug of interest in being more social. She hurried through her chores so she could take the boys to the skating pond. Grant was old enough to learn to skate. Emer was too boisterous to take good care of the little one, so she decided to take Grant with her.

Going to the dilapidated lean-to shed, Ida dug through the clutter of household and farm supplies until she found the little pair of clip-on skate blades she and Emer had first used. She bundled Grant up and led him to the pond on the outskirts of town.

The brilliant midday sun shone on the group already skating. Others were sitting on logs around the blazing bonfire. She strapped the small blades on her brother's feet, and plopped him down to wait while she put on her skates. Taking both his hands in hers, she held him up to get the feel of the slippery ice beneath their feet. His slipping and sliding sent them both into peals of laughter, and she was unaware of anyone else as she carefully steered a safe course around the pond. Her brown eyes sparkled and her cheeks were rosy with both the cold and excitement. She had forgotten how much fun this could be.

A voice behind her said, "That's a mighty pretty laugh you have. It matches your pretty face."

Whirling around, she ran smack into a set of powerful arms which held her up and prevented her and Grant from falling. The blue eyes looking down at her had laugh wrinkles around them, and the smiling mouth was much too close to hers. His grasp tightened as she tried to wiggle free of its confines.

"Whoa there, Miss Oyler, let me help you get steady." He reached down to take Grant's little hand, motioned her to take the child's other hand and pulled them into the main stream of the skaters. He had to skate bent over to reach the child, and the picture of his hunched over skating posture caused her to laugh outright. Grant was squealing with joy from the attention as they whirled him around the icy circle until he couldn't catch his breath. They coasted to the bonfire and sat on the large felled tree trunks while they rested from their wild fun.

"Thank you for helping me with Grant, Mr. Herwick. This is his first time on skates, and he's a handful."

"I'd prefer that you called me Josiah or Si," he said. "Everyone else does. It's only fittin' because I intend for us to be friends."

Ida felt herself blush furiously. How was she supposed to respond to this man? Nothing in her short life had prepared her for this intense emotion. She'd never had the luxury of dreaming about boy and girl things, let alone how to talk to a grownup man. She felt warm from his approving glances, but terrified to talk. She thought that she must appear hopelessly stupid and longed to escape this man who could make her forget her own name.

Josiah rescued her by quietly asking questions about who the various people were. As Ida answered his questions and offered comments about her friends and neighbors, she felt the tension leaving her. He seemed to enjoy chatting about ordinary things. She called to Emer to come get Grant and escort him around the ice a time or two, so she could concentrate on talking with this intriguing man.

She and Josiah were still engrossed in their visit, when she was startled to realize that the afternoon was waning and it was getting colder. "My stars," she said, "my little brothers must be half-frozen by now. I must get them home before they take a chill." Motioning for the boys to come over to her she took off her skates and bent to remove Grant's as well. When she rose, she saw that Josiah had also removed his skates and was waiting for her to gather the boys.

"May I have the pleasure of escorting the three of you home, Miss Oyler? I'd like to meet your father and mother."

Grant spoke up, "We don't have a mama. Idie takes care of us."

"And I can see she's doin' a fine job," replied Josiah, as he looked inquiringly at Ida.

"Our mother died two years ago, so I've tried to take her place, as best as I can," she replied. "Pa works hard to make a living for us, and I do everything I can to make it easier for him."

Josiah looked at her with admiration. "I'd say that you've taken a mighty heavy load on those pretty young shoulders," he said. "I'd like to meet the man who raised such a nice family."

Tucking her hand into the crook of his arm, they started down the lane with the boys trailing along behind. Ida was oblivious to the glances and comments of the people who had never seen her look so gay and animated.

Josiah's easy attitude with Ida and the boys extended also to her father. William Oyler and he were soon deep in conversation about the construction jobs, about farming, and the reports of good land out west.

"There's money to be made out there," Josiah said. "I plan to move down to Kansas after this job's over. My brother Fred, who's in Missouri, has been talking about moving his family out there. He says that there's plenty of work on the railroads and the stock drives into southwest Kansas. The Union Pacific has been advertising good farm land along the right-of-ways. It sounds like a good opportunity to buy some cheap land and settle down."

Ida bustled around making hot cocoa for everyone while she listened to the conversation. She was enthralled by this man. He seemed so sure of himself and of what he wanted out of life. It would be difficult to say no to such an imposing man. She remembered his rock-solid arms around her on the skating pond and realized how good it felt to lean on someone strong for even a moment. How glorious to be able to depend on his strength. Her love-starved eyes devoured him as he sat visiting with her father, who was unaware that his daughter had made a tremendous leap from her caretaker role to that of an average fourteen year old girl in the throes of her first romantic adventure.

During the course of the evening, Ida learned that he was twenty-two years old, one of seven living children, and he had been born in Iowa and raised in Missouri. His father, Frederick William Herwick, was a boatman on the Mississippi until he retired and died in 1869. Josiah spoke lovingly of his mother, Susannah, who had held the family together by teaching school after his father's death. Josiah and his three younger brothers had helped by hiring out on farms as soon as they were old enough to work. It was apparent that he had known hard work and adversity, but it hadn't dimmed his enthusiasm for life. This man was bent on becoming a prosperous citizen.

Ida could depend on Josiah visiting several times a week. She eagerly looked forward to the booming voice heralding his arrival, as he stooped to enter the little cabin. She made special preparations when she knew he was coming, although her available provisions were usually limited. However, Josiah loved her cooking and never failed to compliment her on the fine food, especially her biscuits. This unusual appreciation was music to the ears of a young woman who had grown up with very little recognition.

Pa seemed very comfortable with Josiah's frequent visits. They talked at length about the new promised land in Kansas and further west to Colorado. Pa' s old wanderlust had been reignited by the younger man's enthusiasm for new land. He, too, had sought new lands in his younger years, and he remembered the thrill of settling new territory. Ida wondered if part of his excitement was because he missed Ma and thought a change of scenery would help the pain go away.

Ida's fifteenth birthday was fast approaching. Josiah had promised he would visit her that evening. She hurried through her many household chores that day. It would be nice to have a tub bath, but she didn't have time to haul and heat the water. She had to content herself with freshening up and brushing her long chestnut hair until it shone like bright, rippling satin. She giggled as she dabbed some of her precious vanilla extract behind her ears. She'd smell good enough to eat!

Josiah arrived at her doorstep in time for supper. He was full of excitement about the most recent stories coming from Kansas where companies were begging for strong workers. Ida's heart sunk when she realized he would soon be moving on, and she'd never see him again. The thought of him leaving made her realize how important this man had become to her and how she would miss his presence. Her sadness at his impending departure made her quieter than usual throughout supper. As she cleared up and washed the dishes, she heard Pa and Josiah's conversation from across the room. Her pain seemed to be gathering into a tight ball in her mid-section. Tears welled in her eyes, and she quickly wiped them away for fear someone would question her. She stiffened her back and resolved not to let anyone see how upset she was by Josiah's news.

After the boys went to bed, Ida saw Pa yawn and realized that he, too, was wanting to go to bed. But Josiah lingered on, which was unusual behavior on his part. Pa finally excused himself by saying he had been up very early that morning and was plumb worn out. He left the fire and entered the second room which he shared with the two boys, leaving Ida and Josiah sitting next to the blazing stove. When Josiah finally realized she was not contributing to the conversation, he took her chin in his large hand and turned her head so she had to look into his penetrating eyes. "What's the matter little one? You're very quiet tonight. Is it because of your birthday? I'm sorry I wasn't able to get into town to buy you a present, but I'll try to make it up to you later."

Ida shook her head. "No, I'm not upset over my birthday or presents. I'm just sad that we'll soon be saying good-bye. It sounds like you are bent on going to Kansas, and we'll never see each other again."

The tears in her eyes were betraying her. She averted her head and tried to wipe them away, but Josiah pulled her around to face him once again.

"Dear little girl, don't you know how I feel about you? I don't want to leave you; I want to marry you and take you with me!"

He held out his arms and enfolded her in his strong grip. Her ear was pressed to his chest, and she could hear the strong beats of his heart. How wonderful it felt to be held like this. At last Josiah picked her up in his arms and sat down in the big rocker in front of the stove. She felt so small and protected sitting on his lap. Her mind was fuzzy from all the ardor and tenderness he was showing her. He tilted her head up and brought his lips down in a soft, gentle kiss. His touch sent a warm feeling throughout her body. She felt that she was drowning in this new but delightful sensation. His hands caressed her back while his lips kissed her cheeks, then her forehead and, finally, her lips. She felt weak and limp. She never wanted this feeling to end.

"My little sweetheart," he murmured against her lips, "I love you, but I was waiting until you turned fifteen to ask you to marry me. I was afraid your Pa would run me off if he thought I was courting his fourteen-year-old daughter. Will you marry me, Ida?"

Ida's mind was in a whirl. Everything was happening too quickly, and it seemed that her brain had left her body. She couldn't think about anything beyond the fact that this wonderful, gentle giant was holding her and telling her he loved her. He wanted to marry her! She laid her head in the curve of his neck and trembled with emotion. No one had ever said that they loved her—not Ma, not Pa, not even her little brothers. The word seemed magic and she was immersed in that moment.

They sat for hours touching, whispering, and talking. Josiah planned their future, and Ida listened. She knew that anything this man wanted she would give him. She'd go anywhere, do anything. She stilled the voice of guilt inside her which said that she was abandoning Pa and the boys. She knew she had to follow this man no matter what the consequences. His profession of love had opened a floodgate of yearning in her. Surely Pa would understand that this was her chance for happiness. He couldn't say no, but she was prepared to fight if she had to.

William Oyler awakened the next day at dawn to the smell of coffee and the sound of whispering. He entered the kitchen to see Ida stoking the fire while Josiah sat at the table drinking his coffee. "Idie, what the hell is goin' on? Young man, do you mean to tell me that you spent the night here?"

"Pa, calm down. It's not what you think. Josiah and I have something we want to tell you. Sit down and let me pour you a cup of coffee."

William glared at the big man but sat down across from him. "Well, what is it?" he asked angrily.

"Will, I thought maybe you'd guess by now what my intentions are toward your daughter. I've been coming here for over a month, and I'm sure it's plain that I love her and want to marry her. I realize this is a short courtship, but I have to make plans to move very soon, and I don't have the luxury of a long courtship. I know Ida is young, but she's a mighty strong, sensible woman, and I hope you'll give us your blessings."

William looked from Si to Ida. There was no doubt that these young people felt strongly about each other. "How could I have been so blind," he thought. "If I had known his intentions I'd have thrown him out the first day. What will happen to the boys and me if she leaves? Who will take care of us?"

Ida looked at her father and knew that he was feeling overwhelmed by this news. He had leaned heavily on her for the past two years, and she knew that she would be sorely missed. But little Grant had just turned five years old and Emer was ten. They could help Pa with the chores and maybe find some lady who could do the washing for them. She sat down next to him. "Pa, I know this is a shock to you. I guess I feel pretty surprised, too. I never thought things would turn out this way. But I love Josiah, and I want to marry him and go to Kansas. You've been looking at making another move, maybe we can go scout out the territory for all of us. Maybe we could all end up living in the same town, and I could help you and the boys. Wouldn't that be nice?" She got up to stand beside her young man who was putting on his wraps and preparing to report for work. His arm was around her shoulder, giving her courage that she would never have felt otherwise. "But, no matter what, Pa, I am going to marry him, with or without your blessing. We plan on talking to the minister on Sunday after church."

She and Josiah looked into each other's eyes and smiled. They embraced and kissed in a self-conscious manner before he opened the door to greet the pre-dawn darkness. "Sorry to leave like this," he said, "but I'll see you on Sunday, and we can talk more about the wedding then. So long."

From Wednesday morning to Sunday, Ida lived in a whirl of activity. After several conversations, she and Pa ultimately reached a compromise about her marriage. He could tell that she was hell-bent on having her own way and there wasn't much he could do about it short of locking her up. "You've got your Ma's stubborn streak, Idie," he said. "When she got somethin' into her head, no one could change her mind. You're awfully young, but you've been doing right by me and the boys for going on to three years, and I guess you're as ready for marriage as a lot of girls much older than you."

Ida could tell that he was intrigued by the thought that he and the boys might eventually follow them to Kansas. She shamefully admitted to herself that she promoted these thoughts because it kept him from being so resistant to the marriage.

Sunday morning dawned bright and clear. Josiah appeared at the door an hour before church and sat down with Ida and her family to discuss the wedding. "I've found a little cabin two blocks over with some furnishings in it. I'll rent it for several months until spring and then we can move south to the Salina area. That way you folks will have some time to prepare for our leaving. How does that sound to you?"

Both Ida and her father were relieved about the delay in the departure. Ida was impressed that Si had been busy with so many plans in the four days since he left her. After fifteen years with Pa and his hesitant decisions, it was exciting to have such a decisive man in her life. It was wonderful to be taken care of!

Ida and Josiah stayed after the Sunday morning services to talk to Reverend Olinger. Looking across his study at the couple, the pastor expressed his surprise about their news. Ida seemed to be such a down to earth, common sense girl. It didn't seem possible that she was willing to give up her family life and go off with this young man. "Well, I can see that your mind's made up Ida, and I'll be glad to marry you, but are you completely aware of all the responsibilities that marriage brings?"

As the couple looked at each other, Reverend Olinger knew that it didn't matter whether she did or not, this girl and young man were committed to making a life with each other. One thing was in her favor; the fellow was clean cut and seemed to be an honest, hard working sort. "She certainly could do worse," the minister conceded.

On a Tuesday evening in February, 1876, Ida Oyler and Josiah L. Herwick were married. Pa, the boys, and a few close friends gathered in the church to witness the simple ceremony. After the vows were said and the union blessed, the newlyweds said good-bye to everyone and walked to their small cabin which Ida had cleaned and provisioned from Pa's limited supplies.

Ida built a fire in the kitchen stove making the little room cozy and warm. In the dim light Ida looked at the spare furnishings and the handmade bed with Ma's old quilt. She sighed with satisfaction and turned to her new husband.

Josiah picked her up in his arms like a small child. He gently laid her down on the bed while he caressed her back and arms. His lips met hers with a gentle urgency. She enjoyed the melting sensation it brought. His lips pressed down on hers with increasing pressure. His hands sought the front of her dress, searching for the swelling fullness. His fingers quickly opened the buttons and stroked the softness above her chemise. She lay in a state of contentment with his hands on her skin. Warmth spread to all parts of her body. His fingers started to explore and something inside her sounded an alarm. This invasion was frightening–what was happening? He sensed her tenseness and bent to kiss her again. She made herself relax. This was her husband. It was all right.

"Lie still Little One. It will only hurt for a second." Then sharp, piercing pain coursed through her lower belly, tearing her apart. She struggled help-lessly until Josiah was pulling away from her, and she felt both a physical and emotional emptiness. She'd loved the kisses and caresses and wanted that wonderful feeling to go on and on. She didn't want this other thing. Is this all there was? Josiah was lying limply by her side–silent–trying to catch his breath. At last he casually reached over to stroke her arm and pat her hand.

"Did it hurt you too much? You're so young. It will get better, I prom-ise."

As she lay in the shelter of his large body she wondered, would it really get better? She felt very young and naive, and there was no one to turn to for information. Josiah's gentle snoring finally lulled her to sleep on her first night as Mrs. Ida Herwick.

∽ In 1876 a prairie fire in the Northwest corner of Phillips County, Kansas nearly destroyed the small town of Long Island. In 1877 the area was flooded.

∽ On June 25, 1876 George Armstrong Custer and one-third of the 7th Cav-alry were wiped out at the Battle of the Little Big Horn, resulting in an in-creased military force whose sole purpose was to crush any residual Indian resistance. The Army campaign, which destroyed whole indian villages, lasted well into 1877.

∽ On August 2, 1876 "Wild Bill" Hickok was shot and killed while playing poker at a saloon in Deadwood, South Dakota.

DECEMBER, 1876 PHILLIPS COUNTY, KANSAS

The sun finally came out partially drying the clay soil. It looked like there might be a day or two of good weather, and Ida felt a burst of energy for attacking the constant flow of dirt, rodents, and bugs in her mother-in-law's sod shelter. The sod houses presented an incredible challenge. Ida remem-

bered the nights when she had awakened to the feel of crawling insects passing over her face. Her initial screams had become annoyed mutterings as
she grew accustomed to her new life.

Her wedding day, some 10 months before, seemed to be in the distant
past. They moved in July to Josiah's mother's place in Philips County, Kansas. She felt a tremendous sorrow at the thought of leaving Pa and the boys.
But Josiah had kept at her with all sorts of arguments until she finally gave
in to his demands. She wiped a tear away as she remembered saying good-
bye to her family who stood forlornly waving until she was out of sight.

They had made the trip on horseback. A sturdy mule carried all the
belongings they would need on the 170-mile trip. They had moved west,
following the Platte River for the most part, where they could find forage and
water for the animals, and then headed south at Kearny. The July heat, wind,
and mosquitoes had plagued Ida until she thought she would go crazy. Ida
started feeling ill two days before arriving at Mother Susannah's. She decided
that the cramping was probably a complaint brought on by the trail diet of
beans and bacon and all the unaccustomed riding she had been doing.

Ida remembered the kind eyes of Josiah's mother, Susannah, as she greeted
her and helped her into the cool sod house. She could see that Ida was in pain
and she hastened to assist the young woman to bed while Josiah unloaded the
wagon. During the night Ida's cramps became much worse and Susannah
tried to comfort her. "Ida, when did you last have your monthly time?"

"I hadn't thought about it, but it has been two months."

Susannah sighed, "Ida, I think you are going to have a baby."

"How could I not have noticed?" Ida wondered aloud. Everything had
been so strange and confusing these past few months–getting accustomed to
life as a married woman, feeling such terrible guilt at the thought of leaving
Pa and the boys, and the anxiety of going to a new land with her young
husband. She guessed there had been too much on her mind to remember
bodily things.

In the middle of the night, Ida's womb finally expelled the small promise of a baby and she sunk into a deep, exhausted sleep. Susannah went to
the next room to tell Josiah.

"I'm sorry, son. It was too late for anything to help," she said. "All that
jouncing around on horseback for a week probably brought it on." As he sat
with his head in his hands, his mother silently wrapped the bloody bundle
and, picking up a shovel, went out behind the shed.

Susannah had made a tidy, if poor, home for herself and the two youngest boys when she came to Kansas. After her husband, Frederick, died in 1869 she had taught school to support the children, and times had been very hard. But they had survived. Her children were now scattered throughout the states. John was in Minnesota; Fred in Greenwood County, Kansas; Frank in Idaho; daughter Sarah and her family somewhere in Colorado. Now Josiah and Ida had joined her in Walnut Township. Josiah would be a welcome addition to seventeen-year-old Wes and sixteen-year-old Owen who were helping their mother work the small farm. She was not yet able to afford a hired man and there was always so much to do. Very little of the sod on their land had been broken because they could not find time in the spring when so many other things needed their attention. "It would be wonderful," Susannah thought, "if Josiah and Ida would stay here with the boys and me. Between all of us we could make this little place blossom. Maybe we could even get an oxen so that we could clear it quicker. Then we might have a decent corn crop next year."

In the pre-dawn light Ida woke to the sight of Josiah sitting by her. His eyes were somber. "I'm so sorry my love," he said. "But we're young, and there'll be more children. Don't be sad, it just couldn't be helped."

It all seemed very unreal to Ida, and she needed some time to think about the baby she didn't even know she'd been carrying. She remembered the pain and confusion of the previous night and realized that she was very, very, tired. Her eyelids closed as she felt herself carried along on a golden carpet of warmth and silence.

"I will think about it tomorrow," she promised herself.

Ida's healthy, young body soon responded to the loving ministrations of her mother-in-law and she was up helping with the chores within a week. She was a bit frightened to know that this pregnancy could have happened without her being aware of it. "I am really a ninny." she thought. "I might have known that those nights with Josiah would lead to a baby. Why wasn't I more observant?" She decided that she needed to pay closer attention to her body so that this would not happen again.

Ida was soon learning her first lessons in "soddy" housekeeping. The summer heat of the Kansas plains was partially diminished by the thick earthen walls, but she discovered that other guests liked the coolness as well. One morning she came in to pick up a bundle of dirty clothes for the wash tub full of boiling water in the yard, only to discover a huge bull snake coiled up in the pile of cloth. She was sure that her screams could have been heard in the next county which brought her mother-in-law running into the house. Susannah carefully slid a shovel under the undulating reptile and carried it out by the barn. Then she laughingly explained that snakes, other than rattle snakes, were actually friends to the soddy inhabitants because they kept the mice and bug population manageable. Ida wasn't sure which would be worse, but from then on kept one eye and ear open at all times.

As much as Ida missed Pa and the boys, she found herself happily fitting into the Herwick household routine. Milking, washing, mending, making butter, and all the other daily chores went much faster if there was someone to share them with. She was pleased to resume her housekeeping lessons which had been suddenly curtailed with her mother's death. Susannah was not only a loving woman, she was a learned one as well. She patiently helped Ida find better ways of keeping a tidy house and ministering to her loved ones. Susannah knew the best spices to make a savory stew, or the best herbs to heal a cough. Each day was an adventure in learning, and Ida felt safe, loved, and secure.

The evenings were spent sewing and darning by the light of the lamp while Josiah played the fiddle and occasionally sang. Ida was surprised the first time he took the instrument out of its case and drew the horsehair bow across the strings. "You didn't tell me that you played the fiddle!"

"I guess I just forgot. It's been a while since I was around one. This here is Pa's fiddle. His Pa brought it with him when he came to this country. This is the only thing Pa had left to remember his family, and he was mighty fussy about how it was handled. Mother, 'member how he used to play the old jigs and reels?" Striking up a lively tune, Josiah tapped his toe in time to the music. Ida looked forward to these evening gatherings. The Herwicks were happy people, who loved teasing and pulling pranks on each other. Their cheerful attitudes helped lessen the longing for her own family, and she felt very comfortable in the little group.

Secure in her own happiness, Ida was missing the signs of gathering restlessness in Josiah. While she was enjoying the comfort of a close family, he was looking impatiently toward the south where he heard that laborers were earning good money on the railroad and the farms sprouting up adjacent to them. There was talk of a new steam-powered flour mill being built in Salina, and he was sure that he could do much better down there than working on his mother's farm. When Ida realized Josiah was serious about moving, she became silent and pouty. This had become her home. She was anxious about relocating but the worse part would be leaving Susannah whom she had grown to love as her own mother. It would be like saying good-bye to Ma all over again. It was a rather pleasant surprise when her husband seemed almost relieved by Ida's reluctance to go with him. He suggested that it might be best to go ahead to secure a job and housing before he took her. She could spend the fall with his mother and brothers while he worked and saved up enough to get a little place. This plan was met with approval by everyone.

Susannah missed her only living daughter, Sarah, and she felt blessed by Ida's presence. She encouraged Josiah to go on without Ida. "I think that would be an excellent idea, Son. You'll be able to concentrate more on getting a job and laying away a bit of money. You'll also be able to find a decent place to live, so Ida won't have to stay in some of those houses which are little more than a wet hole in the ground."

Summer moved into fall, with little news from Josiah, who proved to be a sporadic letter writer. The few lines he sent were positive about the job availability and good wages. This was a period of increasing prosperity in Kansas. The horrible grasshopper plague was over. The railroad industry continued to flourish.

The crisp, golden days of autumn in Walnut Township were replaced by frosty mornings and overcast skies. The boys tended the stock, while Ida and Susannah spent more time with their needlework. Ida loved to work on the colored squares of cloth that made up the quilts. Her mother-in-law could tell her the history of each piece, how old it was, and who had worn the garment. Upon its completion, the quilt would be a beautiful display of the family's existence. Ida never grew tired of hearing the stories about Fred and Susannah Herwick, their family, and their ancestors.

Ida found that she shared another thing in common with Susannah. She too, had been married when she was but a week past her fifteenth birthday. She also had left her family in Ohio to follow the man she loved. Frederick was a sea-faring man who came west with the opening of the Erie Canal and continued moving toward Ohio. He longed to head toward that great Mississippi River he had heard so much about. He tried farming for awhile, but was eventually lured to the river and its occupations. He moved Susannah and their son to St. Louis, Missouri and then to Iowa. For close to twenty-five years, Susannah Herwick had learned to make do with limited resources while Frederick was away from home on the river. She was a survivor, and Ida marveled at the tales she shared about her struggles.

*I*da was beating on the rag rugs one day, cleaning them of the ever present dirt, when she heard a yell coming from down the road. A team of horses and a wagon was rumbling down the road, raising little tufts of dust behind them. The driver was standing up, waving his arms and yelling. As she peered at the sight, her heart started racing. "Josiah - I think it's Josiah!" she cried as she ran headlong down the road to meet the wagon and its occupant who had stopped and was running toward her. Josiah swept her up in his powerful arms, while he bent and kissed her soundly on the lips. The male smell of him overpowered her, and she realized how much she had missed him. Here was the man she adored, her love forever. Her lips responded in kind as she welcomed him home.

Susannah and the boys were alerted by the shouts coming from down the road, and they were waiting as the wagon pulled in front of the house. With his arms around both Ida and Susannah, Josiah moved to the front door while instructing his brothers to bring in the parcels and boxes hidden under a canvas in the back of the wagon. "It's getting mighty close to Christmas," he laughed , "and I don't want anyone peeking until I have a chance to look through each one. But here's something that we can all enjoy." Extracting a brown paper bag from the pile on the floor, he opened it to reveal ripe, plump oranges. Everyone exclaimed while helping themselves to one of the fruits.

"I would've warned you that I was coming," Josiah said, "but I figured I could get here about as soon as a letter, so I decided to deliver myself instead." Ida looked at him with love shining in her eyes. She thought she had never seen a grander figure of a man, from his blond hair and blue eyes right down to his considerable feet. But she decided that he could do with some female attention. His hair was growing long over his collar, his shirt was raggedy, and he could certainly use a bath. His tall, muscular frame could stand some fattening up, too. It was apparent that he had been concentrating more on his work than on his appearance.

Josiah spoke excitedly of the wealth of opportunities a hundred miles to the south. He had worked at various jobs which paid well. By careful spending he had been able to save enough to buy the team and wagon and put down some rent money on a few acres in Saline County. There was a small sod structure on the property where he and Ida could live until they were able to find something better. Ida realized with a start that he was expecting her to go back with him when he returned after Christmas. But, she promptly put this at the back of her mind and concentrated on enjoying Josiah's presence while he was at home.

Christmas was a happy time in the Herwick household. The weather continued cold but clear, allowing the family to pile into the wagon on Christmas Eve and travel to the little country school a few miles away where church services were being held. They packed a basket of food so they could share a meal with their friends and neighbors after the services. Ida shyly enjoyed visiting with all the folks that she hadn't had a chance to meet. While she and Susannah chatted with the women-folk about women things, she could hear Josiah discussing his experiences of the past few months. She could also see that his favorable report on the work conditions was exciting to the other men, as well. She remembered her Ma saying that men always seemed to have one foot in the future while women kept one foot in the past. That had been true for her parents, as well as her husband's parents. She wondered if she and Josiah would follow in the same pattern. It certainly looked as if they might.

Christmas Day dawned crystal clear and crusted with heavy frost. The men's footsteps going to the barn could be heard crunching loudly in the glittering stillness. Returning with pails of steaming milk, they sat at the kitchen table to be served a hearty breakfast, after which they exchanged the meager supply of presents. "Let's see. I think there might be one more package in the sack," Josiah said, teasing Ida. He handed her a wrapped parcel which she opened with eager anticipation. Inside was yards of a lovely periwinkle blue-striped material - enough to make a nice full dress and add lots of flounces and ruffles. She rose to give Josiah a big hug and then sat down to stroke the soft material.

"Why isn't that the prettiest dress goods you've ever seen?" exclaimed Susannah. "And it's Josiah's favorite color. If you like, I'll help you cut it out tomorrow, and we can sew on it in our spare time."

Ida thought she had never had a more wonderful Christmas. Josiah pulled out the old fiddle and played some of their favorite Christmas carols. Then he broke into a lively and merry set of reels while everyone clapped and tapped their feet. The joy and happiness of the family gathering drowned out the sound of the cold, howling wind and blowing snow outside.

Later that day, her warm contentment was interrupted by Josiah's conversation. He and Susannah were discussing the farm and what future crops would do the best. "You know Mother, you really need someone to help you out, because Ida and I won't be here to put in the crops next spring. I can't afford to stay here when I can make such good wages in Saline County. I suspect that Wes will soon want to get a paying job, too, which will only leave you with Owen. The place won't support more than one family."

Ida was jerked out of her preoccupation by the painful thought of leaving this warm, cozy, little family. She longed to ask Josiah to reconsider. "We could make a decent living here," she inwardly argued. "If all of us pulled together we could do fine, and maybe even buy another acre or two. Then Josiah and I could have our own little place near Mother's."

But, while this internal conversation was going on, she knew that it was useless to pretend it would happen. This man had his mind made up to go back to Saline County, no matter what argument she might present. He was convinced that the only way to get ahead was to be on their own. She bit her lip to keep from begging him to stay. She could hear Ma's voice telling her it was her duty to go wherever her man went.

Ida restlessly tossed and turned that night with visions of future disasters in her head. She wished that she was as brave as her husband who didn't seem to fear anything. She felt small and powerless to cope with the unknown tomorrows. Fatigue finally drove her to sleep, where she dreamed of a large ball of wire that was chasing her. She ran frantically to avoid being consumed by it.

∾ After years of fruitless gold mining, rich silver deposits were found in the area of Leadville, Colorado in 1877. Prospectors came from all over the United States for this latest strike.

∾ In July, 1877, Charles Bennett and Phillip Pratt led separate prospecting parties across "Hunter Pass" (later to be renamed Independence Pass) to the headwaters of what the Utes called "Thunder River." They were seeking the same geological formations found in the Leadville area, and they weren't disappointed. Before returning to Leadville, both parties had staked out a number of claims.

SEPTEMBER, 1877   SALINE COUNTY, KANSAS

The sun was here! The rains were gone, leaving green shoots of grass and delicate flowers. Everywhere Ida looked, there was a carpet of color. Her few hens and their chicks pecked around in the yard. A stray mother cat, who had been left by the previous tenant, lay under an old wooden box with her newly born kittens who were sucking noisily. The world was producing new life, and she was no exception. She felt a tug in her stomach and stopped to feel the energy of the new life growing within her. This was a healthy babe by the strength of its movements. She smiled and rubbed her distended body. "Be quiet, my babe. Your mother has work to do before your grandmother arrives."

After a few weeks of rain it felt good to leave the soggy house and let things dry out. The roof had started leaking from the excessive moisture filtering into it. It became a constant struggle shuffling things around to avoid being soaked by the constant dripping. She had about run out of corners into which to move the bed when the sun finally came out. She had instructed Josiah to string some rope from the corner of the house to a spindly bush ten feet away so she could hang the bedding out to air. She looked at the garden plot and yearned to root out the weeds, but he'd made her promise not to do such heavy work, saying that he'd do it on Sunday when he didn't have to go to work . She knew that her previous miscarriage had made a big impression on him, and he didn't want to jeopardize this pregnancy. Although Josiah had never admitted it, she wondered if he felt responsible for the loss of that first baby by insisting on her accompanying him south to Kansas.

Ida was somewhat apprehensive about the birth of this baby, but Susannah had promised to be with her when the time came. Although she sorely missed Mother Herwick and the boys, Ida had to admit that there had been compensations to being alone with her husband. They had found a comfort in each other, and she looked forward to falling asleep every night at his side. He was an ardent lover who took obvious enjoyment in being with her. Although she, herself, had never gotten beyond a warm expectant state in their lovemaking, her marital duties were anything but unpleasant. She enjoyed being married and was amused thinking of how she had thought this side of marriage would be so awful.

Living a few miles out of town, she hardly ever saw other people. Josiah usually worked six days a week, so they had little time to visit with their neighbors. She had to content herself with her household chores, occasional reading in the Bible, and the old mama cat whom she had grown to love. Watching Puss Cat feed and wash her kittens was fun, and she found herself talking to the cat as if it could understand her words. "I guess all mothers are the same," she thought as she stroked the soft tan fur.

By the end of the day, Ida had dried their clothes and cleaned as much of the little sodhouse as possible. "It really isn't much," she thought. "I hope Mother won't be upset that we haven't done better." Although Josiah had steady work, there didn't seem to be any money left over for more than necessities. The higher wages were eaten up by the corresponding higher expenses in this booming area. He talked about getting ahead, but it hadn't happened yet. Josiah was working as hard as he could, and Ida was sure Susannah would understand.

The sun was going down in a great red flame when a wagon pulled into the yard. Susannah and Wes stepped down to greet Ida in a flurry of hugs and conversation. Ushering them inside, she hurried about getting supper ready while they visited.

"It looks like I didn't come a minute too soon, Ida," her mother-in-law laughed. "I'd say that baby is not going to wait more than two or three more days. You've dropped considerably."

As Ida felt her swollen belly, she realized that she did have more room to breathe. The baby wasn't pushing against her lungs as much as it had a few days ago. She shivered with an anticipation which was both fear and joy. "What will it be like?" she wondered. The yearning for a child of her own was tempered by the memory of her mother's death struggle. Childbirth was women's most dangerous task. The cemeteries were full of young wives who had lost the battle in this most primitive event. Ida pushed down the fear she felt rising in her throat.

"Mother won't let anything happen to me," she assured herself. "She's wise about birthing. Nine living children are proof of that."

Ida absentmindedly stroked her abdomen and wondered the gender of this baby. Boys seemed to be predominant on Josiah's side of the family. His mother had birthed nine children, six of them males. "I'm sure Si would love a son," she thought. "And heaven knows this country is hard on women. But, it would be wonderful to have a little girl who would be mine. I could teach her all the things that I've been taught. I'd never have to be lonesome if I had a daughter. Boys grow up and go with their father, but girls stay at home with their Ma. I'd like that." With a smile she shook herself out of her reverie and went on with her supper preparations.

Two days later Susannah's prediction came true. Ida woke early that morning with a burst of energy she hadn't felt for several months. She climbed out of bed and stoked up the fire in the kitchen range. Coffee was boiling and bacon was sizzling in the frying pan before everyone else was up. Josiah and Wes had been sleeping in the barn, because the soddy was too small to sleep everyone, and the fragrant hay made a better bed than the hard dirt floor. Susannah had slept with Ida in the one bed. Ida missed her husband's big body next to her. She'd grown accustomed to his warm, male presence.

Looking up, she saw him standing in the doorway, still groggy with sleep, and reaching for the milk pail so he could go milk old Bossy. She was a recent addition to their little farm family, and old as the hills. But she continued to give a decent bit of milk twice a day, which was a welcome supplement to their limited diet. Josiah had taken over the milking duties as Ida's time grew nearer. Before long he was back with the full pail, which Susannah took from his hands and prepared to strain into a large brown crock. "It looks like there's enough cream for us to churn today, Ida. I'll make some biscuits for supper to go with the fresh butter. The buttermilk will taste good, too."

The morning chores seemed to go quickly. Susannah insisted that Ida sit down to churn the butter while she did the heavier work of hauling water, sweeping the dirt floor, and preparing a light lunch. Ida was bending over to put the churn on the table when the first pain hit. She doubled over in surprise at the sharp, stabbing contraction. It was gone in just a second, allowing her to straighten up, but Susannah observed the amazed expression and knew what had caused it.

"Well, Ida girl, it looks like you're going to be a mama today! Now, we've got to get things all ready for this big event. Show me where the extra sheets are. It's too soon to boil water, but I will need your scissors and some string. I'm going to bake those biscuits right now, and put some meat on to stew. That way we will have supper all cooked for the men and they won't have to go hungry tonight."

Another contraction came, stronger than the last. Ida was a little dazed by the sudden on-set of her labor. She had thought there would be more time to prepare for it. But this gripping pain wasn't giving her much relief. It felt like her belly was being held in an iron grip, squeezing harder and harder. Even the moments between the hard pains brought relentless cramping. Fear started welling up within her, but Susannah intervened before she became suffocated with anxiety. "Let's get up and walk a bit. It will help with the cramps and the baby can get in position for it's birth. I know it's uncomfortable, but trust me. I know about these things," she said, her eyes twinkling.

Ida followed Susannah's orders with faith that her mother-in-law knew exactly what needed to be done. Her mind grew foggy as the pains came closer together. She was floating in a sea of discomfort, punctuated by the rising and falling rhythm of the contractions. She couldn't tell how long this child had been tearing her apart in its struggle to escape her womb. She could hear Susannah's voice from a distance, telling her when to relax. Her hands were guided to a cloth wrapped around the headboard. "Hold on tight to this Ida girl, and pull as hard as you can when the pain hits. It will help you to bear down when the time comes."

It could have been days; it could have been mere minutes–Ida lost track of time. Her reality was the capsule of pain which had become more demanding. She began bearing down with each contraction. It felt like she could expel the infant if she just kept pushing.

"Slow down, dear. You'll end up tearing yourself to bits if you keep pushing like that."

Ida felt a sting in her lower region and then Susannah said, "Okay, darling, let's go. Push as hard as you want, your baby is ready to come out."

There was a tremendous relief in being able to bear down hard. Ida's breath stopped as she concentrated on the job she had to do. She felt a movement in her lower body as she bore down one final time. "Ida, look at your beautiful daughter!" cried Susannah.

After the birth of baby Birdella, Ida settled into the little sodhouse near Salina, completely happy with her life. Josiah provided the necessities, if not the luxuries of life, and they were quite comfortable. Ida's days were spent doing her chores, milking Bossy, playing with Puss Cat, and cuddling her baby daughter. She couldn't believe it was possible to love such a tiny mite so much. The pain of her birth faded away in the delight of seeing this child thrive and grow. Each coo and gurgle was cause for new wonderment. She was surprised that Josiah didn't seem to share her level of devotion, but she decided it was because he was a man who didn't know how to act around such a small baby. "That will change when he gets used to being a father," she thought.

Josiah did seem glad to welcome her back into the marriage bed. There were times he became impatient with her if she needed to tend to the baby when he had other ideas, but he usually got over his irritation quickly enough. Ida couldn't have asked for a better life.

∿ *Two prospectors named Kelly and Patton explored the Battle Mountain area in the summer of 1878. They returned with ore samples which contained high concentrates of lead carbonates and silver. Prospectors started pouring into the area over Tennessee Pass from Leadville.*

∿ *A steam-powered flour mill, costing $75,000, was built in Salina, Kansas.*

∿ *The Atchison, Topeka, and Santa Fe Railroad established their general offices in Topeka, Kansas. The railroad workers went on strike, and the Governor called out the militia.*

SPRING, 1878   SALINE COUNTY, KANSAS

At supper one spring evening, Josiah mentioned that he had been talking to some railroaders in town that day. They had discussed a rumor that the Santa Fe workers were talking about a railroad strike. They'd also mentioned that Colonel Cyrus K. Holliday, promoter for the Santa Fe railroad, had established the general offices and machine shops in Topeka.

"This might be our chance to get ahead, Ida," Josiah exclaimed. "My brother, Fred, is doing real well on the railroad down in Greenwood County. If I could hire on with the Santa Fe, maybe I could make enough money to put some aside. The way we're going, we'll be grubbin' on this poor piece of land for the rest of our lives. I think you'd like the country over around Topeka. It's got more hills and trees. Maybe we could even find a little log or frame cabin so you can get out of this damned dirty place."

"Josiah, you needn't curse about it. I think we're very comfortable here, and it's closer to Mother and the boys. Now that I've gotten the walls whitewashed, our little place is quite presentable. I don't really want to move." Ida was trying to hide the plea she felt in her heart.

Throughout the next few weeks, Ida was bombarded with all the reasons a move to the Topeka area would be beneficial. Everyday she looked around her small, tidy domain and dreaded the thought of moving again. But, her husband would not be put off, and she finally gave into his demands. They sold old Bossy and the few chickens to a neighbor, loaded up the wagon with their meager supply of household goods, and headed east 180 miles to Topeka.

Ida hated the noise and activity of the city. She much preferred the quiet of her little prairie soddy. After prevailing upon Josiah to look for a place outside Topeka, they finally found a little log cabin located ten miles away in Jackson County, and Ida started making it their home. As much as she missed the soddy, she did admit that it was a nice change to not have dirt dribbling down from the ceiling all the time, and the shade of the big old tree was wonderful. After living on the barren prairie, she had forgotten what a bit of foliage could do for a place, and it meant she no longer had to depend largely on buffalo chips for heat and cooking. In a short time she had the little place clean and comfortable while Josiah started his search for a good job.

Somewhat to Josiah's chagrin, the jobs were plentiful but usually paid no more than his previous work in Salina. He was good with horses and could always find teamster jobs, but was not able to get a job with the railroad. However, life was good, and with the baby growing so fast, time seemed to fly by.

In the fall, Ida discovered that she was pregnant again. By her calculations the baby was due in June when Birdie would be almost two years old. "Well, I guess it isn't true that you can't get pregnant if you're nursing," she thought ruefully, "but it will soon be time to wean Birdie anyway."

The fall and winter passed swiftly and simply. Ida felt physically well, and her pregnancy appeared to be uncomplicated. She did feel some anxiety, however, that her mother-in-law would not be with her to assist in this delivery. Susannah had written that it was not possible for her to leave, because Wes had gone several counties away to work, and that left only her and Owen to run the small place. So, Ida started inquiring around and found that a highly recommended midwife lived less than five miles down the road.

When her time came, the labor was intense but fairly short. At the end of the day, on June 5, 1879, Ida was able to present Josiah with his first son, William. The baby was a carbon copy of him, with almost white hair and the bright blue Herwick eyes. He was a healthy baby who cried only when he needed food and changing. Ida thought her heart would burst with joy. "We've got a little girl and a little boy and they're both healthy. How blessed we are."

She was up and around very soon after her confinement and discovered that taking care of two children and a home kept her busy most of the time. She was not able to afford the luxury of long summer afternoons spent just playing with the children and Puss Cat. No doubt about it, her life was full of responsibilities.

∾ *In 1879 over $9 million in silver was mined in Leadville, which had a popu-
lation of over 15,000 people. This made it the second largest city in Colorado. The Rio Grande Railroad was busy laying tracks from Pueblo, through
Salida, to the boom town.*

∾ *The neighboring Utes became angry at the invasion of their land by the white
prospectors. On September 29, 1879 they murdered the Indian Agent, Nathan
Meeker, and eleven other men at the White River Agency in northwestern
Colorado. This incident threw all the miners within a hundred miles into a
panic. The good citizens of Red Cliff went so far as to erect "Fort Arnet" on
a rocky outcropping in the middle of town.*

JULY, 1879 JACKSON COUNTY, KANSAS

"Ida, did you hear me? We've got to get on the road before the sun gets up
much higher. Otherwise, we're gonna be boiling in our own juice before we
even get out of the yard."

"I heard you, Josiah," Ida responded, "but your son was hungry, and I
know you don't want to hear him squall so I stopped to feed him. I'm just
about ready. Is Birdella out there with you? I can't find her."

Josiah bent down to pick up his toddling daughter. "Yeah, she's out
here with the cat. Come along, Birdie. We've got to get up on the wagon so
we can start the trip. Say good-bye to the kitty like a good girl."

The dark eyed child promptly set up a howl of rage at the thought of
being separated from her favorite pet. Tears were streaming down her face as
her father plopped her in the middle of the front seat of the wagon. "We'll
find another kitty for you when we get to Grandma's," he consoled her. "I'll
bet she has lots of cats—she always did."

Ida hurried out the door of the little log house with a sigh. Handing her
infant son to his father, she climbed up over the high wagon wheel and then
settled the sleeping child in his quilted bed.

Josiah snapped the reins and the team of horses moved out with their
cargo. Ida looked back at the little house and its big shade trees. "I'm sorry
to be leaving you, house," she thought. "I've been happy here. I just wish
Josiah felt the same way." As the wagon rumbled along, she mentally looked
back over the past month.

News from Colorado had reached eastern Kansas. The second rush was
on to the Leadville area, where lead, silver, and gold were being mined in
abundance. When Josiah had begun talking about the opportunities some
months ago, Ida was too busy with her first child and the impending birth

of the second to pay much attention to the conversation. However, right after the baby's birth, she realized that Josiah brought up the topic every evening. Whenever possible, he obtained Denver newspapers which stated that thousands were heading to the mountains each week. Assay and geology reports confirmed that this was truly another boom, similar to the California Gold Rush in 1849. Stagelines had been formed and roads improved, all leading into Leadville. By the time Ida realized the extent of Josiah's obsession with this newest "Utopia," she also realized that he had already made his mind up to go west.

"It isn't as if I'm asking you to go with me at first," he argued. "I could take you back to Mother's while I'm gone. I'm sure she'd welcome your company and help, especially now that Wes has left the farm. I could work out there for a season and save my money so I could send for you. I understand that the railroad is building south of Leadville. When I've put away enough money, you and the children could come by train. Wouldn't that be an experience?"

Ida knew it was useless to argue with her husband when he had his mind made up. Before she knew what was happening, Josiah had written his mother who promptly answered back. Susannah reported that she had taken in an old friend and a young girl in her teens to help out, so there wouldn't be room for Ida and the children in her house. However, just a few miles away in the next township, there was a nice little place which had been vacant since early spring. Her letter showed her excitement about having Ida and the babies close to her once again. That seemed to clinch the deal for Josiah who immediately started preparing for their trip. He wanted to get to the mountains and settled in before winter. Ida felt it was an afterthought when he mentioned that he also wanted to be sure she and the children were prepared for winter before he left.

Despite the fact that she adored him and was usually ready to make excuses for his perceived shortcomings, she suspected that he did not always place her and the children first. Deep down she heard a small voice saying, "But what about us? What will happen to the children and me while he's gone? How will we live with no income? How can he take care of us when he's miles and miles away?"

Ida hushed the voice inside and prepared for yet another move.

∾ The Rio Grande Railroad reached Leadville, Colorado on July 22, 1880. A special train carrying Ulysses S. Grant and William J. Palmer arrived to a cheering crowd.

∾ In February, 1880, B. Clark Wheeler, Captain Isaac Cooper and William L. Hopkins set out from Leadville for "Ute City" (later Aspen) on long, Norwegian skis. Walking atop five to seven feet of snow, it took them nearly four days to travel the seventy miles.

∾ The "Aspen Town and Land" company was formed in the summer of 1880.

JULY, 1880   PHILLIPS COUNTY, KANSAS

The early morning sun was already beating down on the bare dooryard, promising another day of sweltering heat. Ida decided she had better get busy and hoe part of the garden patch before she talked herself out of it. After that she'd have to lug some water from the well to irrigate the plants. It seemed like a lot of work if Josiah came back before harvest and they moved to Colorado. On the other hand, those vegetables could be a blessing to her next winter if he didn't.

Her husband's sporadic letters assured her that he was doing fine but was out in the hills most of the time and not able to write often. She laughed at his description of those "hills." It didn't sound as if they looked much like the Nebraska and Kansas hills. In fact they sounded downright frightening. But he reported that he was making good money doing some hunting for the various camps. When he wasn't hunting he could usually find some mule-skinner work, or hauling for local companies.

Ida was not able to obtain the Denver papers very often, but the mail carrier brought any he picked up along his route. He knew that she was eager for current news about the Colorado mining boom and any other information about this wilderness to which her husband had gone . Soon after Josiah left she had received reports of a Ute Indian uprising in the Colorado mountains that people were calling the "Meeker Massacre." She was frantic to find out more about the victims of this slaughter. Her relief upon getting the full story many weeks later made her feel guilty. "Those poor women," she thought. "How sad to lose your husband and father and then to be abducted by savages." She silently prayed for both the living and dead of this tragedy. "God, take care of those ladies, and give them comfort in your presence, just as you do me in my moments of sorrow and grief. And please Lord, also watch over my husband and bring him back safely to me and his children."

Other news reports from the infrequent newspapers indicated another big strike had been made in a region north of Leadville called Red Cliff. Josiah mentioned it in one of his letters, and said he had passed through the area on one of his hunting trips down the Eagle River. She could tell that he was taken with this river valley where he said the game was so thick, a man never had to worry about going hungry. The valley was uninhabited except for a few old timers and some hardy prospectors who were hoping to find another big strike in the area.

The newspapers also reported that the Rio Grande Railroad was pushing its tracks north from the towns of Pueblo, Canon City, and Salida. With good luck it was supposed to reach Leadville sometime this month. Ida got excited thinking that she might be riding that same railroad before the first of the year.

Josiah's last letter, which arrived the last of June, reported the conditions in Leadville were deplorable for boarders. The few hotels were charging two to four dollars a day, if you were lucky enough to find a vacancy. The shortage of sleeping space had grown so critical, that "Lodgers" started renting beds for eight hours at a time. And the meal situation wasn't any better. For those who could afford it, the Tontine Restaurant, one of the better eateries in town, provided meals for six to seven dollars a week. Josiah soon found out that this was too expensive for him, although he was getting twelve to twenty-five cents per pound for bear, deer, and elk meat. It was for this reason that he decided to hire out to a man named Nucholds who had driven a herd of cattle up from the south and was intending to summer them in the mountains surrounding the Leadville area. He'd be leaving for the high country and would probably not come back to town until they brought the cattle down in the fall. He planned to live off the land for the summer, which would allow him to save more money than if he stayed in town. He warned her that she should not worry if she didn't get a letter until fall because he would not be able to post a letter where he was going!

Ida felt immeasurable fear at the thought of her husband in those high mountains for so many months without any human contact. "What will happen if he becomes ill or injured? It might be months before he's even found. It would be even longer until I'd get word about him." Thinking of him lying alone, sick or dead, caused such internal pain that it consumed her, causing her breath to come in short gasps and her chest to feel as if were being crushed by a heavy weight. She thought she couldn't stand it night after night, as she cried into the darkness, but come morning, she'd drag herself out of bed and go on with life for the sake of her children.

Birdie, almost three years old, and William, just turned one, were healthy, happy, chubby babies. She immersed herself in the daily, daytime chores of taking care of them. Birdie, true to her father's promise, had gotten another kitty cat which she followed around from morning to night. William was just learning to walk, and he tottered after Birdie falling down frequently, but always getting up and trying again. "He's a sturdy little fellow," Ida thought, "Just like his father."

Susannah usually visited at least once a week to check on Ida and the children. She made sure they had enough to eat by bringing over fresh milk and cheese from her supply. Occasional gifts of ham or beef supplemented the staple diet of potatoes, beans, biscuits, and whatever vegetables were in season. Ida was still nursing William, and Susannah urged her to eat more because she was very thin. "That baby is taking all your strength, Ida. If this continues you'd better wean the child. You've got to stay healthy for the children's sake, and Lord knows he's a strong enough boy."

"Oh, I'm fine. I just haven't had much of an appetite lately. I kind of go in spells that way." Ida couldn't tell her that the real reason for her gaunt frame had nothing to do with nursing her child. How could she eat when her husband might be lying dead or dying at this very moment. Food seemed to stick in her throat, and her stomach ached continually.

Susannah guessed more than Ida realized. She had also spent many youthful nights in fear for her husband's life on the wild and unpredictable Mississippi River. "It's men's lot to explore, and it's women's lot to worry and grieve. I think you need to get out and socialize more. Why don't you come to church with me on Sunday? I think you'd like listening to the Reverend. He speaks a powerful message, and maybe he'll have one for you."

Ida reluctantly agreed to accompany her mother-in-law the next Sunday, although she privately thought that it was really too much trouble to get herself and the children ready for church services. When Ida and Susannah pulled into the church yard there were several wagons and buggies already there. Ida remembered some of the folks from when she had lived there four years before. She shyly greeted them and was introduced to others who soundly welcomed her. The voices quieted as Pastor White stepped to the pulpit and began to read,

The Lord is my shepherd, I shall not want. He maketh me to lie down in green pastures; He leadeth me beside still waters. He restoreth my soul; He guideth me in the paths of righteousness for His name's sake.

As Ida heard the familiar words, she felt a comfort that she had not experienced for some time. She could feel the tension start to drain from her. The minister continued with a sermon taken from Isaiah 26:3,4:

Thou wilt keep him in perfect peace, whose mind is stayed on thee: because he trusteth in thee. Trust ye in the Lord forever: for in the Lord Jehovah is everlasting strength.

Ida was comforted by the words of God's love for each person and His knowledge of each person's needs. It had been quite a while since she had felt a sincere connection with her Creator. She had been so consumed by worry over Josiah, that she had forgotten that he was in the Lord's care. "Father, please do for him what I am not able to do. Take away my worry, and let me grow to trust You more. Help me to have faith in the Divine Plan for me and my family." With a full heart, she joined in the singing of the final hymn, "His Eye is on the Sparrow."

Throughout that summer and fall, Ida worked on her spiritual fitness as well as her physical well being. She looked forward to every Sunday sermon, believing that God was speaking directly to her through the minister. Her prayers each night carried petitions for continued protection for her husband, and the extreme fear began to leave her. As she emerged from her depression, she found it easier to eat and take care of her bodily needs. She even found herself humming fragments of the hymns sung the previous Sunday. One day blended into another as she and the children grew and thrived.

It was mid-October, and the weather was getting cooler before she finally got her first letter from Josiah. He wrote that he was well and had gotten through his summer's experience without any major problems, except he had worn his britches out and didn't have any way to replace them. But he was an enterprising person who managed to fashion a pair of pants out of feed sacks until he came across some prospectors who had an extra pair for which he traded some fresh venison. He reported that he was again working in the Leadville area and thought he might be able to get steady work on one of the stagelines. Even though the train had reached Leadville and crews were pushing the rail bed over Tennessee Pass, there was still a great demand for stage travel. The Georgetown to Leadville route was twelve hours one way. In summer, a "coach and four" was used, but in the winter, sleighs were used if the snow was packed enough to allow the horses to push through. Until the train reached Red Cliff, there was a daily need for stage runs over the pass from Leadville. Josiah also mentioned that the new area around Redcliff was still being explored, and that mining speculators were in abundance. The Herald Mine had recently been sold for $30,000 to a New York mining company. The final news was that he had been successful in finding an old cabin on the outskirts of Leadville which was barely more than a large box sunk in the ground, but it would be warmer than a tent when winter hit. He'd spent a few of his precious dollars to buy a small metal stove. He'd also purchased food supplies which were outrageously expensive. Bacon was twelve to fifteen cents per pound, flour forty cents, and coffee forty-five cents. Fresh produce was out of the question, even if it could be found.

Enclosed with the letter was fifty dollars which Si told Ida to use to buy needed supplies and to save the rest for her trip next spring. "Well, I guess that takes care of my plans for going to Colorado this fall," she thought dispiritedly. But, deep down she had known that this would happen, and she found that her disappointment was much easier to bear than it would have been a year ago. Her life now seemed so far removed from that of her husband in the wild, remote country where murders, suicides, and lynchings were everyday occurrences.

The last newspaper she had read did contain some positive news. A school district committee was actively investigating a site for two more schools. The building of the schools, along with the seven churches already listed in the 1880 City Directory, might tame down the city before she arrived.

The crisp days of fall turned into the chill of winter, and Christmas was upon the little family. It was a bittersweet affair because they were celebrating it without Josiah, but the various holiday events occurring in the community made for a festive holiday. Susannah managed to make sure Ida was invited to some of the parties so she wouldn't have time to feel so sad. One of their neighbors invited them all to a taffy pull, an activity with which Ida was not familiar. Sugar was scarce, but molasses was available in most households. It was boiled to a hard crack stage, and then allowed to set until the mixture was able to be touched. All the participants liberally buttered their hands and, taking a piece of the hot, pliable material, pulled the taffy out and doubled it over, forming another string to again be pulled to its limits. Young people enjoyed having partners, especially those of courting age who picked their sweetheart with whom to engage in the sticky struggle and wound up glued to each other by this honey-brown, amorphous mass. Ida found herself giggling like a school girl as the evening progressed and thought she had never had more fun. As she and Susannah rode home that evening, with her sleepy children between them, she felt that she was truly a member of this little community. The thought warmed her.

On Christmas morning, Ida and Susannah and the children went to church. The children had been diligently practicing for their short nativity play before regular services. Little Birdie was not able to memorize any specific lines, but she was included in the group around Baby Jesus and took this role very seriously. When William saw his sister kneeling on the tiny stage he commenced yelling, "Siser, Siser" to Ida's embarrassment and everyone else's delight.

The traditional Christmas carols were sung by the congregation, accompanied by the lady playing a wheezing pump organ. *Silent Night, Holy Night...* "Yes, it is a holy night," thought Ida. *All is calm, all is bright...* "Thank you, God, for giving me the peace of these past few months." As she took Communion, Ida felt the mysticism of the symbolic act. She hoped to remember this sense of spiritual completeness when she was next tempted to trust in herself instead of God.

part two

1881-1888

∾ In 1881, Holy Cross City had a post office, store, assayer, justice of the peace, and a boarding house. It was located below the major mines, "Little Mollie" and "Grand Trunk." The settlement of Gold Park was down Homestake Creek toward Redcliff. It had a population of 400 people in 1881 and sported two hotels. After Gold Park's demise in 1883, the area continued to offer good fishing for the men providing food to Leadville.

∾ On Sunday November 20, 1881, The Denver and Rio Grande Railroad reached Red Cliff, Colorado. Extra engines had to be put on east bound trains to push the freights up over Tennessee Pass.

∾ Early settler, Joe Brett, froze both his feet while on a hunting trip. He was taken to Redcliff where both feet were amputated. This plucky pioneer lived many more years in the Eagle River Valley, raising his family there.

MARCH, 1881   PHILLIPS COUNTY, KANSAS

When Ida thought about the past three months, it was with wonder. The parting from her mother-in-law that she had been dreading so much wasn't going to happen. Susannah and Josiah's brothers were all going with her and the children to Colorado.

When Josiah had written the first of January, he sent $100 which he estimated would buy her passage via the Kansas Pacific to Denver. Then she'd transfer to the Rio Grande Railroad which ran through Pueblo and Canon City to Leadville. She had used very little of the first $50, so she had almost $150 for the trip.

"It seems a shame to spend that much money for our fare," she told Susannah. "Mercy me, that would buy a year's worth of staples for us. It must be very expensive to live out there in the mining camps. The worst part of going by train is that I'll not be able to take many of my household goods with me, and I expect it will take a king's ransom to purchase them in Leadville."

"Josiah is making good money. You'll be able to buy the necessities. Just get on out there to your husband and quit worryin' so."

But beyond all the worry about her belongings was the sadness she felt at leaving her mother-in-law and the boys. She had grown to love them like her own family and couldn't conceive of leaving them behind. Susannah would be fifty-seven years old in June, and although she was fairly hearty for her age, Ida knew it couldn't be many more years until her mother-in-law would require assistance. Wes would be twenty-one and Owen nineteen years old in the fall, and Ida knew they would soon start thinking about creating a life for themselves. At least Wes would. Owen was one young man who didn't get very far away from his mother's apron strings. Ida supposed it had something to do with his being the youngest.

The more Ida discussed the impending trip, the more reluctant she was to go. "It would be wonderful if we had the money to go with you, Idie," Wes sadly declared, "but there's no way we can come up with $225 for train fare. Even if we sold off all the stock and farm equipment, I doubt that we'd get more than $100. It's too bad we can't pile all our plunder into the wagon and take off for Colorado." Ida absently patted Wes's hand and silently prayed that she be given some divine guidance about reuniting with her husband.

A week later the answer seemed to be forthcoming through a letter Susannah received from her son Frank in Idaho. It seemed he was tired of ranch-hand life and reported that he was leaving soon to return to Kansas for a visit before going on to Colorado where he had heard there was great promise. He figured it would take him a week to get to the railhead and dispose of his horse and tack before boarding the train for home. He wanted the boys to meet him in Elm Creek, Nebraska, which was about seventy miles due north of Phillips County, on the last day of February.

"Wes," Ida squealed, "that's it! We can all travel by wagon to Colorado. Thank heaven Josiah made sure we had a good sturdy wagon when we left Jackson County. The team is young and in good shape, and Frank is an experienced teamster who shouldn't have any trouble getting us there. We can pack up both our households in the wagon and buy two tents for us to camp in. We'll have everything we need to make a home when we get to Leadville, and the best part of it is that we can all be together. If we start out in late March, the grass should be up far enough for the stock to feed on, at least until we get to the mountains. With a little bit of grain to supplement, they should do fine."

The newborn plan soon started to take shape and was expanded upon with Frank's arrival. Although Susannah displayed little of the youthful enthusiasm of her sons and daughter-in-law, she was glad that they would all be going. She admitted that she had not looked forward to staying in Kansas without Ida and her grandchildren. She had no real reason to stay in Kansas. Heaven only knew where her oldest son, John, was at this moment. It seemed that he had inherited the wanderlust of his ancestors. Fred was still with the railroad in Greenwood County, and she supposed she could move down there to be closer to him and his family, but she realized that she would be happiest with Josiah and Ida. There was a certainty that she would be taken care of when the time came for her to slow down. Not that she was planning to anytime soon. An added incentive to her going was the fact that her daughter and son-in-law, Sarah and Will, were somewhere in the western part of Colorado. "Yes," thought Susannah, "it's good for me to be going to Colorado. I'll have five of the seven children close to me, and that will be a blessing."

Ida quickly posted a letter to Josiah in Leadville, praying that he would frequently check at the post office. To her surprise, a letter of response arrived in a month. Josiah was very pleased that they were planning a wagon trip. He also wrote about the high cost of supplies in the mountain areas, and he asked that Wes pack plenty of saws and lumber tools, as well as good hunting rifles and a supply of ammunition. He also suggested they include gardening tools for the abundant garden they'd be growing this year on the Eagle River.

LATE MARCH, 1881   PHILLIPS COUNTY, KANSAS

The day dawned for their departure. All the spare stock had been sold, including the cow and chickens. Susannah and Ida had agonized over this decision, because they knew that milk and eggs could be a vital part of their diets on the road, as well as after they arrived. But the early departure with little forage available would be too hard on the cow, and they didn't have the room or money for extra feed. So, the stock was parceled out to neighbors for a few dollars each.

Frank had packed the wagon to its capacity, refusing to stash any additional cargo. "Ma, you know as well as I do that the horses will have a hard enough time without loading them down even more. You and Ida will have to make up your minds on the most important things because that's all we can take."

The women, bowing to his wisdom, packed and re-packed time after time trying to prioritize each article so they could be sure of taking every piece necessary for their existence. This journey would take them through long stretches of uninhabited land, and they had to be sure emergency wheels, harnesses, and food supplies were available. Then there were provisions for the children, feed for the horses, canvas tents, cold and wet weather gear. The list seemed never-ending, but they finally had everything packed to their satisfaction.

Finally the team was hitched and the children were stowed between Susannah and Frank. Ida mounted the gentle old mule while Wes and Owen climbed on their saddle horses. The little caravan headed west with the weak March sun at their backs. "How many years has it been since I last set out for an adventure like this?" wondered Susannah aloud. "Land sakes, it was almost forty-two years ago when Fred Herwick took me from my home in Ashtabula, Ohio to Illinois." She reminisced, thinking of all those past years when she had been younger than Ida and filled with the joy of youth. "I don't think you'd like this land very much, Fred," she silently told her dead husband. "You'd feel lost without a boat deck under your feet, and I haven't seen a river big enough to float anything larger than a canoe. This is a strange land. God protect us on this journey."

LATE APRIL, 1881   BUENA VISTA, COLORADO

The wind blowing up-valley chilled their backs and caused the children to whimper. As she soothed her grandchildren, Susannah decided that this did not feel at all like springtime. Their trip had been uneventful, if long and tedious, until they reached Trout Creek Pass. Then the weather had turned cold and cloudy. Snow still heavily blanketed the surrounding mountains, with smaller patches visible in the lower elevations. It was apparent that there had been snow and ice in South Park just a few weeks before. The brown grass was still bent over from the weight of its winter burden, with only a few stalks of green poking up through the drab landscape. The road became muddier, with the low spots turning into a boggy mess which the team struggled through. "We might as well be back up on the Erie," Susannah thought. "I don't believe I've been this chilled since I left the north."

The sun was casting its last hour of light when the wagon pulled through the town of Buena Vista. The lights of the few buildings beckoned to Ida. "How wonderful to be able to sit before a real fire and sleep in a real bed," she said. "Lord, I'll be so grateful when we have a home once again." Ida felt guilty complaining when she knew the children and Susannah had suffered just as much as she had. She couldn't imagine what it would be like to make this trip when she was almost fifty-seven years old. Mother Herwick was a strong woman, and Ida prayed that she'd be half the woman that her mother-in-law was. No matter how difficult the trail, the older woman never complained. In fact, her cheerfulness had set the tone for all of her family, whether it was cuddling little William, keeping Birdie occupied, or quietly tempering the impatience of her three young sons. Ida's love and admiration for Susannah knew no bounds, and she was so pleased they were sharing this new adventure.

The snowy mountains which surrounded her on all sides sent a shiver throughout Ida's body. She felt like she was suffocating, and she had to keep reminding herself she was not in danger. Never had she seen anything as massive and foreboding as these mountains. The thought of moving further north into the heart of these rocky beasts set her heart pounding uncontrollably. "How can Josiah enjoy living up here?" she agonized. "Surely he doesn't intend to make the children and me live in such a primitive place." Nothing in her short twenty years of life had prepared her for the sight of this wild country. As they made camp on the outskirts of town that night, she despaired that she would ever again have the few comforts she once had, and for the first time she found herself doubting the judgment of her husband.

Josiah had written that he would meet them in Buena Vista on May 1, giving Ida and the family a few days of rest before pushing on. She and Susannah spent the time repacking some of their provisions and washing all the clothes they hadn't had time to wash while on the trail. The weather had turned out clear and sunny with only a mild chill in the air. Ida was amused by a few blue-gray birds which hovered about their camp site and squawked raucously for bits of food. "What bold creatures," she laughed to her mother-in-law. "I've never seen better beggars. Maybe this country makes them more courageous. I hope it does the same for me." She was feeling slightly less intimidated than she had two days ago, but the fear still bubbled inside. She knew it would not take much for it to surface.

Ida looked up from the campfire and saw a lone rider fast approaching from the northwest. At first she didn't recognize the visitor. Then as he came closer to camp, she looked up and saw the same incredible blue eyes that she had fallen in love with and her heart raced until she couldn't breathe. Josiah was dismounting and gathering Ida into his strong arms, overwhelming her with the smell and presence of him. The children stood by, big-eyed and fearful of this giant who was twirling mama until her feet flew around in circles. Then he turned to them and reached down to sweep them both into his arms as they kicked and screamed with terror. But Mama was laughing and her eyes sparkled with joy. "This is your daddy. Don't be frightened. He won't hurt you."

Then everyone was crowding together for hugs and handshakes of welcome.

"Mother! Frank! Wes! Owen! It's good to see you. How was the trip? I had to hold back from coming to meet you down the trail, but I decided it would be best to finish up a hauling job before I came, so we can pick up my supplies and head right over the mountain to the Eagle River. I've got so much to talk to you about."

Through Josiah's eyes their new land became one of magnificent opportunities. It was apparent that he was completely absorbed in this wild country with its extreme challenges. That night in their own tent, Ida shyly tried to explain her fears. Josiah laughed and replied that she'd soon get over the "Mountain Fears."

"I can't believe that people are actually afraid of these towering beauties," he chided. "Have you ever seen any sight more magnificent?" It takes strong men and women to tame this country, and I plan on being one of them."

Ida was mesmerized by his confidence and enthusiasm. The past two years melted away as she yielded to her husband's ardent caresses. "It's been a long time, little one. I've missed you so much." Ida's fears evaporated as she responded to the hands which could make her forget anything beyond their touch.

"I've missed you, too," she sighed.

Josiah's impatience to get over the mountain pass, which separated them from the Eagle River Valley, caused the family to speed up their preparations for the final leg of the trip. Supplies were cheaper in Buena Vista than in Leadville, so he made sure that they had a sufficient amount of flour, coffee, bacon, and other staples which would have to last them for some time because there were no stores or trading posts where they were going. Josiah was anxious to get settled so they could start planting the huge vegetable garden he envisioned. It would provide fresh produce for the bustling town of Red Cliff, as well as supplying a large portion of their winter diet.

The road north of Buena Vista continued through a narrow valley with the high range of mountains to the west, and a slightly lower range to the east. The Denver and Rio Grande Railroad tracks shared the middle of the valley with the old wagon road and the Arkansas River. Although the stream was not currently swift, it would soon become swollen from the snow melt in the high mountains. The wagon road meandered west of the railroad tracks for the most part, connecting to the various train stations which had been established along the route to Leadville.

The weak spring sun was high overhead at noon of the first day when the little caravan approached Riverside, the first station north of Buena Vista. There was nothing but an abandoned depot and an empty water tank, so the wagon rumbled on until they found a river access where the stock could be watered.

Ida was relieved to be stopping for the night. She felt the tightness in her muscles begin to loosen as she set about making up beds for the children. The sun was going down behind the tall peaks, and the blazing campfire felt very welcome. After Ida had tucked the children into their bedrolls, the adults sat by the fire and talked about their future in this land. "Those miners are going to always be needin' supplies. There'll be quick cash for good hunters, and I'll bet we could pull a good profit from sellin' our garden vegetables, too," said Josiah.

"That's something we can all help with, putting in a big garden. We just have to be sure to keep enough to feed all these hungry mouths," laughed Ida.

The fire crackled and sent glittering sparks into the cool night air. Josiah continued to talk about how all of this mining activity was bringing hordes of people into the area, and how they would need wood for the smelters and mine timbers, as well as for building homes, putting up telegraph poles and building flumes. Josiah was convinced that logging could be a rich source of income in the Eagle River Valley.

Ida looked at his face in the firelight and couldn't help being energized by her husband's enthusiasm. She could picture their future home where they would raise their family in the coming years –a place where they could settle down and stay. She daydreamed about the large log house they'd eventually build, the livestock they would butcher each fall, the big root cellar where she'd store the winter provisions. "It will be worth all the difficulty in getting there," she thought. "It will be a blessing to have Josiah home with us each day. The children and I need him so much."

The campfire was burning down into red hot embers. "Hey, where's my fiddle?" asked Josiah. "This is a good time for some foot stompin' music, don't you think?" The group collectively held their breath, waiting for one of them to summon the bravery to give an explanation.

"Son, I've got a bit of bad news for you," his mother replied. "The fiddle was laying too close to the campfire one night, and the side got singed. But I think it can be easily repaired," she hastily added. "It may have to be re-glued in some places."

"Who the hell was the idiot who left it too close to the fire?" Ida flinched at Josiah's outburst.

"I guess that'd have to be me," Frank replied. "I'm really sorry, Si. I know you set a great store on that fiddle, and I'll do whatever I can to fix it for you, but I'm not too good at that sort of thing. Maybe we could find someone in Leadville to fix it on our way through."

By this time Josiah had found the violin case and pulled the instrument from its velvet lined confines. "God damn it, Frank. You always were reckless with stuff, especially when it belonged to someone else. It looks like the whole top is loose, but maybe I can fix it when we get over the mountain. But you keep your hands off it from now on, Frank, you hear?"

The family heaved a sigh of relief, and silently thought that Frank had gotten off easy. At one time Josiah would have mopped the floor with him for such stupid behavior.

The next morning, they took up camp and set out for the second day's journey. To pass the time, Josiah told stories he had heard about some of the people and events in and around Leadville. One of the more interesting stories was of Horace and Augusta Tabor who came to the Cache Creek area from Kansas in 1860. Josiah's voice was tinged with awe as he described how this couple and their small baby had traveled over the same Trout Creek Pass from Colorado City in an ox-drawn covered wagon. But there had been no road in 1860 and trees needed to be chopped down in order to get through. Leaving the Cache Creek area after a short period of time, the Tabors then went north to California Gulch where they slaughtered the oxen, set up the wagon bed as a table, and Augusta started feeding the miners. From that humble beginning, the Tabors had risen to the highest prominence of Leadville society, thereby proving that anyone could strike it rich with hard work and a little luck. Josiah did not share the information that Horace Tabor's reputation had taken a dramatic downturn recently because of a highly publicized romance with an enchanting lady by the name of Elizabeth Doe. He didn't think his young, naive wife was ready for that sort of information about the residents of her new homeland.

They passed Balltown at the entrance to the Twin Lakes area and Ida heard about the luxurious Lakeside Hotel which graced the southwest bank of the lower lake. It boasted a dance pavilion, an ornate stable with fine riding horses, sleigh rides, ice skating, and many other features. There also were other resort residences scattered around the perimeters of the two lakes which had been built by the newly endowed mining barons from Leadville. Ida shook her head in disbelief. "Josiah, I do believe you are teasing me. Why it's not possible for there to be such luxury in the midst of this primitive country. We've seen very few places along the way that are much better than what we had back home. Are you sure about this?"

Her husband laughed as he assured her he was telling the truth. "Not only that, my dear, Leadville already has a telephone system. What do you make of that?" Ida couldn't comprehend a town, built at 10,000 feet, where snow often fell eight months out of twelve, having these accouterments. She'd have to see it to believe it.

They made camp the second night on the outskirts of Leadville, at Malta. Their sleep was interrupted by the sounds of the trains coming and going, as well as the freight wagons which seemed to run all night. The fifteen smelters belched sulfur-laden smoke into the air, causing a permanent gray fog over the entire area. The previous peace and tranquillity of the trip was replaced by the noisy, boisterous sounds of this burgeoning city and its outlying regions. Ida slept poorly, jumping awake with each new sound. When morning came she was more than ready to move on north to Tennessee Pass. She was secretly glad when Josiah decided not to take the time to stop in Leadville because they needed to get to the top of the pass by mid-afternoon.

As the wagon passed through the mud-bogged streets, she could see the teeming life on Harrison Avenue. The Tabor Opera House stood side by side with the Clarendon Hotel. Ida could see an upstairs ramp connecting the two buildings and wondered why in the world Mr. Tabor's patrons would need such an entrance. Across the street from the Opera House was the Saddle Rock Cafe. At this early hour of the morning it was crowded with a blend of miners, promoters, and other assorted citizens. Did these people ever get used to the awful din of this city? Her ears felt assaulted from all sides. Although there were saloons along Harrison Street, she was fully spared from seeing the multitude of saloons, gambling halls, and houses of ill repute off the main street. No one was quite sure exactly how many existed, but a rough estimate indicated there were at least forty and probably closer to one hundred houses operating in Leadville at that time. Ida's strict Methodist upbringing would have led her to believe that Josiah Herwick had brought her to the depths of degradation–indeed even Hell!

Ida was very relieved when they reached the outskirts of the city and turned northwest to Tennessee Pass. The sun was warm and bright. The road had dry patches of dirt on the higher ground but miserable bogs in the lower swales. The team struggled to plod through some of the worst ones, but they were still making good time. Although most of the snow was melted along the road, Ida could see that it was still fairly deep in hollows on the adjoining hillsides. The high mountains looked like they had been frosted with her mother's famous egg white frosting, and she wondered if the snow ever entirely left the peaks. A cold breeze reminded her that they were headed into an area which hadn't yet experienced springtime.

When the sun was high in the sky, Ida would dismount the mule and walk for a while. They traveled through a large park which would soon be beautiful with its deep green meadow grass and low growing brush. Although there were a few groves of trees, Ida could see that most had already been cut down. The stumps were sticking up as lone memorials to the greed of the fiery charcoal ovens which were burning continuously in order to supply the area smelters. An eastbound Rio Grande train was slowly making its way back to Leadville. It would return tomorrow with supplies for the track crew which was hard at work laying track toward Red Cliff. It was at Red Cliff that the family planned to arrive the following day.

As they traveled, Josiah pointed toward the west. "Ida, that there is the Mount of the Holy Cross. There's a snow field on the mountain that is shaped like a cross. Seems almost like it was planned, doesn't it?"

"Oh Josiah, what a lovely thought."

The slow but steady pace finally brought the little group down Iron Mountain into Red Cliff, and they shivered even in their heavier garments. The bustling town sat in a rocky bowl surrounded by mountains, except for a narrow rocky canyon entrance. They had passed the Rio Grande Railroad track crews coming down the pass and it appeared that the railroad would arrive in Red Cliff by the end of summer.

As they pulled into the town and forded the Eagle River, it looked to Ida as if every square foot of land had been used in the small area. Newer wooden buildings were built along the river which ran through the middle of the town. The Star, Southern, and Pacific Hotels, several stores, a barbershop, and Golding Clothiers were located near the water course. And, there were at least two saloons, which caused Ida to look contemptuous. Numerous smells assaulted her nose; wet earth, newly cut lumber, animal dung, and rotting garbage. Debris of various and sundry description floated down the river, and Ida averted her eyes so she couldn't identify them.

Josiah finally found a small clearing a short distance up Turkey Creek into which they could pull the wagon and unhitch the team for the night. Wes and Owen led the horses down to drink while the others started setting up camp and hastily built a blazing fire to take the chill off the night. As darkness descended, the sounds of the saloon patrons could be heard. If the town had churches, Ida had failed to see them on the way through town. She felt some trepidation about raising a family in such Godless surroundings, and she yearned for the known safety of the Nebraska and Kansas farming communities. She and Mother Herwick would have to work extra hard to give the children a good upbringing without proper churches and schools.

As she burrowed down into the bedroll to escape the night chill, she realized how exhausted she was. The air was so thin at this elevation that it seemed she had to gasp for each breath, and any exertion caused her heart to start racing. The Eagle River Valley was lower, with a better climate, and Ida was glad about that. She worried about Mother Herwick who had developed a serious cough back in Kansas, and she observed that the rarefied air wasn't helping her breathing.

"Come on everybody," Josiah said the next morning. "The sun'll be up soon. Let's get a move on. Sooner we get started, the sooner we get to the Eagle River Valley. We oughta be there by nightfall. Come on now." Josiah's excitement was enough to get them all moving.

Ida was still fatigued, but the thought of finally arriving at the land Josiah had chosen for them last fall lifted her spirits and her energy level. She said a quick prayer that no one else would claim it before they could get there.

Josiah took over the team for this stretch of the journey, while Frank, Wes, Owen and Ida rode the horses and mule. Susannah and the children stayed in the wagon for the switchbacks up Battle Mountain. As the wagon topped out on the rocky plateau that housed a settlement, Josiah stopped the team for a rest after the long hard pull, and Ida got her first look at this town setting on the top of the world. "Dear Lord, protect us!" she exclaimed as she looked toward the edge of the cliff a short distance away. She felt like she was being sucked toward that vast abyss whose bottom she couldn't even see. Her head was dizzy and she felt faint from fear. For the past seven days she had been afraid of the mountains looming over her, and now here she stood on the very brink of one! Ida felt her mother-in-law's reassuring hand on her back.

"Take a deep breath, Ida, and enjoy God's handiwork. Did you ever imagine such an extraordinary sight existed? Makes one feel a mite insignificant, doesn't it?"

As Ida responded to the soothing voice, she stilled her fears and struggled to stand up on the slanting land. She was terrified that she might fall down, and roll clear to the bottom of that yawning rock-solid crevice. Her steps were hesitant until she became more confident, but she held Birdella tightly by the hand so the child could not escape her grasp.

"What is the name of this town, Josiah?" she asked in a tremulous voice.

"This is Cleveland," he replied, "named in honor of Grover Cleveland, an up and coming democratic contender for the Presidency of the United States. In case you can't guess, this camp is overwhelmingly Democratic."

The camp was divided into two sections. The lower, more level one was named "Poverty Flats," while the other portion upon which they stood was perched on a steep hillside above the road. Ida was awestruck by the energy that it must take to build such dwellings and to work on such an incline. "How does one learn to walk on this mountainside?" she wondered.

After the horses had a chance to rest, Josiah started them west across the rocky ridge. A short distance away was another clump of houses, located toward the western edge of the plateau. Once again Ida saw all manner of buildings perched on the rocky out cropping, even down into the deep canyon. A structure was built on whatever space could be utilized. "Who could live in a place like this, hanging off the sides of cliffs?"

"It's mostly workers from the local mines, so they don't have to go back and forth to Red Cliff everyday," Josiah explained.

As they left the settlement, they curved around a gulch which shot straight down into the canyon. A small stream called Rock Creek ran across the road. Looking forward from the back of the wagon Ida couldn't see where the road continued, and she leaned out so she could get a better look. The resulting sight so astounded her that she was speechless. **There was no more road!!** Instead, a rocky path extended on around the hill, so narrow that a man couldn't stand beside a wagon without being in threat of falling over the edge. In addition, the trail slanted so drastically toward the cliff that she could not imagine how a wagon would stay on it.

Josiah yelled to the team and stopped on the last piece of moderately wide shelf road. "Everyone out," he said, "We've got some work to do in the next hour or so." Ida climbed from the wagon, clinging to the mountain side of the road while she helped her mother-in-law and Birdella down. She then lifted out the sleeping toddler, William, and stepped to the widest part of the road.

Josiah was issuing orders to his brothers as he unhitched the horses and started unloading the most important goods from the wagon. Ida, Susannah, and the children found an outcropping of rock to sit upon and watched the mysterious goings-on. Even the intrepid Susannah seemed to be daunted into a contemplative silence. In a half-hour the men had successfully accomplished unpacking much of the more fragile goods that Susannah and Ida had spent countless hours making sure were packed just so. When that was done, Josiah motioned for the brothers to help him remove the larger wheel from the right rear of the wagon, while he removed the smaller one on the front. With the wagon axle balanced on several large rocks, Josiah placed the larger wheel on the left hub, toward the cliff edge, while Wes and Owen put the smaller on the right side toward the hill. Then they repeated the procedure with the other two wheels. When they were finished, the wagon, with two big wheels on the down-hill side, sat more evenly on the sloping mountainside, and Ida had a faint hope that it might actually make it over that non-existent road. Josiah motioned for the men to hitch up the team. "Now folks, just sit back and wait. I should be back in several hours."

Before Ida could recover her senses, he had mounted onto the wagon seat and, flicking the reins over the team, started them around the curve of the hill and out of sight.

She started running after the wagon, yelling for Josiah to come back. Tears were streaming down her face from stark terror that she would never again see her husband alive. Wes ran after her and pulled her back to the group where she collapsed into Susannah's arms. Her mother-in-law said, "There, there, Ida. Si is very resourceful, and he's accustomed to these mountains. I'm sure he has often thought about this part of the trip and knows exactly what he needs to do."

Birdie and William watched their mother with big eyes. At the sight of her tears, they too started puckering up. "It's all right, darlings," she tearfully soothed them. "Mama's not hurt. See, my tears are all gone. It's going to be all right. Daddy will be back soon." As she gathered them to her breast she wanted to believe her own words, but all she could see in her mind was the wagon and its cargo laying at the bottom of that horribly deep canyon.

True to his word, Josiah was back in less than two hours, riding one of the horses, and leading the other. He, Wes, and Owen started packing the work horses with some of the goods. Then Si put a pack saddle on the sure-footed mule. To this he lashed a small open trunk on one side, and a boot box on the other. "Ida get some blankets to pad the bottom of these, will you?" As she searched for padding, Ida uncovered two very special possessions. Snatching them up she came back to the mule with some of Susannah's quilts. Josiah reached down and lifted Birdie into the trunk. Then he plucked William up and deposited him on the other side in the boot box. Handing the reins to Ida, he turned to pick his mother up and place her on the saddle horse. "All right now, let's start down. Take it easy, and stay to the inside of the path as much as possible. Frank, I'll watch out for Ida, and you take care of Mother. The Utes have been traveling this trail for many, many years. I don't see any of their bones in the canyon, do you? Wes, you and Owen stay here for the next load. I think we'll be able to get all of it in one more trip." He picked up the reins of the team and started down the mountain.

Ida's fear threatened to overwhelm her again, but she realized that she could not give in to it for the children's sake. Looking down, she realized that she was still holding her most prized possessions. Going to Birdie's side, she placed her mirror in the child's hands. "Hold on tight to this, darling. You'll want to see how pretty you are when we get to the bottom of the mountain." Going to the other side of the mule, she tucked a framed embroidered motto into the box beside William. "Dear Lord, let it be true. Please 'Bless Our Happy Home.'" Picking up the reins, she followed her husband down the mountain.

JUNE, 1881   THE EAGLE RIVER VALLEY, COLORADO

When the Herwicks arrived at their future home site just east of Buck Creek on the Eagle River, the job of hewing a home out of the wilderness became their primary concern. There were no houses to move into—not even a one-room cabin. The family continued to live in their tents for the bulk of the summer while Josiah and his brothers went to the hills to cut logs and snake them down to the valley floor. While Susannah tended the children, Ida hitched the old mule to a hand plow and dug up a large garden plot close to the river so they could easily irrigate the ground. Then she planted the precious seeds which had been brought from Kansas and commenced to wait for the bountiful crop a few months later.

The growth of the garden and the cabin were parallel that summer. As Josiah and his three brothers laid one log layer after another, Ida and Susannah were busy hoeing, watering, and harvesting. By mid July the Cabin was ready for the rafters to be put on, while the first of the tender lettuce, peas, new potatoes, and onions were ready to be eaten.

Ida discovered that the garden and cabins weren't the only things growing that summer. One morning in June she had awakened to run outside and retch by the side of the tent. "Oh no. It can't be. I can't be expecting so soon! There's so much to do before winter sets in, and besides I'm not ready for another baby. It takes most of my energy taking care of Birdie and William, or Widdum as Birdie calls him. What will I do with another one?"

At the end of another week she had resigned herself to the fact that she was indeed pregnant, and realized she would have to make the best of it. "It certainly doesn't take much for me to get that way," she ruefully thought as she rubbed her soon-to-be swollen belly.

Josiah seemed pleased about the news, but he was more preoccupied with all the building and hunting and didn't say much except that they could always use another good ranch-hand. Despite Ida's ambivalence regarding this new life within her, she physically felt very well and found that increasing size did not diminish her energy or enthusiasm for getting her household settled. "It must be an omen," she thought. "God is truly blessing our new home."

The walls of the cabin were up and ready for the two cross-layered sets of poles which would make up the foundation for the dirt roof. When it was available, canvas was used to lay on the logs before placing the heavy chunks of grassy sod. The Herwicks had to be content with a layer of smaller branches and twigs which would help catch some of the loose dirt before it cascaded down on the heads of the cabin's occupants. Once the first cabin was ready to inhabit, the men would move west several miles to erect a similar structure on the land Owen had picked for his homestead. Susannah, Frank and Wes would be living there with the youngest brother.

The cabins were done and the family began to move in by the end of August, just as the garden started sending forth its abundant crop. Everyone gorged on the fresh produce and declared it had never tasted so good. Wilted lettuce, sliced tomatoes, and green beans flavored with bacon rind now became part of the daily fare, along with the earlier creamed peas and new potatoes. "If we only had a cow and some chickens," proclaimed Susannah," we couldn't want for anything else."

While Ida was busy preparing their snug little cabin for the winter, Susannah was equally busy on the lower place. She knew that Frank would soon get tired and move on, but this would be a nice home for Owen, Wes, and her. And, the best part was that she and Ida were within spittin' distance of each other. The George Townsend place had prevented Josiah and Owen from settling on adjoining land, but they were less than two miles away as the crow flies, and often found time to visit each other two to three times each week.

By late fall of 1881 all members of the Herwick family were snugly ensconced in their cabins while the horses were stabled in the new barns. Everyone had worked hard to get everything completed before the first snow. Wes and Owen had put up a fair amount of wild hay for the horses. Josiah and Frank had gone on a hunting trip which netted four deer and one elk. The river ran right through their property with its prodigious supply of fish, and the small root cellar was over flowing with potatoes, pumpkins, carrots, beets, turnips, and other assorted bounty from the garden. Strong odors were emanating from a kraut barrel where the fermentation of the cabbage and salt mixture was rapidly taking place. It looked like the Herwick family would make it through the winter in fine shape.

As the days became shorter, and the frost came every night, Josiah went out on another hunting trip and returned with three deer. Ida had set aside the surplus food which they would not need, and she contributed this to the foodstuffs that her husband took to Red Cliff. He'd been able to trade for flour, sugar, coffee, and other staples they'd need during the next four or five months. Always in demand, the fresh produce and meat were enthusiastically bought before he could even unpack it from the horse's panniers. To his surprise and pleasure he came out with a few dollars more than he had to spend on their supplies.

When Josiah arrived home in the late afternoon, he discovered Ida and the children were gone. Assuming they had gone over to his mother's, he unloaded their provisions and started west with the remainder for his mother and brothers. In route to the ranch, he stopped at George Townsend's to make a deal for something that he had seen last week when he was visiting there. He knew it would thrill his mother.

The family stepped to the dooryard as Josiah rode up, and they started helping him unpack the provisions. Perched on the back of one horse was a wooden crate lashed to the pack saddle. Stepping closer in order to see the contents, Susannah started clapping her hands and laughing. "Si, where in the world did you get those chickens?" she asked. Pulling one rooster and two hens from the crate she started for the barn to make a nice little nesting place for the fowls. "As soon as the hens get over their fright, we are going to have some fried eggs!"

∾ The Rio Grande Railroad reached Rock Creek, northwest of Red Cliff, Colorado by March 10, 1882. The Belden Mine was shipping 50 tons of ore to Leadville every day.

∾ Marshall Sam Townsend was killed on the streets of Leadville on March 28, 1882. His killer was attorney Thomas Early, who had a grudge against Townsend. Sam's widow, Allie, and their six year old son, Sam Jr., moved to the Eagle River with Sam's brother George Townsend who had homesteaded on Beaver Creek in 1876 or 1877.

∾ Orion Daggett took up land on Gypsum Creek in the western part of the Eagle River Valley. He hunted game for the Leadville and Aspen markets. On one occasion, he brought back two wagon loads of elk from the Flat Top area.

∾ Josiah Herwick, Pierce Crane, and Thomas Campbell filed incorporation papers with the Secretary of State of Colorado for the Astor City and Grand River Toll Road Company. It was capitalized at $10,000 with 100 shares for $10 each.

∾ On September 18, 1882 a huge fire consumed most of the buildings on Water Street in Red Cliff, Colorado.

JANUARY, 1882   EAGLE RIVER VALLEY, COLORADO

The Eagle River Valley had few women inhabitants when the Herwicks arrived in 1881, and the closest doctor was in Red Cliff some twenty miles away. The lonely frontier life was made tolerable by Susannah's presence, and Ida thanked God for her every day. She was the one who helped bring Frederick, the first white child born on the Eagle River, into the world on January 29, 1882, while a winter storm raged outside the small cabin.

When Ida's pains had started late in the afternoon, Si had wrapped up

Birdie and Wid in heavy quilts and started out for his mother's place. Leaving the children with his brothers, he started back to his cabin with Susannah just as the first of the storm hit. By the time they had traveled the two miles, they were grateful for the dim glow of light in the window and hurried inside to the warmth of the cabin. By the next morning, Ida and her new baby boy, Fred, were snuggled down into the warm covers of the bed, while Susannah and Si sat close to the fire and listened to the wind howl outside.

Although constantly busy, their life had settled into a nice routine. The fall and winter days of 1881 and 1882 were spent doing all the house and outside chores necessary for their existence. The long nights were welcome after the exhausting days of summer, but the men were busy several hours each day just getting water and feed to the horses. Susannah fussed over her chickens, worrying that they would get too cold in the barn. She took warm water to them and made sure they were able to roost in the warmest part of the barn. In response, the hens still produced a few eggs each week, which seemed more precious than gold.

On clear days, the two families would travel to see each other, and it was during those times that Ida was eternally grateful to her mother-in-law for exercising such patience with the children. Susannah's experience as a school teacher was invaluable when it came to keeping the little ones occupied and giving Ida a welcome respite. The uncles were always welcome sights for Birdie and Wid who delighted in their attention.

Because Ida and Josiah's cabin was the first one encountered when coming down the valley, they occasionally had visitors who were fed and housed overnight, if necessary. Two men who arrived during a temporary thaw in February become the catalyst for an idea that had been germinating in Josiah's mind for some time. Although he had settled his whole family down on ground that was prime agriculture land, he was much more ambitious than just aspiring to have a productive ranch. During his travels over the Astor City Trail, he had thought about the possibility of creating a toll road company to improve the trail so more people could travel that route rather than the existing one over Belly-ache Mountain, which came into the valley miles west of their place. Pierce Crane and Thomas Campbell had been over the toll roads between Red Cliff and Leadville, and they commented how much revenue someone could derive from a relatively small amount of work. Ida remembered coming over the tortuous toll roads last summer and thinking that it was a sin to take money for the barely improved Ute trail.

As Josiah and the gentlemen discussed the possibility, Ida could see he was becoming more enthusiastic. "Just think, we could be right there collecting all the fares from those folks who are going to be pouring into this valley come summer. Now that the railroad has reached Rock Creek, all we'd have to do is blast away some of the rock face to make a wider road up there. And once we get off the mountain it will be clear sailin' down-valley. I hear tell there's gonna be more mining activity up Brush Creek come spring, and a guy was through here several weeks ago who plans on doing large scale hunting for the mining district."

By the time Crane and Campbell left for their western destination, firm plans had been made for Josiah to accompany them to Red Cliff on their trip back, where they could get someone to help them draw up the papers of incorporation which would have to be approved by Summit County and the State of Colorado. The application was signed on March 11, 1882. The Capital Stock was set at $10,000 with 100 shares at $10 each.

When Josiah returned, Ida could see he had become consumed by this recent scheme. He spent most of the long evenings discussing all of the plans he had for himself and his brothers, who seemed to be glad to be his disciples in this venture. He figured that Wes and Owen could keep the ranches going, while he and Frank started the road improvement as soon as the spring thaw hit. In the meantime, he'd make a trip to Red Cliff and try to scare up stockholders who could provide some funds to start the work. Ida finally brought him back to reality by informing him that she had used up the last bit of meat in the evening stew, and he'd better become the family hunter again if he wanted to have meat at every meal.

March brought another visitor to their valley, and this time it was a female. Allie Townsend had lost her policeman husband when he was gunned down on the streets of that Godless town of Leadville. This was a terrible tragedy for the woman who had also lost her lawman father in a gunfight several years before. She had no way of making a living for herself and her small son, so her brother-in-law, George, who had been in Leadville when the homicide occurred, brought her back to his ranch. Ida and Susannah were both sympathetic and loving friends for Allie during those first grief-stricken months. It became an established routine of stopping by whichever direction they were traveling, and the women formed a warm and loving bond. Sam Jr. was about six years old and was a welcome playmate for Birdie and Wid.

~ *Eagle County was formed from part of Summit County on February 11, 1883. The County seat was Red Cliff, Colorado. Garfield County was also formed on that date, with its county seat being the newly formed mining camp of Carbonate. On August 21, 1883, the Garfield County Seat was moved to Glenwood Springs, Colorado.*

~ *Fifteen hundred miners camped at the banks of the Colorado River, near Dotsero, Colorado during the spring of 1883. They were waiting for the snow to melt in the Carbonate area so they could start prospecting. When the snow did melt, the Colorado River became so high, the flimsy bridge was destroyed. Many of the disgruntled men turned back to the established mining camps in the Red Cliff and Leadville areas.*

AUGUST, 1883   EDWARDS, COLORADO

Susannah had taken Birdie, Wid, and Fred back to her place for the morning so Ida could concentrate on the thriving garden. And here she sat, crying in her rocker under the big shade tree. She recently suspected she was with child again, and the thought was anything but pleasant. The thought of having a baby every twelve to eighteen months caused her to panic, but what was a woman to do? She loved her husband, and she enjoyed being with him. The memory of his caressing hands caused a warm flush to spread throughout her body.

"It's not fair that I have to pay such a high price for a few special times," she sobbed. "Surely there must be something a person can do to keep from gettin' that way." But if there were, she didn't know about them, nor did her mother-in-law, who had also struggled with frequent pregnancies during her married life.

Ida thought lovingly about the older lady, and her brow furrowed with worry lines when she remembered Susannah's bout with lung fever during the early winter. Although she had recovered in a month or so, it seemed her lungs were further weakened from the illness. On several separate occasions, Ida had caught her mother-in-law surreptitiously spitting into a rag following a coughing fit. She'd never been able to see the contents because Susannah always made sure it was promptly burned, but Ida suspected that there may have been blood in the discharge. Ida knew she could do nothing but pray for Susannah to get better.

*T*he Herwick family's first year had been moderately successful in their mountain valley. Wes and Owen's mares had a couple of new colts in the spring, which would eventually contribute to the prosperity of the ranch. Susannah's two hens had hatched out some chicks which would seed a future flock. Josiah had not been as successful in finding stockholders for his toll road venture and had eventually gone back to his earlier plans of supplying the mining camps with food and timber. He and Frank were gone a good share of the week, either in the mountains or hauling to Red Cliff. Occasionally one of the Herwick men would run into someone who was willing to trade a range cow or two for something else. They had acquired a few head of cattle, along with a few more horses.

Susannah was ecstatic when Josiah came home from one of his trips leading a bony old milk cow. Once the animal had a chance to put a little weight on and was rested up from her trek into the mountains, she started giving a respectable amount of milk everyday. Ida and Susannah were delighted with this newest addition to their little colony. Not only would the children have fresh milk, but they'd also have butter, cream, and all the other wonderful dairy products.

Ida's garden had flourished during the summer, and she regularly sent produce into Red Cliff, as well as preserved as much as she could for their winter use. She felt a little like an industrious squirrel as she stocked the root cellar with bins of vegetables. Her only regret was that there were no fruit trees from which she could harvest apples, peaches and pears, but the wild berries were almost ripe on the hillsides, and she planned to spend several days harvesting as much of the fruit as possible. "I can just taste the berry jelly on a nice batch of biscuits," she thought. "That will be a treat for all of us."

One night Si and Frank left to go hunting so Ida and the children were alone. She could hear the coyotes howling up on the hill, and she shivered a little at the mournful sound. The children awoke and toddled over to crawl upon Ida's lap. As they snuggled their sleepy bodies into hers, she chided herself for the display of pity she'd shown when she realized she was pregnant again. "You're the luckiest woman in the world. You have three sound younguns, a man who takes good care of you, and a family who loves you. And here you were, bawling like a baby over something that's normal and natural. You're going to have children because that's God's plan. Be thankful that you aren't one of those poor ladies who can't have babies. You'd feel terrible if that happened. Squeezing the children tightly, she kissed them soundly before putting them back down on their bed and pulling the covers up to their chins.

DECEMBER, 1883   EDWARDS, COLORADO

All of Ida's years on the plains of Nebraska and Kansas had not prepared her for this amount of snow. She was accustomed to blizzards, but one steady storm after another was something else. It had started in the fall with very few days of let-up. Just before Christmas, their neighbors to the west, Orion Daggett, Henry Hernage and several other men had arrived at the Herwick homestead on horseback. They told the family they needed to get to Red Cliff for supplies but decided that the horses couldn't make it much further because the snow kept getting deeper as they came up the valley.

Ida invited them to share the Herwick's noon meal and maybe spend the night before turning back to their homes. Afterwards, while sitting around the fire, the men agreed they could probably travel the twenty-one miles to Red Cliff on snow shoes, but they wouldn't be able to carry enough supplies back to make it worth the effort.

"What about making a sled?" Josiah asked. "I've got some pieces of thin lumber, and we might be able to steam them enough to put a bend in one end so we could pull it through the snow. We could either lash the boards together with rawhide, or nail some wooden strips over the top. I've got a piece of beeswax that we could melt on the bottom. That should make it slick enough to slide."

As the men considered this idea, they became more convinced that it might work. "Let's see that wood, Si," said Orion. "I've used a sled a time or two to get some meat out when I've been hunting, but I've never had to haul it twenty-one miles. Do you suppose we can build it strong enough to hold together that long?"

"I don't know, Orion. I guess we'll just have to try. How bad do you need to get to Red Cliff?"

That seemed to clinch it for the men, and they set a good-sized kettle on the stove to boil water. The rest of the afternoon was spent joining, steaming, and bending the boards into a curve so they would glide over the snow instead of digging into it. Firm but gentle pressure was steadily exerted on the wood in order for the curvature to become permanent. Once the bend was complete, the boards were tied with wet rawhide to dry overnight by the fire. As it dried, the rawhide tightened up and kept a proper tension on the board.

After a hearty breakfast the next morning, they removed the rawhide, planed the rough edges down, and waxed the bottom. A trial run around the snow-covered yard proved that the sled would glide properly, whereupon the party set out for Red Cliff. They planned to spend the night there and come back the next day, if all went well. With two men pulling the loaded sled at one time, they should make good time, especially since it would be downhill all the way from Bell's Camp.

Ida rather crankily waved good-bye to the party. "I don't know why Josiah had to go, too," she complained to her mother-in-law who had ridden over to see how everyone was faring. "We have enough supplies to last for a few more months. Besides, he could have sent an order with Orion rather than going himself."

"I suspect that Si is starting to get cabin fever, and this was a good chance for him to get out and blow off some steam," Susannah replied. "I'm sure that by now you know your husband does not like being idle for very long. He will always look for an adventure. It seems he was born that way. I can recall that he was the one I had to watch the closest when he was young. He was the chance-taker who caused more than a few of my gray hairs." Ida smiled, but wished Josiah would lose some of his wanderlust.

Josiah and his friends made it back two days later, exhausted but happy because of their great adventure. They reported that other men were also coming into town from all over the region with their homemade sleds. Will Duplice was down from Gold Park, and he intended to haul 500 pounds of supplies back by himself. Ida could hear the admiration in the men's voices as they voiced the hope that he'd make it back in good shape. When the others had gone, Josiah surreptitiously slipped Ida a sack of sweet treats to hide for the children's Christmas. She realized that he might be an adventurer, but he also loved his family a great deal.

∾ The winter of 1884 was very severe. Over 80 feet of snow fell at Frisco, Colorado, just over the mountain from the Eagle River Valley. Red Cliff, Colorado, was snowed in on April 5, 1884. The newspaper editor, Warren, printed the weekly Shaft on wallpaper because he had run out of newsprint. Grain and hay were getting scarce. Snow was ten feet on the level.

∾ Thirty-one ranches were being cultivated in the Gypsum area, many having been settled by disgruntled miners who realized they could make a better living supplying hay, grains, and farm produce to the mining camps.

∾ A bridge was being built over the Eagle River at Gypsum. Bridges were also being built or re-built at Dotsero and the settlement of Castle.

∾ In 1884, Dr. Wallace DeBeque and three companions settled on ground at the eastern edge of the present DeBeque Canyon. Dr. DeBeque called this area Ravensbeque. He later settled three miles east of the original homestead and this settlement became DeBeque, Colorado.

∾ The first bridge over the Grand River at Glenwood Springs was taken out by high water in the spring of 1884.

MARCH 25, 1884 EDWARDS, COLORADO

January and February had brought more and more storms. There had been a few warm days which settled the snow into a rock-like hardness before the next deluge hit. Frank, Si, Wes, and Owen were kept busy almost everyday keeping the paths to the barn and woodpile cleared. The stack of firewood that had looked so big in the fall was diminishing at an astonishing rate, and Ida prayed that it would last long enough until a thaw occurred so the men could go down river for another load.

Ida's pregnancy was advancing, and she felt suffocated by both the close living quarters and the bulk of her body. Susannah kept Birdie and Wid at her place much of the time and occupied their attention with reading and numbers, but two-year-old Fred was easily bored. He required more patience than Ida felt she had at the present time, and she continually thanked God for the blessing of her mother-in-law who had such a soothing effect on every one.

As her time drew near, Ida was resigned to the fact that there would not be any outside help during this confinement. "I wish there was some way of taking part of the load off Mother Herwick. It's going to be hard on her to take care of the family and house while I'm down. I'll just have to get up sooner, so she won't be burdened any more than I can help."

If the weather was better she could probably count on a few of the neighbor women coming by to see what they could do. But, with this horrible snowy bombardment, they were holed up with their families, and you certainly couldn't blame them. She hadn't seen Allie Townsend much this winter, but she smiled as she thought that might have something to do with Allie being a bride. Everyone rejoiced when Allie and George had gone to Red Cliff in January to finally tie the knot. It had been obvious that George cared deeply for Allie, and once she recovered from the grieving for her husband, it became apparent to Allie as well.

Ida continued to be concerned about her mother-in-law's health. Susannah's cough had not gone away, and there were times when she seemed to be strangling from the intensity of the coughing fits. None of the home remedies seemed to help, and Ida sensed that the illness was much more serious than Susannah would have one believe. Since the weather had turned bad, the spells seemed to be worse. "If only the sun would come out and melt all this miserable snow so we could get outside for a few days and Mother could soak up some warmth. I'd love to take a deep breath of clean air. This cabin is not only about as big as a bear's den, it's startin' to smell like one, too!"

But the weather hadn't lessened. Storms continued to put down more white flakes every day or so. Ida woke up in the early hours of March 24th and laid there wondering if last night's snow had covered them completely. As she allowed her imagination to run wild with all sorts of horrible visions of being entombed, the first birth pain hit. By mid-morning the children and Josiah moved to the far corners of the cabin so the women could concentrate on the task at hand.

An insistent nuzzling at her breast woke Ida. Her mother-in-law was standing over her smiling. "Good mornin', my dear. How do you feel?"

"All right, I guess. Mercy, I must have slept soundly. Did the baby cry?"

"No, he was worn out, too. The rest did you both good. But it sure looks like he's hungry now."

As she guided the child's mouth to the swollen nipple, Ida looked up to see Josiah standing in the doorway, his heavy jacket coated with snow and ice crystals. "Good mornin', little one. How're you doin'?"

"I expect I've felt better. Is it still snowin'?" She turned to the small window, although she knew it was useless to look out. The snow had long ago covered the pane, creating a cave-like atmosphere in the cabin. "How are the stock?"

"Yea, it's still coming down and the horses are doing better than we are," Josiah replied. "All they have to do is stay in the barn and eat the hay we bring them. But I have to do all the shovelin' to get out to 'em. I figure it's about ten feet on the level now. We can't see the top of the barn any more, and all that's sticking out of the cabin is the chimney." Josiah touched the golden fuzz on the top of the baby's head. "What are we gonna name this one?"

Ida looked at the sleeping infant and wiped a drop of milk from his mouth. "I don't know. I've always been partial to the name Paul. It's a good Christian name. Would you mind?"

"Not if you've got your heart set on it. What about his middle name?"

"Well, let's see. Robert? Yes, that has a good ring. Paul Robert."

"Paul Robert it is then. When I can finally get to Red Cliff, I'll let the county clerk know about his birth since there wasn't a doctor to attend you. Here, let me take the little fellow so you can get some more rest."

Josiah took the baby into the next room and placed him in the cradle so the rest of the family could meet the newest member of the family. Birdie stood enthralled by the sight of her new baby brother. "Can I hold him, Grandma. Please, can I hold him?"

Her grandmother assured her that there would be plenty of time to hold him after he and Mama had a good rest. Five-year-old Wid looked pretty unimpressed with the red-faced infant, but two-year-old Fred was very interested. What was this thing who had taken him away from his Mama? Reaching into the cradle, he found Paul's tiny pink toe which he promptly pinched, causing the newborn to howl and Fred to be bodily ejected from the area by Daddy!

Ida thought to herself that she would try getting up for a while later on so that Mother could rest for a little while. But right now she'd just close her eyes for a few minutes. She was so tired, and she slept.

FALL, 1884   AVON AND EDWARDS, COLORADO

The sun was sinking into the hills earlier every day and the nights were getting cooler. Ida gathered up the children and herded them into the cabin before she shut the door against the chill. She looked longingly at her garden and knew that it could well be gone in the morning from the first frost. "Oh well, nothing lasts forever. We've got plenty stored up to get us through to next spring. I don't think I could get another smidgen of food into the root cellar. Even Mother's cellar is bulging. Those boys won't go hungry this winter."

Another bountiful year had passed. The children were healthy and growing. The Herwick brothers' stock was increasing to the extent that Owen and Wes decided they'd better apply for their stock brand before some of the cattle began disappearing. Susannah's little flock of chickens continued to grow, and Ida looked forward to the day that there would be enough so they could butcher a few. What a treat fried chicken would be!

Another member had been added to the family when Frank brought his new wife home. Ella Stevens, from Red Cliff, was a sweet, quiet young lady who obviously adored her tall, rangy husband. They had added a small lean-to to Susannah's cabin and settled in with the rest of the family. Ida and Susannah enjoyed having another woman around, and it was nice to have an extra pair of hands, especially since Susannah seemed to have so much less energy these days. Not that you'd ever catch her complaining. But Ida noticed that her mother-in-law seemed more content to sit quietly and tend the children while the two younger women did the harder chores.

And the chores seemed never-ending. Ida could not think of a single day when all of her tasks were completed. Tending the large garden, washing clothes, preserving food, making soap and candles, baking, cooking, taking care of the children's needs, and cleaning the cabin demanded every waking minute. Most nights she crawled into bed so tired that she wondered if she'd be able to get up the next morning. Josiah and Frank were away much of that summer, which was a relief to Ida. She didn't have to worry about getting a big meal on for a hungry husband. She could feed the children bread and milk and send them to bed, thereby gaining a precious hour to tend to some other chore.

"Josiah's being away saves my energy in other areas, too," she thought as she permitted herself a wicked little smile.

ﾟ The 1885 Special Census for Eagle County listed 1,423 residents. Of that
   number, 342 were female, many of them children. One hundred ten citizens
   were listed on the agricultural schedule.

ﾟ The "Tabor Grand Hotel" opened its doors to Leadville's visitors in 1885.

ﾟ The Battlement Mesa water rights were filed by early settlers to the area who
   could not file for homesteads because the land had not yet been surveyed.

MARCH 10, 1885   EDWARDS, COLORADO

"Please Mother, try to take a couple of sips of the mint tea. It will help your
throat to relax and maybe you can get some sleep." Ida forced the spoon into
Susannah's mouth, trying to get as much fluid as possible down the woman's
throat. "If that tastes good, maybe you'll be up to drinkin' a little bit of
broth later on. You haven't eaten enough to keep a small bird alive for
several days, and you know you have to preserve your strength so you can
get well."

Ida felt like she was chattering to the air. Her mother-in-law was not
responding as she usually did, and Ida was terror-stricken. "What more
should I be doing?" she worried. "I've used every remedy I know, and nothing seems to be working. Mother is so thin she looks translucent. I imagine
I could see right through her if I tried." Susannah dropped off to sleep, and
Ida roused herself to check on baby Paul. Thank heavens the day was warm
enough for Birdie, Wid, and Fred to be outside with their father and uncles.

The household work had come to a halt when Susannah had taken a
turn for the worse several days ago. Ida felt guilty because she had been so
busy that she failed to see how sick her mother-in-law really was. The four
children demanded much of her time, and perhaps she had not seen the
warning signals soon enough. Between nursing Paul and doing the bare
minimum of cooking for the family, Ida sat by Susannah's bedside. In the
beginning she believed her strength could forestall the progression of her
mother-in-law's illness, but now she sat because she could not stand being
away from her. It seemed that she drew comfort from Susannah, even now,
sick as she was. "Oh, Mother, don't leave me. I can't think what my life will
be like when you are gone. You have been the best mother a woman could
have. I've learned almost everything I know about life from you: patience,
your loving ways, your courage. I can never be half the woman you are, but
I pledge that I will try to be the best person possible. Just don't leave me yet.
I'm not ready. I have so much more to learn from you." Holding Susannah's

frail hand, Ida shed silent tears of sorrow for the parting that she sensed was coming very soon.

She thought of the past nine years since Susannah had welcomed her into the Herwick family that dreadful night when Ida had lost their first baby. The older woman had been there for her through times that Ida knew she could never have survived alone. Ida had found the courage to make the long wagon trip from Kansas to Colorado because she knew Susannah would be by her side, guiding and teaching her about all the things she had not yet experienced. It was impossible to think about what life would have been like without Susannah. It seemed they had always known each other. Her mother-in-law had taken the fifteen-year-old raw lump of a girl and helped to mold her into a strong, capable woman, wife and mother. "I owe so much to you, my dearest friend and teacher. I pray that I will never let you down."

Throughout the night Ida kept her bedside vigil. Susannah's four sons quietly came to check at intervals but soon left, feeling that somehow they were intruders on this most personal moment of separation. Frank's wife, Ella, hovered in the background wanting to help but knowing that little could be done to lessen the pain of this passing. She wisely decided to take charge of the meals and the children, allowing Ida to continue her lonely vigil. A cold dawn was breaking when Ida heard a faint sound from her mother-in-law. Susannah's eyes opened ever so slightly and she focused on Ida's face. Her fingers curled around Ida's hand and a loving smile came to her face. She closed her eyes and issued a drawn-out breath—almost a gentle sigh. And she was gone.

Ida continued to sit quietly by her mother-in-law's side, not wanting this moment to pass. In some inexplicable way she could feel Susannah's spirit merging with hers. While feeling grief, she also felt a quietness penetrating her being. It was as if Ida could hear Susannah's voice. "You are a strong person, Ida, my dear, who'll be called upon to show courage many times in your life. I have given you all the tools you'll need to carry on. Be a loving mother, but more importantly, be a loving woman. Let the Golden Rule be your guide. I will always be in your heart and mind when you need me."

Rising from her mother-in-law's side Ida went to prepare warm water for Susannah's bath. She didn't want anyone to see her until she was presentable. She combed the long silver hair and coiled it into the bun which Susannah had always worn. Slipping a clean dress onto the body, she arranged the hands upon her chest and bent over to kiss the cold lips for the last time. Only then did she slip out of the cabin and go to the family with the news of Susannah's death.

That day was a busy one for the men. While Ida kept her death watch and Ella tended the children, they prepared a coffin out of the available rough lumber but took pains to plane it down into a semblance of smooth grained wood. Josiah came to sit quietly by Ida. "Where do you think we should put Mother? I don't think that anyone has set up a cemetery around here. Shall we bury her on our place?"

"Josiah, I'd like her to be close to us, but I think I know where she would choose to rest. She and I used to take the children up the hill from her cabin to pick the pretty flowers in the springtime, and she always admired the view from there. I think she would be happy resting where she could keep an eye on the boys, and we can visit her often." Her husband looked at Ida and nodded. He went to talk to his brothers who also agreed this would be a proper place for their mother.

There were few neighbors living close to them but they were by the family's side to say farewell to Susannah Herwick. The small group sang "Rock of Ages" and, in the absence of a minister, they recited "The Lord's Prayer" as the coffin was lowered into the ground.

Walking down the hill to the cabin, Ida felt numb. "This can't be real. Mother isn't lying up there. She'll be waiting for me at the cabin like she has for so many years." She could see her husband and brothers-in-law furtively wiping away dampness on their cheeks, and she wondered why she could not cry. She hadn't shed a tear since yesterday when she had said her personal good-bye. She felt she was moving in an unreal world where everything had a confusing softness rather than the black and white reality of a week ago.

Ida put water on to boil for coffee when she reached the cabin so everyone could have some refreshment before leaving. The neighbor ladies had all brought a food offering which they helped Ida to lay out on the table. The men were down at the barn seemingly to look at the stock, but she knew there would probably be some hard pulls from the "medicinal jug" Josiah kept out there.

As the neighbors gathered Ida into their circle of feminine conversation, she felt befriended by those caring women. Their quiet, unpretentious talk about home and children gave her a sense of reality. She rocked Paul to sleep while listening to the conversation and was almost lulled to sleep herself. She couldn't remember how many hours she had slept in the past two days, but it couldn't have been much.

The men came trooping back into the cabin, filling every empty space. This was the signal for the women to start rounding up the children outside and preparing for the trip home. Before long the last wagon had pulled out of the yard, and the family spent a little time together before Si and Ida bundled up the children for the trip to their place. As they headed east, up the road, Ida turned to the hill where she could see the small bare patch of earth. How could she ever take up her life that had been shattered two days ago?

In the coming days, Ida held long conversations with her dead mother-in-law. She continued to communicate very much the same way she always had with Susannah and could hear in her mind answers to the questions she posed. "Let me think, Mother, what would you suggest we put on Birdie to draw out that nasty infection in her eye? Oh, that's right, I'll shred a potato poultice for her tonight. And I mustn't forget to brown some flour for Paul's diaper rash." Although she moved through the days doing her household and maternal chores, Ida was more often in another world with the woman whom she couldn't bear to give up.

As the spring days turned warmer, Ida often took the children up the hill to "visit with Granny." It gave her a sense of comfort to know that she was so close to the grave which overlooked the lower homestead. The spring flowers were pushing up around the site. Brilliant red Indian paint brush, white pasque flowers, and delicate sand lilies adorned the earth around the bare plot. "I hope they spread well this year so Mother will have blossoms next spring," Ida told the children as she showed them how to pluck the white lily and suck the one drop of sweet nectar from its long white tube.

As the demands of the summer season increased, Ida was not able to climb the hill as often, but she could look down-valley, wherever she was in her front yard, and see the east slope of the hillside. She'd send a silent prayer to Susannah in heaven that she'd continue looking out for them as she'd done in life.

At the end of June, a wagon went by late one evening. Josiah commented that more and more people were coming to the valley each year. There would soon be ranches sprouting up everywhere. As the family was stirring the next morning, a horse and its rider pulled up to the door. A gaunt, sorrowful-looking man dismounted and was invited into the cabin.

The man introduced himself as the owner of the wagon which had passed the house last evening. "Would you folks happen to know if there's a cemetery around here? Our little boy died last night, and my wife has her heart set on him being laid to rest in hallowed ground. I told her that it's doubtful such a thing exists, considering how new this country is, but she wants me to ask before we bury him by the roadside." It was obvious the man was having a difficult time controlling his tears.

As Josiah steered the man to a chair, Ida poured a steaming cup of coffee and pushed the plate of biscuits toward him. "You're right," said Josiah, "there is no regular cemetery around here yet, although I think there's a plot down around Brush Creek which is ten or fifteen miles west of here. The few people who've been killed have usually been buried at the site or taken to the Red Cliff Cemetery. But that's twenty-one miles back the way you've come, and I doubt you want to back track that distance. Maybe I can offer another possibility."

Josiah explained that his mother had died just a few months before and that she was buried up on the hill overlooking his brother's cabin. Going to the door he pointed out the piece of land, and told the fellow that he'd be welcome to lay his son to rest up there.

The man looked at the hill, bathed in the soft light of the early morning. "I reckon Mary would rather have her boy buried up there than along side the road," he replied. "I'll take you up on the offer Mr. Herwick, with my thanks for your kindness."

That morning, while they awaited the arrival of the migrating family, Ida helped Ella bustle around Owen's cabin preparing some food and drink. But she was silently talking to Susannah the whole time. "Mother, there's a little boy coming to keep you company. I hope you'll look after him in heaven the same way you took care of your grandchildren here on earth. Now, when I look up at your resting place, I won't feel so bad that you're all alone."

Ida realized the sorrow was still within her, but something was pushing her beyond the pain. She had to take charge now as the woman of the family. A lot of people depended on her, and she couldn't let them down. If she did that, she'd be letting Susannah down, and she mustn't let that happen.

With Susannah's death, Frank and Ella made a decision to leave the valley. It was almost like Frank couldn't bear to be reminded of her. They headed north up to the Middle Park area where they'd heard there were plentiful jobs on the big ranches there. Left on their own, Wes and Owen seemed at a loss to take care of themselves. Ida finally decided it would be easier for her to include them into her family circle rather than feel guilty about how they were faring.

The men started eating meals with her family, and eventually made a sleeping lean-to against the side of Ida and Si's cabin. They also seemed to be haunted by the memory of their mother's death and journeyed to the lower place only to tend the stock.

As more of their land was cleared for hay fields, the brothers made plans to increase the size of their small herd of cattle. Si had also applied for a stock brand. He was beginning to see the possibilities of raising horses as well as cattle and had made several trades for some decent stock.

By mid-year, Josiah had fifty-five acres cleared and plowed on his place, while Owen had thirty-five. The rest was in permanent pasture for their increasing stock. Si had dug a ditch from the small stream running through his place and was planning on planting alfalfa next spring. The place was prospering, although Ida could tell that Si hadn't given up his visions of making a fortune in other enterprises. Down-river a wagon road was being built to the end of the valley to accommodate the increased activity in that region, and he frequently discussed all sort of venture possibilities with visitors who stopped by their place while going east or west.

Orion Daggett, who had settled in the Gypsum area, was hauling wagon loads of elk and deer off the Flat Tops area for the voracious human hoards in the mining camps. He also occasionally hauled some freight over Cottonwood Pass to the new town of Glenwood Springs. The lower part of the valley was settling very fast, due to the easy access to game, the more moderate climate, and the availability of land. There were thirty-one ranches being cultivated in the Gypsum Valley, and more people coming every day. A bridge was even being constructed over the Eagle River in the town to replace the ferry that had been operating for several years.

With the influx of people, one of the most needed commodities was timber. It was needed for railroad ties, mine supports, fuel to burn, and finished lumber for the feverish building going on between there and Leadville. The forests in the vicinity of the mining camps were being rapidly depleted, and there would soon be an invasion into the hills surrounding the Eagle River Valley. This was not lost on Josiah Herwick, the inveterate promoter.

～ Construction of the Hagerman Tunnel between Leadville and the Frying Pan
River area was started in 1886 by the Midland Railroad Company, which was
competing with the Rio Grande Railroad to see which line would first reach
the mining town of Aspen, Colorado.

～ The wagon road from Russell Siding (later Wolcott) to Steamboat Springs was
completed. From 1886 to 1906, a six-horse Concord Coach left every day,
hauling passengers, mail and gold, bound for the North Park area.

JULY, 1886 AVON, COLORADO

"Oh please, Josiah, don't tell me we have to move. Isn't there some way we
can keep the ranch?" Ida tearfully beseeched her husband to tell her he was
just teasing. Surely he didn't mean to uproot her and the children from the
only home the youngest ones had known.

But his face told her he was very serious. "Look, Ida, we're never going
to get ahead here. The big money is being made in timber cuttin', bridge
buildin', and freightin'. If we can get some money out of this place we can
put that with the two hundred dollars Owen got for signing over the lower
place to John Terrell last fall, and maybe buy a small sawmill outfit. With
the three of us working hard next winter, we should have a fair amount of
timber cut come spring. It looks pretty sure that the new president of the
Rio Grande Railroad intends to start the line down-valley from Rock Creek,
and if that happens all hell is goin' to break loose for timber cutters. We've
started over before, we can do it again."

Ida knew it was useless to argue with her husband when he had that
stubborn set to his mouth. Si Herwick was usually an easy-going man, but
when he made up his German-Dutch mind, no one was going to shake
him–not his brothers, and certainly not her. She looked around her little
nest and wondered if he would ever get the wanderlust out of his blood.
There always seemed to be another valley, another bend in the river, another
mountain to explore. "How in the world am I going to manage this move
with no help?" She held her tears until he'd left the cabin, and then allowed
them to fall unrestrained.

"Isn't it enough that I'm taking care of the household work for all of us
and tending to the children? Now he wants me to pull up stakes and start all
over again."

Ida was thankful for Birdie who was almost nine and a real help to her.
And Wid was growing into a serious little fellow who had done a lot of the
weed pulling in the garden this summer. Birdie watched out for four-year-

old, impish Fred, and two-year-old Paul, which relieved Ida from her constant vigilance of them. With the cabin located on the river's edge, she lived in fear that the boys would toddle away and fall in.

Ida felt some guilt that Birdie was having to share the care of her younger siblings instead of going to school, but until someone was able to start a school, Ida taught her the best she could with the few books that Susannah had left them. There weren't yet enough children to warrant building a school in this area. Sam Townsend, Birdie, and Wid were the only ones old enough to go. Ida hoped that their new home would have an established school.

The next month sped by at a rapid pace, probably because Ida willed it to go by so slowly. Her usual tasks were interspersed by thoughts of what she'd need to prepare for the trip down valley if, God forbid, they really did move. The garden was burgeoning with its summer crop, and Ida plunged into her preserving chores, trying not to predict whether she'd have a big garden next year. Josiah said they'd probably settle down around Russell Camp because that would be the jumping-off place for the stage road, once it was completed. It would also be handy to Milk Creek, and some of the other tributaries draining south into the Eagle River, which possessed uncut stands of timber.

Josiah planned on getting settled before the first freeze, so he, Wes, and Owen could get their camp set up before other tree cutters got there. That way they'd have the best pick of the timbered ridges.

One day in the middle of August he came home from Booco's Camp upriver, and he was grinning ear to ear. "I've got a buyer for the place," he yelled triumphantly. Ida stopped in her tracks, dreading to hear the rest. "Will Nottingham is offering to pay me two hundred dollars for the section. That will give us four hundred dollars to put toward the saw mill. I'm going to ride down to Russell and look around for a place for us to live. That might take a little time because I hear that people are movin' into the town everyday. But surely there's an empty cabin somewhere around there. Will Nottingham and I agreed that we'd be out of here by the twentieth of September, so we've got about a month to get everything harvested and ready to move." With that he turned and hurriedly left the cabin to go tell Wes and Owen.

Even though Ida had tried to prepare herself for the news, she discovered that resignation had nothing to do with acceptance. She'd go with her husband because that's all she could do, but she didn't have to like it! This had been her home longer than any of the others, and she would sorely miss its comforts. She wondered how the children would handle the move. "They're young and this will probably be an adventure to them. I wish I could feel the same way."

One day in mid-September, a little caravan wound its way down the Eagle River. Ida and the little ones rode in the wagon with Wes. Si, Owen, Birdie, and Wid were mounted on the family horses. When they reached the Townsend place, Wes stopped the wagon so Ida and Allie could say good-bye. "I'll miss you, Ida," Allie said with tears in her eyes. "It seems you've always been here for me, and it'll be so lonesome without you." Ida hugged Allie and took a deep breath against the tears which were threatening to spill from her eyes. "Well, my friend, you'll just have to make George bring you down to see me. Josiah and the boys will be out in the hills most of the winter so we will have plenty of time to visit. Come stay overnight. That will give the children a chance to play and me a chance to hug little Charlotte."

Ida hurried back upon the wagon seat so that Allie couldn't see the pain she was feeling. "Well, Wes, we'd better be on our way if we're to get settled in before nightfall." As they moved down the road she was afraid to look back to see the solitary figure still waving to her.

When the family pulled into the little settlement of Russell that afternoon, Ida could see the place was bustling with activity. The supplies needed for the road construction were being brought in from Red Cliff, so there had been more than the usual number of wagons on the road coming west. Once they reached Russell, the wagons had to wait for their turn to be ferried across the Eagle River. A few buildings were already constructed on the north side, along with some corrals farther up the river.

As they waited their turn to be ferried across the river, Ida scanned the other bank, trying to locate the cabin Si said he'd secured for them. He'd warned her it wasn't as big as their present cabin, but he assured her she and the children would only have to stay there for the winter months while he and the brothers were out in the timber camp. Then, come spring, he'd have the money from their first sale, and they could find something that would be more comfortable. As usual, her husband was full of optimism about the possibilities.

"Josiah, point out the cabin to me. I can't see it." Her eyes followed the direction his index finger was pointing, but she still could see nothing against the bare hillside, except a pile of logs. Then her eyes focused again, and she exclaimed, "Josiah Lafayette Herwick, is that what you call a cabin?" The structure was positioned half in, half out of the hill and looked much more like her root cellar at home than it did a cabin for four adults and four children. The front portion was log, but the back was walled up with the sandstone rock that was laying all over the area. There were no trees. A few straggly sage bushes adorned the bare landscape, but all else had been trampled or eaten to the ground. She couldn't take her eyes from this scene of utter desolation which she watched in growing apprehension while the wagon was towed across on the ferry.

Josiah, to his credit, decided to keep still while Ida climbed down the wagon wheel and surveyed her new home. As she crossed the threshold and stepped in, the stench of rotting food assaulted her nostrils. The cabin had been used during the summer by a number of construction workers and various other men who were passing through Russell. It was obvious that none had cared about having anything other than a roof over their heads for a night because it looked like there were still remains of meals eaten two months ago. Tin cans littered the dirt floor and there were signs that rats had been feasting on the leftovers from each meal.

Holding her breath, Ida approached the back part of the cabin. A small room had been dug out of the hillside and rocked up with the same sandstone she'd seen outside. It was barely large enough to hold two beds, let alone any other furniture. The earthen floor of this room was littered with dirty old mattresses which the rats had also used for their comfort. The smell of rodent droppings and the lingering scent of unwashed bodies caused Ida to turn and run outside, retching. The men and children stood silently watching her, waiting for the explosion to occur. But it didn't happen.

Once she was able to catch her breath, Ida straightened herself up to the regal height of 5 foot 3 inches and looked at the speechless family members. "Josiah, I want you and Wes to pull everything out of that cabin but the cook stove. Owen find the pails and get to the river for some water. Then I want you to build a good hot fire, because *we* are going to need lots of boiling water and soap. Birdie, you look after Fred and Paul. Make sure you keep them away from the river. Wid, you climb up in the wagon and find the barrel with the soap, rags, and brushes. And find the broom while you're at it."

Was this determined, steely-eyed woman their mother, sister, wife? The silence was acute as they all jumped to her commands with mute obedience.

Ida seemed to enjoy the sight as the filthy household items became fodder for the blazing fire. Never had the men in her family considered doing anything that resembled women's work, but if their pride was wounded, they wisely kept it to themselves.

The little cabin had probably never displayed the cleanliness it did by the end of the day, although it was still a pathetic excuse for a proper house. Two of the bed frames had been set up in the back room with their clean mattresses, and two more had been placed along the walls in the front room. When the table and several benches were added, the room looked like it was wall to wall furnished! The old door, if indeed there had ever been one, was gone, so Ida hung one of her heaviest quilts over the gap. "Well," Ida commented, "it might be small, but at least it's clean. Now, if someone will get a fire started in that cook stove, I'll put a skillet of potatoes on and fry some meat. I imagine everyone has worked up an appetite."

∾ In August, 1887, a sheriff's posse from Glenwood Springs and a contingent of soldiers from Aspen went on a wild goose chase after Chief Colorow who was supposedly on the war path. In the melee, west of Meeker, the founder of Newcastle, Jasper Ward, was killed along with Lieutenant Folsom and a cowboy named "Curley."

∾ The Rio Grande Railroad pushed its railhead from Rock Creek to Russell Siding, Castle, Gypsum, and on to Glenwood Springs, Colorado, by October 5, 1887. The celebration banquet was held in the very hotel where the infamous gunman, Doc Holliday, lay dying. His death, on November 8, 1887, heralded a new era in which the wild and wicked west was being tamed.

∾ The Midland Railroad, via Hagerman Pass and the Frying Pan River, reached Glenwood Springs on December 12, 1887

MARCH, 1887   RUSSELL SETTLEMENT, COLORADO

A draft of wind coming down the chimney caused the fire in the stove to sputter and smoke. "It looks like another storm is moving in," Ida said as she ladled out the children's cornmeal mush. "I think we'd better walk over to the store this morning to get a few supplies in case it's a bad one. The walk will do us all good. We've been holed up in this place too long. Don't dawdle now, children."

An hour later the family members were all bundled up and trooping through the foot deep snow to the tent and lumber store which had been thrown up a few months before.

This was a company settlement, owned by the Eagle River Mercantile and Forwarding Company. As such, the store carried mostly items needed by the road construction crews, but that wasn't a problem for Ida, who did not have the means to buy anything other than the bare essentials now. The equipping of the sawmill camp had taken most of the family's ready cash. By the time the Herwick brothers had purchased the necessary saws, axes, and other sawyer equipment, plus the food and camp items, most of the money was gone. Ida had been left with just enough to get her and the children through the winter, if it didn't last too much longer.

It seemed to her that Josiah and his brothers had been gone for years. One winter day folded into another, until Ida really couldn't say just what day it was. She reminded herself that she really should keep track of the current date, although she'd be at a loss to say why. Her world had shrunk to the four walls of this miserable cabin and her four children. Four and a half with the baby due in May. It seemed the only thing that punctuated the awful sameness was the terror-filled nights when she stayed awake listening to the wolves and coyotes nosing around the blanket covered door, looking for food. On those nights, she would keep the fire blazing while she sat with an old rifle across her lap. Perhaps it was the smell of humans, whatever the case, not one animal came through the blanketed opening. Each morning Ida would utter a prayer of thanksgiving that her children had been spared one more time.

The small supply of meat, which Josiah had left, was almost gone and she was rationing out small portions everyday. Most of the daily fare consisted of the cornmeal mush with canned milk and soups made from the small bits of meat and the remainder of her garden vegetables which she'd preserved last summer. That, combined with her bread and biscuits, kept the children fed. She didn't have an appetite, so it really didn't matter much what she ate. This pregnancy had been a very difficult one. She had been sick to her stomach most of the time. It was just as well that it was wintertime with little demand for physical exertion because she feared she would not be up to anything more than the slightest effort.

As they neared the tent store, a figure approached them. "Good morning, Mrs. Herwick. How you be today? Lands sake, you'd better start eatin' more. Y'all skinny as a rail. That youngun you 'bout to have is gonna need to be fattened up if he's gonna be healthy."

Ida looked warmly at the large black woman who so presumptuously confronted her. "Good morning to you, too, Miss Rose. You're right, I know I should eat more, but I've been poorly with this one. I just can't seem to keep anything down. I've tried all the remedies that I know of, and nothing to seems to work."

"I bet I've got somethin' that'll help. Yes sir, old Rose knows just what will fix you up. Ginger and wild yam sure takes the misery out of women in the family way, and I'll be over this evening, after I deliver all the laundry. You just rest and take care of those younguns. Everythin' gonna be okay." She turned and hurried away before Ida could respond.

"Mama, why is Rose so dark?" little Fred asked. Ida sighed as she thought about how to respond to his question. The children had not been exposed to people of various races, and it was expected that he would be curious about people who didn't look like him. But did he have to be so open about it? Birdie and Wid would never think of asking such embarrassing questions, but Fred was another matter. He was an inquisitive child who didn't hesitate to ask for information about things he didn't understand and to make comments at the most inopportune times. Ida had tried to tell him it wasn't polite to discuss certain things in public, whereupon Fred looked at her and simply asked why.

"Well, Fred, the Lord made people in lots of different colors. The Negro people have dark skin, Indians have red skin, and Chinese people have yellow skin. It depends on what country they are from."

"But Mama Rose is from here, so why is she dark and we ain't?" Thinking to divert him, Ida said, "Aren't Fred, not 'ain't.' We'll talk more about that later on. Right now, let's hurry to the store. I'm getting cold, how about you?" Grabbing his hand, she quickened her step.

There were a few men in the store when the little group arrived. Most were surrounding the pot-bellied stove which was positioned in the center of the room. "Good morning Mr. Hughes," Ida greeted the store keeper. "I need five cans of milk and ten pounds of flour. I'd appreciate your putting the flour into two five-pound sacks so the children can help me carry it back home. I guess I'd better have a pound of sugar, too, and that should do it."

She could see the children eyeing the big glass candy jar on the counter, and she thought how good they were, and how little they asked for. "I guess we'd better have four pieces of the hard candy, too." The youngsters smiled and eagerly examined the jar which Mr. Hughes held out to them. Each one selected their choice and happily popped the hard sweet ball into their mouth. "I guess four pennies aren't going to spell the difference between life and death," Ida argued to herself as the five of them divided up the packages and started their walk home.

True to her word, Miss Rose stopped at their cabin later that afternoon with her herbal remedy. Ida was grateful to her for her kindness and used the mixture exactly as ordered. Unfortunately it did little to help her queasiness, and Ida still had to force food down each day.

MAY 9, 1887   RUSSELL SETTLEMENT, COLORADO

The ankle-deep mud had finally dried out around the cabin so the children could all go out to play in the sunshine. Ida sat on a bench and watched them. April had been miserable with the spring thaw. She thought she had never seen such a sticky mess. The oozing reddish-brown earth clung to everything, and the task of keeping the cabin swept became a monumental one. For the past month, Ida had seen wagons and horses slogging through the hub-deep muck in the road and it was good to see that traffic was moving much better. That meant that Josiah and the boys would soon be able to get all the railroad ties moved which they had stockpiled up on Milk Creek. The job of timber cutting was carried out in the winter, but the logs couldn't be moved down the mountain until the road bed ceased being a bog.

The Herwick brothers had been fortunate to get a railroad tie contract for the tracks being built down from Rock Creek. The contractor was offering twelve cents a tie delivered. The three men had been able to cut and flat shape one side of 2,800 ties throughout the winter months and were just waiting for the hauler to come get them.

They'd come down the mountain just before the big thaw to find things were not well with Ida and the children. Her strength was depleted from nausea and the poor food intake, and Josiah was genuinely concerned for her welfare. The household had used up the last piece of meat, so Wes and Owen went back into the hills to do some hunting. Game was getting scarce, so they all hoped they would get lucky. The years of slaughter for the mining camps were taking their toll.

Josiah stayed with his family and sent word to Dr. Evens in Red Cliff that he needed to stop by on his rounds down valley. He put Ida to bed and took charge of his young family with Birdie's assistance. Ida's guilt about being taken care of was outweighed by her illness. She slept for twenty-four hours, only waking up to take small sips of broth from Josiah's hands, and then closing her eyes again. When the doctor arrived two days later, she was feeling some improved but still very weak from malnourishment. After his examination, Dr. Evens motioned Josiah outside to tell him the serious news. Ida's condition had left her in a very weakened state, from which she would probably recover. But the doctor was concerned about the physical condition of the unborn child. It had possibly been affected by the lack of food, but there was no way to determine to what extent the baby might be damaged. They would just have to wait until its birth. He sternly warned Josiah that there was much that could be done for his wife in the month before her expected delivery. He left some liquid medication which was to be given in drops to her several times each day. The medicine would help reduce the nausea, and she was to be fed as much, and as often as she could eat. She needed to get some fat on her bones before the delivery, for her sake, as well as that of the baby. After some rest, medication and good food, she was feeling much better, and the warm spring weather helped, too.

As she sat under the warm sunlight, she felt the first twinge of labor. Ida knew that she'd better quickly make some arrangements, in case the labor was as short as it usually was. She sent Wid to the general store to fetch Josiah, who came hurrying back to the cabin. Ida had already started gathering the necessary items needed for delivery, and she asked him to go warn Miss Rose that she might be needing her sometime today. "I'll send word to Doc Evens, too," Josiah said as he left for the settlement. "Maybe if we're lucky, he's already in the area."

By evening, the tiny, red mite, who was to be called Collins Owen Herwick, arrived in the world. Both Miss Rose and Dr. Evens were with Ida during the delivery, and they shared a long sad glance as they examined the child. It was apparent that this little fellow would have a real struggle to survive. He was severely underweight, looking more like a tiny gnome than a baby. As Dr. Evens applied his stethoscope to the chest, he could hear serious heart murmurs and the respiration was rapid. Weak mewing sounds came from the infant as Miss Rose bathed and wrapped the skinny little body for presentation to his mama. Ida was exhausted from the day-long ordeal but very anxious to see her new baby. "Is he all right, Dr. Evens? Tell me—is he healthy?" She could see by the doctor's serious expression that something was not right. It was the very thing she had been worrying about for so long.

"I won't lie to you, Mrs. Herwick. The baby is very sick. Maybe he'll pull out of it, but I can't give you much hope. It sounds to me as if his heart is severely damaged. There really isn't much we can do except wait and see if he grows out of the condition. If you're a praying woman, I suggest you do a lot of that from now on."

"God won't let this child suffer because of the sins of his mother," Ida said under her breath as she cuddled the tiny bundle to her breast. "He'll get better, Doctor. I'll take such good care of him that he'll grow up healthy and strong. Just you wait and see!"

AUGUST 12, 1887

The ever present breeze blowing over the little mesa helped to dry the perspiration of the people gathered around the open grave in the Edwards Cemetery. Many of the friends who had stood there with Ida two years ago when they buried Susannah, were with her now. Josiah stood with his arm bracing her back as the tiny casket was lowered into the grave. She thought she would never again feel such wrenching pain as when the first shovel of dirt was thrown upon the wooden box. Her friends gathered around to draw her away from the scene and help her mount the wagon which would take them all down to the Townsend Ranch. Allie and the other ladies had prepared a lunch for everyone before they departed for their various homes. The Herwick family would be going back down to the Russell Settlement today, and it seemed to Ida that she had been away for a long time, although, in fact, it had only been three days since she and Josiah had made the decision to take the baby by train to Red Cliff. The infant's breathing was becoming much more labored and his lips, fingers, and toes were constantly blue. He was becoming too weak to suckle, which hastened the worsening of his physical condition. Ida knew, but was unwilling to believe, that her son was near death, and it was her insistence that finally convinced Josiah to take them to Red Cliff.

If it had been any other occasion, Ida would have enjoyed her first train ride up valley. The railroad had reached Russell Siding just a few days before, and they were among the first passengers to journey to Red Cliff. But, her mind was consumed by worry and guilt about her baby. She had not been able to rid herself of the thought that she had created this problem by her illness and malnourishment. Ida's life for the past three months had been devoted to making baby Collins well. Even on the last day when it had become apparent that he would be dying soon, she desperately searched for another solution.

When Dr. Evens examined the infant, he just shook his head. Placing the baby back into Ida's arms, he told the parents that he believed Collins wouldn't last through the night. He guided them into a spare room in his office where there was a bed and several chairs. He instructed his nurse to help make them as comfortable as possible while he attended to the rest of his patients. Late in the evening the little soul ceased breathing as Ida held him, and Josiah held them both. How could such a little babe, here such a short time, carve such a deep hole in their hearts?

After the funeral and dinner at the Townsends, Ida, Josiah and the family started down valley to their home. Passing south of the cemetery on the mesa, Ida felt that a piece of her heart had frozen. How could she accept the fact that her tiny little boy was lying under six feet of dirt up there? The worst part was knowing that it was probably her fault that he died. If only she'd taken better care of herself, this wouldn't have happened. She felt like screaming but took a deep breath and restrained herself. No matter how sad it was to say good-bye to other loved ones, nothing could compare to the misery of letting your own child go. She doubted that she would ever again feel any deeper agony than she was experiencing at that moment.

part three

1888-1898

∾ Dotsero and Gypsum, Colorado, each had fifty residents in 1888.

∾ The Avon School, first in the Eagle River Valley, was built in 1888.

∾ In 1888 the Denver and Rio Grande Railroad reached Newcastle, Colorado.

∾ The Grass Valley Land, Loan, and Irrigation Company was formed between Ferguson and Rifle, Colorado in 1888.;

MARCH, 1888   CANYON OF THE GRAND

The huffing and puffing of the narrow gauge engine, called the "Little Giant," spewed forth black smoke and cinders as it clickety-clacked over the newly laid track to Glenwood Springs. The children were enthralled by this new experience. Imagine going over thirty miles an hour! It was a far cry from anything they had seen before, and they were too excited to sit down and be quiet. Ida finally allowed them to move around the car and visit with the other passengers as long as they were polite. She really didn't have the energy to keep them contained. She was five months pregnant and tired out from all the preparations for the trip. It was a treat for her to just sit and rest. Birdie was keeping watch on little Paulie, but no one could contain Fred who was striking up conversations with anyone who would talk to him. He was, as usual, full of curiosity about his fellow travelers and not reluctant to ask all sorts of questions.

Josiah would be meeting her and the children in Glenwood Springs, where he was hauling the last of the ties he and his brothers had cut during the winter. The Denver and Rio Grande had blasted a rail bed through the solid cliffs of the rock-walled canyon and entered Glenwood Springs in October. The Colorado Midland Railroad, due to arrive sometime in December, 1887, had lost in its race to beat the Rio Grande. The D&RG tracks were now being laid close to the coal mining town of Newcastle, and the demand for the wooden ties continued, but Josiah wouldn't be able to furnish them. He had been fortunate to get another contract for ties to be delivered down the Grand River Canyon, which had kept him and the brothers busy for the winter. But then the railroad had gone too far down valley for him to supply the contract from the Eagle River Country.

After the first of the year, Josiah's sister, Sarah, had written to the family. She and her husband, Will Huntley, had been living on Battlement Mesa, south of the town of Parachute for several years while Will constructed the Huntley irrigation ditch. Through several mail exchanges, Sarah told her brother about the many opportunities in her area which were opening up to farming and ranching, as well as the railroad. She told Josiah that they were living in a snug little cabin on Battlement Mesa and Will thought he could get Josiah and his brothers work helping to build or enlarge some of the ditches, if they wanted to come further west.

People had started arriving to the area shortly after the Ute Indians had been removed to their new reservation in September, 1881. The former reservation was officially declared public lands the following August, although pre-emptions could not yet be filed because the lands hadn't been surveyed. The pioneers were anxious to settle on the most desirable locations, and they went about building dugouts or cabins, digging ditches, and making other improvements, although the properties weren't technically theirs.

Josiah knew that for the land from Glenwood Springs and west to be arable, a web of irrigation canals would have to be dug. He figured that he could make good money working for the irrigation outfits, and then when the water was available, he could get a piece of land and do his own farming. He felt sure his family's future was down valley.

Ida, growing accustomed to her husband's wanderlust, had made no complaint against this move. Her sister-in-law's letters indicated that the climate was more moderate than that up country. And, it would be nice to see Sarah and her family. She didn't know her very well, but the few times they'd met, her sister-in-law seemed to be a very loving woman, and Ida was certainly starved for some female company. Perhaps the best piece of news was that Battlement Mesa had its very own medical doctor, C.L. Hayward.

The doctor and his wife were a welcome addition to the small rural community located so far from any type of medical help. Ida looked forward to having a physician close by for the coming baby, due in July. She had taken much better care of herself during this pregnancy, but there was still the fear that the child would also be damaged in some way. So it was that the Herwick clan prepared for their move some eighty miles west. They had pitifully few belongings, all of which had been brought with them on the train. The remainder of their things had gone with Josiah and the brothers when they left with the load of ties.

As the train exited the tunnel and rounded the last curve into Glenwood Springs, Ida could see that construction was occurring at a steady pace. The town, snuggled into a triangle of ground between the Grand and Roaring Fork Rivers, was a bustling settlement of 2,500 or more people. Steam was rising from both banks of the Grand River, and she remembered hearing that the area hot springs were very healing. A huge hotel and spa were being planned in the near future for all the newly wealthy miners and investors from Leadville and Aspen who sought rest and recreation. A brick bath house with separate facilities had already been constructed on the north side of the river, where males and females could soak in the therapeutic waters for twenty-five cents.

Josiah, Wes, and Owen were waiting when the train pulled into the station. The children were bubbling over with information about their experience, and they pranced up the muddy street in front of the adults, taking in all the sights and sounds of this lively town. Fred and Paul had never seen so many people or so much activity in their young, isolated lives.

Josiah led them to the Inter-Ocean Hotel on Cooper Avenue, which was clean but much cheaper than the Glenwood and Barlow Hotels. Once again the children were awed by the size of the two-story building, which had rooms for forty guests. Fred's wonderment even rendered him silent for a few minutes. Ida was thankful for the lull.

The next morning, the family walked to the livery stable and mounted the freight wagon which had been provisioned for their trip fifty miles down the valley. "This might take longer, depending on how deep the mud is," Josiah said. "I figure it will take most of the day to get to New Castle. Tomorrow we should spend the night at Rifle, and, with luck and dry roads we should be at Parachute day after tomorrow." Ida, Birdie, Fred, and Paul rode in the wagon with Josiah, while young Wid and his two uncles trailed along on their horses.

Despite the jouncing around in the heavy freight wagon, Ida found herself enjoying the trip. Just a few miles out of Glenwood Springs, they crossed Mitchell Creek and then entered the infamous "Hell's Canyon" which had been such a barrier until 1886. Huge red slabs of sandstone had extended into the river-bed, blocking all access into the canyon. Before tons of dynamite had blasted a narrow passage through it, travelers had to go over the Flat Tops, to the north, or Divide Creek, to the south, in order to get to the new county seat, unless they were willing to walk or ride through the Grand River in certain places. Ida admired the beauty of the sheer red cliffs, although she still felt some the old fear of being engulfed by these dangerous pinnacles.

Once past the rocky canyon, they encountered flatter, but much muddier land where the four horses struggled to pull the heavily-laden wagon. When they finally pulled into New Castle in the late afternoon, the team was exhausted from their day's work, and Ida was glad to be rid of the constant bouncing around, which was making her back ache something terrible.

The streets of the little coal mining town were crowded with men leaving their work shift in the dangerous, gas-filled mines surrounding the town. Ida heard foreign languages being spoken as the men passed by. It was difficult to tell their national origin because they all looked alike with black encrusted faces, but Ida guessed that many might be Italian. The cottages and businesses were crowded into the narrow valley and continued up the hillside as far as it was possible to build. Ida was dismayed to see that the bustling business district of New Castle included twenty-two saloons where the miners could spend their few evening hours. Adding to the hubbub of the town was the new railroad which had reached New Castle and was busily engaged in hauling coal eastward to Leadville.

After a welcome night's rest, their journey continued with the team slogging through the hub-deep mud between New Castle and a town called Silt. They had passed the crews busily laying railroad track toward the small settlement. Continuing west, the Herwick family passed through Cactus Valley where the Grass Valley Land and Water Corporation hoped to be soon diverting water to thousands of arid acres. The only homesteads they saw were located along the banks of the Grand River where water could be gotten to the crops. In mid afternoon, they encountered a homestead with a blacksmith shop and small store. There was also a ferry spanning the Grand River to another homestead on the south side. A mile further west was a stage stop located at the base of a bare hill. "I don't think we'll stop, 'cause it shouldn't be much longer to Maxfield's Ranch. We need to find a place to camp and get the team taken care of. They've had a hard haul today, and it looks like they have another pull coming up," said Josiah.

Josiah directed the horses onto the road which wound its way up a steep, bare gulch to the top. The gummy mud stuck to the wheels, making the climb even more difficult for the animals. But after a brief, hard pull they topped out on Graham Mesa and started down another winding road to the bottom lands.

Maxfield's Ranch was located on the east side of Rifle Creek north of where it flowed into the Grand River. A log and adobe structure, it was surrounded by a variety of buildings, most of them barns and corrals maintained for the stage operating between Meeker to the north, Grand Junction to the west, and Glenwood Springs to the east. Other ranches, adjacent to the Maxfield place, could be seen from the top of Graham Mesa. Josiah drove the team to the forks of Rifle Creek and the Grand River to a small dug-out. A thin, almost emaciated, man came to meet them.

"Howdy, Mister, my name's Josiah Herwick, better known as Si. Me and my family are on our way down river to Parachute, and I wonder if you'd mind us finding a spot beside the creek to camp tonight."

"Pleased to meet you, Si. I'm John O'Brien. You're welcome to find a place to unhitch for the night, and you're welcome to share my quarters, too, if you'd like. I'm afraid the accommodations aren't much, but they might beat a tent or the ground. This must be your wife. How do you do, Mrs. Herwick."

Ida painfully crawled down over the wagon wheel. Her back hurt from the constant adjustments she'd made to the swaying and bouncing of the wagon, and her belly was slightly cramping. Disregarding the pain, she smiled and thanked Mr. O'Brien. "Thank you for your kind offer. I'm afraid I can't repay your kindness with much more than an invitation to share our meal, but I'd be right happy if you'd join us."

"Mrs. Herwick, an invitation to a home-cooked meal is never a small thing, and I'd be glad to eat supper with you. Please, come inside and tell me what you need. I apologize for the scarcity of my supplies. I don't do much fixing for myself. I teach school during the summer months in exchange for my room and board, and the rest of the time I try to do work for my keep. You've just caught me at home for a few days, which I guess is lucky for both of us."

The next morning a more refreshed Ida climbed aboard the tall wagon and looked eagerly west to her new home. It would be good to arrive and get acquainted with her sister-in-law before the end of the next day. She really had no idea of what the accommodations would be, but she knew that anything with a roof would be a blessing.

Leaving Rifle Creek, the small caravan followed the Grand River on its westerly course. The first five miles were through relatively flat, arid land, dotted with sagebrush, greasewood, and cactus. Several gullies had to be crossed, but the mud was drying out, and the team had less trouble pulling the heavy wagon.

Reaching Webster Hill, the team leaned into their collars as they started up the steep eastern slope. Mr. O'Brien had warned them that the hill was dangerous when muddy, and Ida was grateful that they didn't have that problem to contend with as well as the normal challenge of the winding trail. She shuddered slightly when she saw some debris at the bottom of one of the switchbacks which looked like remnants of a wagon. They at last emerged from the last curve and started a gentler descent to the bottom. Previous travelers going through while the road was muddy, had left deep ruts in the route, which provided bone jarring bumps when the wagon wheels went over them.

"Maybe when more people move into the area, the roads will be better. I don't know though, some folks say they won't work on the roads until they see what happens when the railroad finally gets laid clear into Grand Junction," Ida mused.

"I don't believe the day will ever come when the train takes the place of good roads," Josiah replied. "There's no way the railroad can do anything but supply the places along the tracks. Why, just look at this country. You've got all these mesas and creeks where there are homesteads. They have to get to town and, in order to do that, they need roads and bridges. I think, Ida, that road and bridge construction would be a good business to be in. With some good teams, a few men could scrape out a road in no time. And the best part is that we'd be contracting with Garfield County instead of trying to raise capital for a private toll road like we did up-country. Maybe I'll look into that when we get to Parachute. If I can build reservoirs and ditches, I can also learn to build roads and bridges."

Ida was less than impressed by her husband's optimism and enthusiasm, and she wished she'd never said anything about the roads. Thus far their marriage hadn't often been a very prosperous one. Everything depended on Josiah's work or lack of it. "It's chicken one day and feathers the next," she ruefully thought as she pondered what it would be like for him to have steady work so they could put down roots in one place. Maybe this was the opportunity he needed. She'd pray that it was, for her family's sake.

The day seemed never-ending as the Herwicks plodded through the barren landscape. Ida had never seen anything more desolate, and she was beginning to wonder about their decision to come here. The mountains surrounded her again, but their bare cliffs were farther away and weren't as majestic as those in the high country.

South of the Grand River, to her left, one land bench after another rose toward the high mountains. Ida could see places where meadows flourished during the summer months and correctly guessed that these areas must be fed by natural springs. The remainder of the land was dotted with the twisted trunks of juniper trees, which local folk called cedars. Tall cottonwood trees grew along the river banks, but there was little else to diminish the drab brown landscape.

To the right, the sagebrush and greasewood ended at the base of the barren hills leading to the top of the equally bare mountain. Some of the spires rose in eroded magnificence, seeming to defy the constant wind's pursuit. In other places, the multi-colored hills looked as if they had been dropped from a giant spoon. She could see evergreen trees dotting the upper reaches of the desolate hillsides and wondered how they managed to grow in such rocky, arid conditions.

"Mr. Hayden warned me of this country," Josiah said, as if reading her thoughts. "He said this was part of the Great American Desert and that it was useless unless water could be gotten to it. See those white patches that look like snow? That's called alkali, which won't let a thing grow, except what you see. I'm not exactly sure what it is, but you have to find ground that doesn't have it or you'll never grow any crops. Looks to me like most of it is on the north side of the river, so maybe there won't be so much of it on Battlement Mesa on the south side."

Late that day, the group arrived at a small settlement located a quarter mile or so from the confluence of the Grand River and a small stream flowing from the north. A log cabin on the east side of the settlement boasted a sign stating "General Store, F. Fisher, Prop." Further on, there were several cabins, as well as barns and corrals, which housed both people and the stock for the stage line which operated between Grand Junction and Glenwood Springs. Adults and children were moving about the area and stopped to look over the new arrivals before going on about their work.

A bearded man stepped forward. "Howdy, folks. My name's Hurlburt—John Hurlburt. Looks like you've come a ways today. Get down and come inside."

"Pleased to meet ya, Mr. Hurlburt. I'm Josiah Herwick, but everyone calls me Si. This here's my wife and younguns, and my two brothers, Wes and Owen. My team's pretty well played out, and I'd like to get them fed and watered, if you don't mind."

"You bet, Si. Just pull them over to the barn, and we'll take care of them. Your missus can visit with Mrs. Hurlburt. She's inside fixing supper. Rebecca, go tell your Ma we've got company."

As Ida wearily crawled over the wheel and climbed down to the ground, a pleasant-looking woman stepped to the door of the largest cabin. Children surrounded her on every side, and she gently directed them aside as she made her way toward Ida. "Hello, my dear. I'm Martha Hurlburt. Do come inside. The girls and I are just ready to put supper on. Will you join us?"

The smells from the cabin were enticing, and Ida looked to Josiah for acceptance of the invitation. It would be wonderful to sit at a table and eat something she didn't have to prepare. He interpreted her pleading look, and said, "Well, I guess we can afford to have a ready-made meal tonight. Thank you, Mrs. Hurlburt. We'd be glad to join you if you have enough."

"Oh, this meal's not for charge, Mr. Herwick. I'm inviting you to be my guests, if you're not too fussy about how it's served. As you can see, we've got a full house, and we generally have to eat in shifts. I see you've got some younguns, too. We'll feed them first and then we adults can sit down and enjoy the meal without too many interruptions. Come inside, Mrs. Herwick. It looks like you have had a hard day."

Ida gratefully followed the woman into the cabin. The first room, packed wall to wall with beds, led into a central room which served as the kitchen and dining area. Ida could see a door leading to another room beyond the eating area. Two young girls were busy frying meat at the big Monarch stove. "Mrs. Herwick, meet my two oldest girls, Francis and Minnie. Pour her a cup of that coffee. It looks like she could use some."

"Thanks for your kindness, Martha. Please call me Ida, and this is my daughter, Birdella, or Birdie, as we call her. I guess the boys went down to the barn with their father. Can we give you a hand with supper?"

"No, Ida, we've just about got it done. Besides, it looks like you're plumb wore out. Riding a freight wagon in your condition must have been hard. Just sip your coffee and tell me what brought you folks to this area."

Ida blinked back tears at the unexpected and welcome attention from another woman. She had forgotten how soothing that could be. "My husband's sister lives on Battlement Mesa, and she's been urging us to come over from the Eagle Valley. Maybe you know her. Her name is Mrs. Will Huntley–Sarah Huntley."

"Land's sake, of course I know her. She and her husband have been posting those letters to you the past few months. You see, I'm also the postmistress so I get to meet about everyone who settles here. Of course, I don't see folks on Battlement Mesa too often, except in the fall and winter months when the river is down. That river crossing is real dangerous, and no one tries to ford it unless there's a real need. Most go down river to the Indian crossing around Wallace Creek, but that's ten or so miles out of their way. I expect you folks will have to go down there tomorrow when you cross over to Battlement."

Throughout that evening Ida, Josiah, and their family learned more about the local people and the country. Josiah and his brothers listened while J.B. told them about the early days of 1882 when he had trailed 2,000 head of yearling ewes from Fall River, California to Meeker and then down to the Grand Valley. "This land's made for sheep grazing," Mr. Hurlburt said. "Of course, there are ranchers hereabouts that get all riled up over the thought of sheep mixin' with their precious cattle. But I contend that there's room for us all if they'd just listen to reason."

Ida and Martha Hurlburt discussed their children, childbearing, and making a home in this new frontier. The Hurlburts were already the parents of eight children, the last one, Fred, having been born a few months ago. She sensed that this kind woman was truly a colleague in regard to a lifetime of struggle. As Martha related stories about her childbirths and challenges to raising all those children, Ida felt a true kinship with this lady who seemed to have such a positive outlook on life.

Birdie had been welcomed into the giggling world of the two adolescent Hurlburt girls, while the boys had gone to the barn with the men. Wid and thirteen-year-old Luther Hurlburt hit it off just fine. Fred, as usual, was busy asking questions about all sorts of things to whomever would answer, and little Paul and Mae Hurlburt, both four years old, were busy playing with stick Indians and cowboys.

At bedtime, Martha appropriated one of the beds for Ida and Josiah and suggested that Birdie could sleep with the girls. The Herwick men and boys were sent to the old dugout, which the Hurlburt family had lived in when they first came to Parachute. For the first time in ages, Ida went to bed that night without the feeling of being so alone in the world. Her prayers included thanks for the kindness of Martha Hurlburt.

By late morning of the next day, the Herwick family arrived at the Indian crossing over the Grand River, having complied with the suggestion of J.B. Hurlburt who encouraged them to go the extra miles in order to make a safer crossing. He thought it would be too risky to take the heavily loaded freight wagon through the river ford a mile southeast of his place. The

Grand River spread itself out in a more shallow path at this location. There was a small island where they could stop to let the team have a breather between the main channels of the river. Josiah halted the heavy wagon and started giving instructions to his brothers. "Wes, why don't you go across and check out the bottom, then come back. You and Owen can ride along side the team while we get them across. Wid, I think you'd better hitch your pony to the back of the wagon and ride with us. We'll have enough to look out for without worrying about you."

The team wasn't accustomed to fording a body of water this large, and the whip had to be snapped over their backs a few times before they plunged into the icy river. The first channel was shallow enough that they could keep their footing, and they came to the island in short time. After giving them a few minutes on the island, Josiah was flicking the reins and sending them into the main stream again. Ida tightened her hold around Paul and took a deep breath. Her early memories of coming to Nebraska from Iowa flashed back through her mind, when her folks had lost their much loved mare. She held herself rigid as the team lost their footing, and started to swim. Josiah was yelling encouragement to the big horses while Wes and Owen swam beside them on their horses, giving them reassurance. At last they found solid ground and were starting up the river bank. Ida was a little dizzy from holding her breath. Birdie, Wid, and Paulie were all silent, but young Fred was laughing joyously. "Jeepers, Pa, that was great. Let's do that again!"

"Not today, son," Josiah laughed.

Mr. Hurlburt had drawn a rough map of the Battlement Mesa area for Josiah and pinpointed where he thought the Huntleys were presently located. By mid-afternoon the little group climbed the last hill and topped out on the mesa and headed south toward their new home less than a mile away.

Sarah came flying out the cabin door as the wagon stopped in front. She embraced her brothers and then gathered Ida and Birdie into her arms. "Oh, it's been so long since I saw you, Ida, and this here girl was just a babe. Where has all the time gone? And these must be your sons. My, such handsome young men! Come in, come in. I didn't know when you'd be arriving, but I sort of figured that it would be soon. Let me stoke up the fire and put a pot of coffee on, and we'll have some biscuits and my own squawberry jelly."

As Sarah bustled around the neat little cabin, Ida thought about Susannah. The mother-daughter resemblance was striking. The same loving ways, the same positive attitude, even the same expressions on her face.

Yes, Sarah was surely Susannah's daughter. It brought back so many wonderfully sharp memories of the time she had spent with her mother-in-law.

After their coffee, the men decided to take a short ride to look over the mesa land, especially the irrigation ditches that were in various stages of completion. Sarah and Will's teenage boys, Lewis and Will Jr., were working east on the Shutt Ditch which was being enlarged. The ranchers who could get water to their fields were harvesting abundant crops of hay, grain, corn, and vegetables. As each new squatter came to the mesa, they immediately started finding ways of bringing the water to their property. This involved buying water from the men who had wisely filed for water rights as soon as they arrived. The Battlement and Huntley Ditches were the first rights filed in 1884 and 1885. The Battlement flowed eastward bringing water to the Morrisanna Mesa Colony, while the Huntley, which Will had dug, flowed along the western part of Battlement Mesa, bringing irrigation to some of the ranches in that area.

While the men were gone, Sarah and Ida discussed possible living arrangements. Sarah said the family was welcome to camp out on their property as long as it took to get a cabin built, but she knew that Ida would want to be in her own home soon so she could prepare for the new baby. "You know, Ida, I just had an idea. There's a dugout a couple hundred yards away which you folks could probably use. It's not very big, but it would do while Si is putting up something better. He might even be able to expand it so you all could fit in. I haven't seen it for a while but, as I recall, it's pretty tight. These old cedar logs make a good sturdy roof and, if you leave the bark on it makes a cushion for the dirt. 'Course we've got plenty of rocks up here for the foundation." Sarah pointed out to the west field which had been fenced in by a rock wall four feet high. Cedar posts had been installed at intervals to hold the rocks in place. Ida couldn't recall ever seeing such a fence, but she admired the ingenuity of the people who built them.

That evening, while the entire family crowded into the small cabin, Sarah brought up the availability of the dugout. Perhaps the close living quarters at his sister's caused Josiah to be more impulsive. Whatever the case, he enthusiastically endorsed the possibility of moving into the dugout. If they could stay there for the summer, maybe come fall they could find something better, or they could build onto the structure. By the time the family had found spots on which to bed down for the night, they'd decided to look over the dugout the next morning.

AUGUST 1, 1888   BATTLEMENT MESA, COLORADO

Birds singing and the normal noise of an early morning household brought Ida out of a deep sleep. Shifting her position so the nuzzling infant could find her swollen breast, she lay listening to the sounds coming from the next room. Birdie's voice rose over the others. "Fred Herwick, quit teasing your brother and eat your oatmeal. And, when you get done with that, Pa said you're to start pulling weeds out in the garden. They're gettin' higher than the vegetables. Wid's been up and gone for an hour already, you lazy boy! Here Paulie, take the rest of this oatmeal out for the chickens. And then come back in for a pan of milk for the kittens."

Ida couldn't help smiling at her daughter's bossiness. At almost eleven years of age, Birdella was a good little mother for her younger brothers. Of course, there were times when her temper exploded, and then the boys ended up with knots and bruises. "That girl sure does have a hot head," Ida thought, "and nothing I've said seems to make a difference. She's such a good worker, and she helps me so much, but she'd better learn to control herself or she's goin' to end up an old maid. I can't imagine any man wanting to put up with that."

Sarah's voice interrupted the moment. "Good morning, you dear young people. How's Mama and baby doin' this mornin'?"

"I haven't looked in, Aunt Sarah. I'm trying to get this lazy bones brother started weeding. Maybe she's still asleep. I haven't heard the baby cry."

Ida looked up to see her sister-in-law standing in the doorway. "Good morning my dear, you've got more color in your cheeks. I think the rest has done you good," Sarah said. "Let me take that sweet little boy, and then I'll help you wash up some and braid your hair. That will make you feel better."

"Oh, thank you," Ida said handing the baby to Sarah. As she laid back and allowed herself to be pampered, Ida thought about how important Sarah had become to her. From the moment she, Josiah, and the family arrived, her sister-in-law had taken charge of their welfare. Although the dugout was no bigger than the one at Russell Siding, Sarah had helped Ida get settled within the first week. Ida and Josiah had the back room dug into the hillside, and Birdie's bed was along one of the walls in the kitchen area. A heavy piece of canvas had been tacked over the doorway. The men and boys were sleeping outside in a tent while the weather was good, but they would need to build another cabin or dugout before the first snow.

The four months since their arrival on Battlement Mesa had been busy for all the Herwicks. Owen and Wes had found work on several of the ranches, while Josiah had started working on enlarging some of the irrigation ditches which couldn't carry as much water as the permit allowed. As more ranches were settled, the demand for water kept increasing.

Ida and Birdie kept busy planting a garden and settling into their new home. They saw Sarah almost every day, and the time passed quickly when she was around with her keen sense of humor and loving ways. Her boys were full grown, and she enjoyed being around Ida's young family. When time permitted, she and Ida went visiting to some of the other wives on the mesa. One of the first visits was to Dr. and Mrs. Hayward on their place north of the Huntley ranch. Sarah guaranteed Ida that the good doctor would be there when she went into labor with her sixth child and thought that a visit would set her mind at ease. She knew that Ida still grieved over the tiny baby lying in the Edwards Cemetery.

Dr. Hayward assured Ida that she and the unborn child appeared to be healthy, and he saw no reason for any concern. Mrs. Hayward also promised that she would be available to assist her husband when the time came. Ida wasn't used to all this attention. She had forgotten how wonderful it was to have such loving support, and when the time did come for her to have her baby, Dr. and Mrs. Hayward were there just as they had promised they would be.

Several days later while resting and taking advantage of Sarah's tender ministrations, Ida thought that her life couldn't get any better. She had a snug little cabin, another healthy baby boy, a loving family around her, and a circle of friends who would be there in troubled times. Maybe this move would be the lucky charm. Maybe Josiah would be content to settle and put down roots. She had grown to love this mesa in the few short months of her stay. It seemed you could see for miles across the mesa to distant Parachute Creek which lay north beyond the valley floor. There were few trees to block the view, except for the cedars bordering each field. When spring arrived even the sagebrush took on a brighter green color. The newly plowed fields were sprouting with shoots of grain, corn, and hay, looking for all the world like the soft fuzz atop a baby's head. It seemed that anything would grow in this rich volcanic soil as long as it had water. Summer had followed with its hot midday sun and cool evening breezes. By July, Ida's garden was beginning to offer up its bounty, and the family thrived on the good wholesome vegetables it produced.

The family had gathered around her bedside to talk about names for the little boy. Wes laughingly suggested that they would start running out of names pretty soon, at the rate Ida was producing Herwick babies. Ida blushed and ducked her head to the laughter of the boisterous family. "Well, I have a suggestion," chimed in Sarah. "I had planned on naming our next boy Guy, but it doesn't look like that's going to happen, so feel free to use it if you like it."

The children mentioned other names, the most ridiculous, of course, suggested by Fred who remembered the Bible story about Nicodemus.

As Ida and Josiah looked at their newest son, they both realized they would like Sarah to have the honor of naming this babe. She had been so loving and helpful, it seemed the least they could do. Thus was chronicled the birth of Guy Wilson Herwick, born July 29, 1888.

CHRISTMAS DAY, 1888   BATTLEMENT MESA, COLORADO

Everyone sat in a semi-stuporous state from the bountiful feast they'd just consumed. What a Christmas this was! Ida especially savored the day because they had not been able to celebrate the holiday for the several years when the men were on the mountain cutting ties. It was just wonderful having all the family together, although the walls were bulging from all the bodies crammed into Sarah's small kitchen.

The women had outdone themselves planning the Christmas feast. The only thing missing was a big turkey, which was a foreign item on Battlement Mesa. They had to contend themselves with a venison roast, but the side dishes were wonderful. Mashed potatoes and gravy, carrots, peas, winter squash and light rolls were the first course, followed by mince and pumpkin pies. Ida had also made her mother's old favorite, Harvest Apple Cake.

Sarah and Ida had been busily working to knit some mittens and scarves for the children. In October the family had all gone to Parachute, which was a two day trip by way of the Wallace Creek ford, to stock up on their winter supplies. At that time, the women had been able to purchase some woolen yarn from Mr. Fisher's store. Ida ran her hands over a few bolts of bright calico and thought how nice it would be to have a new dress for Birdie and herself. She pulled her hand away, knowing that there wasn't money for that sort of foolishness. But she did manage to buy a bag of candy to put back for the children's Christmas. That would have to do this year, but she promised herself that someday they would all have a more generous holiday.

The late fall had been cool, but not very stormy. In fact, there was not much snowfall for the entire winter. It made life much easier for the families and their stock, but men grumbled that they needed more snowpack in the mountains, or else the irrigation water would be mighty short next summer. Once again the subject was raised about constructing several reservoirs on top of Battlement Mountain, which would hold some of the spring run-off and allow the irrigation season to be extended. Without a dam system in place, some of the ditches were dry by the first of July, and the crops withered from the lack of precious water.

The Huntley and Battlement Ditches had the first water rights, and everyone else had to take their water after those permits were fulfilled. The Clark, Jenny, and Morris ranches were flourishing, while the ranches irrigated by the Shutt Ditch usually ran dry in midsummer. Clearly something had to be done to increase the volume and duration of the Battlement water.

Although she heard the men's grumblings, Ida was too busy raising her family to be very concerned about something as removed as irrigation rights. Her days were filled with cooking, cleaning, washing, ironing, baking, and mending. In addition, she tried to spend a few hours each week educating her children as best she could. Sarah, who remembered the hours spent with her mother, Susannah, while she learned to read and write was a willing helper in this venture. Sarah soon took over the bulk of the lessons, which pleased her and the children, and allowed Ida more time to spend with little baby Guy. Although Ida could read and write, she was not as adept as Sarah, and certainly didn't enjoy it as much. She much preferred to do other things, although she still read her Bible every day.

Guy was eight months old, and March winds were howling around the cabin when Ida discovered she was probably pregnant again. "I can't believe this is happening," she exclaimed to herself. "I'm still nursing Guy. This is too soon." She was reminded of Wes's comment after Guy's birth, and was embarrassed at the truth of it. Josiah's lustiness had not diminished, and she had never felt right telling him no. Now, here she was, going to have two younguns less than fifteen months apart! "But it could be worse," she reminded herself. "At least I'll have Sarah here to help me, and Dr. Hayward will be here, too, so I guess I can manage." That thought was shattered several months later.

~ *The Denver and Rio Grande Railroad reached Rifle, Colorado, July 20, 1889.*

~ *In June, 1889, the name of Wolcott, Colorado became official. A post office was created.*

~ *Railroad fares dropped to $1.25 for a ticket from the Eagle River Valley to Denver.*

~ *A church service was held at Minturn in August, 1889. Sixty-three people attended the outing afterward.*

JUNE, 1889   BATTLEMENT MESA, COLORADO

Wes rode into the dooryard. "Hey, Josiah. Mr. Hurlburt sent a letter to you. Come get it, cause I've got to get on over to Sarah's."

Josiah, washing up before supper, dried his face and hands before taking the envelope from Wes's hand. He tore the flap open and quickly scanned the two pages.

Their old friend from Russell Siding was writing to say that the little settlement was really booming these days. The name had been changed to Wolcott recently as a tribute to a new senator or representative, and an application had been made for a post office designation. Six-horse Concord stages were daily covering the territory between the Grand River and Steamboat Springs. As much as $10,000-12,000 of gold was being periodically sent overland to the banks in the Steamboat Springs area. And ranchers were driving their stock down to the railhead to be shipped on the Rio Grande Railroad to eastern markets. He said that almost two thousand head of cattle had been held in the new corrals and shipped out in the past twelve months. His friend wrote that Josiah and his brothers might be interested in all the activity, especially because they were fine teamsters who would certainly be able to get on with the stagecoach company. He closed with another tidbit of information. It seems that state dollars had been appropriated to build a bridge over the Grand River about six miles south of McCoy. Once this bridge was completed, a road through the canyon could be built, rather than taking the ridge route which was a hazard in the winter months because of its elevation. The construction contract had been let to A.J. Tullock of the Missouri Valley Bridge and Iron Works and was expected to be completed by August 1, 1890. Teamsters would be needed to haul in the materials for the bridge, and word was being sent out that a man could make top wages working on the project.

Ida didn't like the gleam in Josiah's eyes as he read the letter to the family. She'd seen that same look too many times, and it always meant that she and her children would be moving again. Later that day, she shared her fears with Sarah, who failed to give her much encouragement. "I wish I could say it won't happen, Ida, but truth to tell, Will Huntley is also gettin' itchy feet. Now that most of the ditch work has been done on Battlement Mesa, he's thinking about moving to the LaPlata area where he hears there's lots of work going on. He heard about a Mr. Otto Mears building a railroad line from Durango to Dolores which will connect all of the Rio Grande Southern Railroad. Will, Lew and the boys are talking about moving out of here in the next month so they can hire on the construction crew and get us settled in before winter."

"Oh, Sarah, what will I do without you? I haven't felt so happy since your mama was with us. Being here with you and your family has been one of the happiest times of my life. Why can't Josiah be content to just settle down and stay put? I know that the wages aren't as good here, but we'd manage just fine. All I really want is a little piece of land where I can sink my roots. I'm so tired of moving around from one place to another."

"I wish I knew the answer to why men are always lookin' somewhere else," Sarah replied. "Mama always said it was the seafaring blood in her men that made them want to move from place to place. I think it's a lot like all those crazy prospectors who think they're goin' to strike it rich any day. Our men believe that a better life always lies around the bend. You and I know that probably won't happen, but try to convince them of that! In the meantime, we go where they go, unless we want to live alone. I can't speak for you, but I'd much rather share a tent with Will Huntley than live in a mansion alone."

Ida acknowledged the truth of what her sister-in-law was saying. She remembered the long months that she had been left alone and decided that she, too, would live almost anywhere as long as her husband was with her everyday. Besides, no one else seemed to complain about the frequent moves. The children were healthy and always eager to have new adventures. "They must have inherited their father's roving blood," Ida said, as she heaved a resigned sigh.

True to predictions, the Herwick and Huntley families said their good-byes at the end of June and headed separate ways; Sarah and her family south to the La Plata region and Josiah northeast to the Eagle River Valley. Ida had blinked back tears for miles after the sad good-byes were said. She felt somehow that she had lost her mother-in-law all over again. She didn't dare express that to Josiah who would have just told her she was being a silly female.

As they retraced the road which they had first traveled only fifteen months ago, she took one last look at the Battlement Mesa shimmering in the early morning light. "Someday, if I have anything to say about it, we'll be coming back." With that promise in mind, she turned her face resolutely to the east and to whatever experience awaited them.

SEPTEMBER, 1889   STATE BRIDGE CONSTRUCTION SITE

The midday sun shone through the walls of the canvas tent, illuminating the gloom within. Ida had just taken a breather from her morning chores before starting to prepare the noon meal. Josiah would be coming home soon for his dinner, and he always wanted it right away, so he had time to take a cat nap before going back to the job. She stoked up the little camp stove and started slicing cold potatoes into the skillet which already contained bacon grease. She also pulled a pot of beans closer to the flame so they'd boil good by the time the potatoes were done. The biscuits from breakfast would round out the meal.

As she kept an eye on the stove to make sure the potatoes and beans were cooking, Ida reached down and picked up baby Guy who had just awakened and was starting to fuss from hunger. She was trying to wean the little fellow because of her impending confinement in October or November, but Guy wasn't a willing participant. At fourteen months, he still wanted nourishment from his mama and usually refused to drink the diluted canned milk she offered him. The end result was a very frazzled mother and child, who were both determined to win in the battle of wits. "If only we had some fresh cow's milk," she wearily thought to herself, "maybe he'd drink better."

As Ida stirred the food with one hand and cuddled Guy with the other, she heard Josiah and the children's voices coming near. Birdie, Fred, and Paul had walked down to the river bank to accompany their father home, and they all trooped into the cook tent just as Ida was ready to dish up the food.

There wouldn't be as many around the table today, because Wes and Owen had gone on a freight haul to Wolcott and had taken Wid with them. That boy couldn't think of anything except being with the horses. He was already a good horseman, even at ten years old, and would make a great driver once he got a bit more muscled up. He spent every available moment with the teamsters, watching them groom and tend to the stock, as well as learning from them all the secrets of being the best driver. Ida never had to worry about where he was. Her greatest concern was getting him to come home for his chores and meals! She plainly didn't like him hanging around that bunch of rowdies, but Josiah had over-ridden her objections and allowed the boy to spend his spare time over at the barns. However, Josiah cautioned Wid that he wouldn't be able to help if his mother ever heard Wid uttering any of the foul language teamsters were wont to use. Being a smart young fellow, Wid made sure that any *damns* and *hells* were saved for the barn yard and not his mother's house.

Birdie was a tall slim girl, just shy of her twelfth birthday. Ida looked at the dark little beauty with love in her eyes. What a joy she was and yet, what a trial. Birdie had learned to curb her temper somewhat, but she still occasionally let her anger fly. It was usually directed at young Fred who seemed to delight in tormenting her to distraction. When he finally succeeded in making Birdie mad, Ida could see the satisfied gleam in his eye. Now, that was a boy who needed watching all the time. He was so different from Paulie, who was quiet, polite, and obedient. If she instructed Paul to stay within calling distance, she could be sure he would be there when she went to seek him. Fred would as likely be under the horses feet in the corral or asking questions of the bridge workers. Several times his father had sent him home crying from the proper spanking he'd received for being so far from the tents. But the next day it was all forgotten, and Fred was thinking up the newest devilment.

When Wes, Owen, and Wid arrived late that evening they brought mail and the *Eagle County Times*, printed at Red Cliff. The newspaper recounted the formation of the "Knights of Labor," a miners' union in Leadville. And there was an account of sixty-three people attending a church service and picnic held in Minturn. "How wonderful it would be if we could attend church," Ida exclaimed. "It's been eight years since we left Kansas, and I still miss the Sunday services. I feel so bad that the children don't have any religious upbringing except Bible reading and prayers. Josiah, couldn't we just go once in a while to where they're holding services?"

"Listen, Ida, that's a long way to travel just for church. It'd take at least two days up and back, and I can't afford to take that much time off. Be patient. Someday a preacher will move closer to us, and then you can go all you want." Ida noticed he didn't include himself in that statement, and she sighed with disappointment. She'd always known that Josiah was not a church-going man, and it didn't look like he was going to change. He insisted that God had made the great outdoors, and he could be as pious as church-goers when he was out in the hills. Ida couldn't find any rebuttal for that statement, but secretly she questioned whether her husband really took the time to speak to his Creator as he said he did.

The *Times* also had a report on the Rio Grande Railroad's plans to start a four-mile tunnel under the southern portion of Tennessee Pass and how it would be shored up with redwood brought in from California. "Those bastard conservationists are making it impossible for people to provide local supplies for the railroad any more," growled Josiah. "It says here that a joint memorial has been sent to Washington, D.C., asking for the creation of a Timber Reserve on the west slope. How the hell do those people expect us to make a living if we can't cut timber off the federal lands? I wonder how they think we were able to settle this land. They're just a bunch of damned rich guys who have nothing better to do than stir up trouble for us poor working folk."

Ida was alarmed by Josiah's vehemence and not a little concerned by his use of profanity. She wasn't so naive that she didn't know all men used that language when they were away from their wives and children, but no one spoke like that around his family. "Josiah, do calm down, and watch your language. For pity sakes, I don't recall seeing you so worked up in a long time."

"Of course I'm worked up, woman! If we can't use the government lands to cut timber and graze our stock, we might as well pull up stakes and move back to Kansas and Missouri. Ranchers and saw mill owners can't make it if they're forced to buy grazing and timber off private lands. We're barely making a living now, and there sure as hell isn't any extra money to pay for more. That's why we came to this country, because we didn't have to be all hemmed up in property boundaries out here. Now these damned fools are trying to take our rights away from us. But I'm betting nothing that stupid will ever be signed into law–not in my lifetime anyway. Surely President Harrison won't let those jackasses ruin this country."

Josiah stopped grumbling and went back to reading the paper. A short notice caught his attention. The Eagle County Commissioners were seeking bids for a bridge to be constructed over the Eagle River at the town of

Wolcott. "You know, Wes, we should bid on that there bridge. I think we could do as good a job as Mr. Tullock is doing on this one, plus it's a much smaller span which won't require so much reinforcement. All we'd have to do is line up some workers, and I'd probably be able to recruit some of the men off this job, if the pay is right. We'd still be able to use our local timber, unless those damned crazy people in Washington push through that Federal Reserve in the next few months. Yes sir, I think I should work up some figures and see what kind of profit we could make."

True to his word, Josiah worked up a $1,000 proposal and took a few days off to take it to the county seat at Red Cliff. He was told that the commissioners likely wouldn't approve the contract until late November or December because the funds would be coming from the 1890 county budget, and work couldn't start until after the first of January. So Josiah, having done all he could do, picked up some supplies and headed home.

As her time drew near, Ida actively searched for someone to assist her with her childbirth. The little settlement by the bridge was merely a construction camp, with few women inhabitants, and certainly no physician, except for the intrepid Dr. Evens who might be found any where from Wolcott to Steamboat Springs. Some of the so-called "wash-women" did more than just taking in washing, according to Josiah, and she steered clear of those females. That left very few women who might be able to help during her delivery. "If I could just find someone to help out for a few days, I'm sure I can manage all right, with Birdie doing most of the cooking and cleaning," she planned. That day, with Guy on her hip, she walked down to the other tents along the Grand River and inquired about women who might have midwife experience. Several ladies suggested she try Mrs. Hilton whose tent was located the farthest along the river.

A pleasant, smiling woman greeted Ida. "Good afternoon, my dear. It looks like you have a heavy little bundle there. It's a boy, isn't it? Will the little fellow come to me? Do come sit down and take the load off your feet."

After she caught her breath, Ida explained her need for a midwife, or at least someone who had been at other childbirths. She mentioned her concern that Dr. Evens would not be available when her time came, and she wanted to make sure that she and the baby were properly tended to.

Mrs. Hilton assured Ida that she not only had six children of her own but that she had been present at a good many birthings. "I believe I could manage to help you for a few days, Mrs. Herwick, but I doubt I could do it much longer. My man isn't too happy when I leave him to do his own cooking. Not that I blame him, he's a terrible cook! Let me talk it over with him, and see what he says I think I can safely promise I'll be there at least for your confinement. There aren't many God-fearing women in this camp, and I know I'd be concerned if I was in your place."

Afterwards, resting in warm quilts, Ida was very grateful for the ministrations of the kind, caring woman following a brief, but exhausting labor on November 1, 1889. The child, with its head of downy blond hair, yelled lustily when he entered the world and was pronounced a healthy baby boy. Josiah, a proud father for the seventh time, said "Ida, you sure are good at producing those boy babies. I wouldn't mind, though, if you were to have a girl or two for yourself," he joked.

"That's very considerate, Josiah, but what makes you think I want any more children, girls or boys?" Ida retorted.

"Oh, I'll bet there'll be a few more, Mrs. Herwick. Seems like all I have to do is hang my pants on your bedstead, and you get in the family way. What are we gonna name this little fellow?"

Ida had been thinking about that very thing. "Well, I like the name Oren. There was a very nice old gentleman by that name in Nebraska, and I've always thought it has a good sound. What do you think of it?"

"It's okay by me, if you like it. What about a middle name?"

"You choose the middle name; I chose the first."

After a few days of choosing and discarding middle names, the baby was finally named after the lady who helped bring him into the world, and Oren Hilton Herwick was welcomed into their pioneer home.

The winter was a mild one, so far, and Ida was thankful. The tents were so cold, even though they kept the fires built up day and night. In fact, the tents would probably have been warmer if there was snow to insulate the thin canvas walls. Ida put layer upon layer of clothing on herself and the children, and still shivered most of the day. Her concern was keeping the little ones from getting frost bite, and she was constantly searching their appendages for any tell-tale white discoloration.

Christmas, 1889, came and went without much notice; a far different celebration than the previous one on Battlement Mesa. The family was in a survival mode at this point, and did not think much beyond keeping a full belly and a warm body.

∾ *The first bore of the four-mile Denver and Rio Grande Tunnel under Tennessee Pass was started in January, 1890. It was cleared and lined with redwood by November.*

∾ *The Busk-Ivanhoe Railroad Tunnel Company was organized June, 1890, to drive a drift which would be lower, shorter, and less dangerous than the Hagerman Tunnel. The project wasn't completed until 1893.*

∾ *The Denver and Rio Grande Railroad reached Parachute.*

∾ *Alfalfa hay sold for $4 a ton - Native Grass, $7 - Timothy, $9.50*

∾ *The Atchison, Topeka, and Santa Fe Railroad purchased all of the Colorado Midland stock for a total price of $6,805,500 on October 25, 1890.*

∾ *The ore from the Molly Gibson Mine in Aspen was averaging 600 ounces of silver to the ton.*

JANUARY, 1890 STATE BRIDGE, COLORADO

On their first freight haul after the first of the year in 1890, Wes and Owen returned from Wolcott with a letter for Josiah. Eagle County had awarded him the contract for the Wolcott Bridge! The terms of the contract called for the bridge to be completed by the first of July, which meant that the Herwick brothers had about six and one-half months to finish it.

Everyone was excited about the contract. Josiah, Wes, and Owen saw it as a way to make some fairly easy money. Ida looked forward to moving into a dwelling, even if it was a dugout like before. Nothing could be any worse than living in a tent! Birdie thought it would be wonderful to live in a town once more where there would be other girls. She was sick of taking care of her little brothers, and she yearned for the companionship of young ladies her age. Wid hoped that Ma and Pa would let him try to get a job at one of the three livery stables, mucking out if nothing else. The four youngest boys really didn't care much where they were because they knew they'd be cared for, no matter what or where.

The next few weeks passed in a flurry of activity. Josiah and his brothers were frequently on the road to Red Cliff and Wolcott lining up labor and materials. Josiah found a big three-room house constructed of green lumber on the outskirts of Wolcott, so the State Bridge camp was dismantled, much to Ida's delight.

It was cold but clear when the Herwicks started their trip twelve miles south to Wolcott. The children and Ida were nestled between the household belongings in the back of the freight wagon. Each was wrapped in several quilts from their beds, and they were as comfortable as possible under the circumstances. Birdie was cuddled up with little Guy and made sure his nose and ears stayed covered. Ida snuggled baby Oren to her breast and covered them both with quilts. If he became fussy she'd be able to nurse him without leaving their little cocoon. Once the team pulled to the top of Windy Point, it would be downhill all the way, and they should make good time. The fact that the road was frozen also helped. In the springtime the twelve miles could take as long as twelve hours.

The weary team of horses pulled their heavy load into Wolcott late in the afternoon. Ida thought she had never seen anything quite so welcome as the bare little house. Wes and Owen had ridden ahead and built fires in the cookstove, which was the only source of heat in the dwelling. When Ida opened the door, a warm rush of air brushed her face, and she joined the others around the blazing fire. As soon as everyone was thawed out, Ida put them to work bringing in the household items so she could cook a hot meal. That night they went to bed in unaccustomed warmth, vowing they'd never take that comfort for granted again.

The next months went by at a pleasant pace. Ida was busy from dawn to dark tending to the needs of her family, while Josiah, Wes, and Owen worked equally long hours on the bridge project.

One month after they arrived, a school was started in the schoolteacher's home. This was a dream come true for Ida, who immediately sent Birdie, Wid, Fred, and Paul off for their classes. Everyone enjoyed the novelty except Wid, whose dream of working in a livery was postponed for the present time. He was a bright ten-year-old but hated the confinement of the four school walls and used every excuse he could to escape that environment.

Birdie was thrilled to see other girls near her own age. It was a new experience for her to be free of the many responsibilities she'd had for the past six years and to actually behave like any other twelve-year-old girl. Of course that ended at her cabin door, when she once again became her little brothers' second mother. So, she grew to relish the few hours each day when she could leave her tasks behind.

Six-year-old Paul was a studious little fellow who delighted in learning to read and write, but, his brother Fred was another matter! The teacher, while admiring Fred's quick wit and mind, was constantly provoked by his antics. The corner offered a regular seat to the young man, who spent many hours writing, "I will not talk in class," on his slate.

Ida was equally excited by the prospect of soon having regular church services in their locale. Reverend W. W. Winne, newly arrived to Red Cliff, was proposing a preaching circuit. He planned to preach at Gypsum on Sunday morning, at Eagle River Crossing in the afternoon, and at Wolcott on Sunday evening. This tireless theologian furthermore volunteered to conduct services throughout the week in other neighboring areas. His schedule would have intimidated a less devoted man!

Ida waited impatiently for the first service in Wolcott. When that evening finally arrived, she was in the congregation along with all six of her children, several of whom had never set foot in a church before. Fred had been warned with threat of life and limb to behave himself. Unfortunately, she was not able to convince her husband and brothers-in-law to attend. They pleaded overwhelming fatigue from their long and busy day.

Ida was transfixed by the religious ritual which she had missed for so long. As she joined in the hymn singing, it was as if she was again being nourished by the same loving atmosphere she had once known.

Nearer my God to thee, nearer to thee.
E'en though it be a cross that raiseth me.
Still all my song shall be,
Nearer my God to thee, nearer to thee.

Reverend Winne stepped forward to the pulpit for his sermon. "My sermon tonight is taken from Isaiah, Chapter 40, verse 31. 'But they that wait upon the Lord shall renew their strength; they shall mount up with wings as eagles; they shall run, and not be weary, and they shall walk and not faint.'" Reverend Winne continued, "As children of God we are given the strength to do his bidding. Yes, even in the midst of this wilderness we can bring the word to His children and turn non-believers into good Christian souls."

As Ida listened to this silver-tongued man of the cloth, she was mesmerized by the sound of his magnetic voice.

"I know it is not an easy life that God has chosen for you in this unsettled country. But take heart, for hasn't He promised you peace? Matthew, Chapter 11 says, 'Come unto me, all that labour and are heavy laden, and I will give you rest. Take my yoke upon you and learn of me, for I am meek and lowly in heart: and ye shall find rest unto your souls. For my yoke is easy, and my burden is light.' God has chosen all of you to tame this country and help it to become fruitful. He has instructed you fathers to hew out a home for your family. And mothers, He wants you to bring forth the children which will till this land for generations to come, and to praise Him for their good life."

Ida felt herself re-committing to what she believed her Creator wanted her to do.

"It's so easy to lose sight of one's spiritual goals when there's no one to remind us of our obligations," she thought, as the minister's voice washed over her. "I needed to be reminded that what I'm doing is God's wish, and not be discouraged when life seems so hard."

Her reverie was broken by Fred squirming in his seat. As his eyes intercepted her threatening look, he whispered, "But I've got to go, Ma. I've really got to go!"

"Be quiet for just a few more minutes, son," she quietly replied. "Reverend Winne is just about through with his sermon. Can't you wait that long?"

"No, Ma, I can't!" With that, Fred bolted from his seat and headed for the door, amid many glances of disapproval. Ida sighed, as she watched her son disappear into the night.

The days following the first church service were especially bright and happy for Ida. She often remembered the sermon and was buoyed up by the thought that her life did have meaning. Everything she did for her loved ones was part of the holy plan God had for her. That thought was comforting.

SEPTEMBER 1, 1890   WOLCOTT, COLORADO

"Oh no," Ida exclaimed as she leaned against Josiah's chest. "Please God, tell me it isn't so! How could such a horrible thing happen to Sarah?"

Josiah had just arrived home from the post office. When he came through the door, Ida knew something terrible had happened. His face was pale, and his customary smile was gone. He held out a letter from Will Huntley which told of Sarah's death on August 1, in La Plata County. She and Will were sleeping in a tent in the vicinity of Parrot City when a bolt of lightening had struck and killed her. She and her family had been living in the construction camp along the newly-built railroad, which had reached Parrot

City at the mouth of the La Plata Canyon. Will reported that he'd been shaken but not hurt from the terrible accident, although he wished that it could have been him instead of his wife that was taken. His grief was almost audible in the words of his letter. Sarah had been laid to rest in the little cemetery close to the settlement

As Ida sobbed into Josiah's shirt, a jumble of thoughts ran through her mind: Sarah welcoming them on Battlement Mesa, Sarah playing and reading to the children, Sarah's presence when Guy was born, the Christmas dinner they celebrated together. She thought she couldn't bear the pain she was feeling at that moment.

"Just cry it out, Idie," Josiah consoled her. "I know how close you were to Sarah. She was a special lady." His voice broke as he reminisced about his sister. "She was my big sister, but she was also my best friend. We were five years apart, and mother said when I was born Sarah thought I was her special gift. She was always there when I needed her, and now she's gone. I can't believe it. Poor old Will. I wonder what he will do now? Maybe we should invite him to come stay with us for a while."

Ida agreed that Will should come live with them, and they sent a letter in the next mail inviting him to become part of their family. A month later the letter was returned to them unopened. It seems Will Huntley had disappeared from the La Plata area.

Ida's newly rejuvenated religious fervor suffered a severe setback as a result of Sarah's death. She sought out Reverend Winne after the Sunday night services and asked to speak to him privately. "Reverend, I need you to explain how the God you talk about, the God whom you say loves us so much, can allow so much sorrow in this world. Sarah was such a good woman, just past her forty-second birthday. She never did a mean thing in her life. No one was ever turned away from her door. How could God take such a wonderful person and leave others who are so cruel and mean spirited? Tell me, Pastor, I need to know."

"Ida, did it ever occur to you that God took your sister-in-law precisely because she was so kind and caring? Maybe He had far greater need for her in Heaven than on Earth. I know that our faith is sorely tested at times, especially when we lose someone we love so much, but I want you to know that there is some divine reason for this sorrow. Maybe it's to test our spiritual strength; maybe it's to give us lessons in bearing pain; maybe it's to prepare us for a future time when our faith will be tested even further. We don't know those answers, but God does, and we have to trust that He is working out the perfect solution for each of us. Remember the old hymn 'His eye is on the Sparrow.' Well, His eye is on you now, Ida, and all you have to do is ask Him for strength to see you through this present sorrow. Would you like to pray with me?"

As Ida knelt beside the minister, she desperately prayed for Sarah's safe passage into Heaven, while she was also asking for peace and strength for herself.

CHRISTMAS DAY, 1890   WOLCOTT, COLORADO

Ida looked lovingly at the sleepy-eyed children gathered around Josiah and her, as they looked to see if there were any presents under the small tree which had been decorated with popcorn and other homemade ornaments.

"Well, let's see here what we have," teased Josiah. "I do believe this one is marked for little Guy. Here you are, young man. Open it and find out what you've got."

The two-year-old-didn't know quite what to think about all this ceremony, but he obligingly opened the box to reveal a soft fabric dog, which his mother had sewn from old pieces of coat material and stuffed with bits of rags. Clutching the toy to his chest, he laughed and giggled while he ran around the room.

"It looks like the next one's for Paul. And here's one for Fred. I bet this has a piece of coal in it! Wid, come get yours. And last, but not least, Birdella, I think this one had your name on it."

The children were excitedly tearing open the plain brown wrapping paper concealing each gift. Paul was soon quietly absorbed in practicing his letters on the new tablet with his store-bought pencils. Fred was tearing around the room issuing alternate war cries and bang-bangs as he played with his metal Indians and soldiers. Wid was admiring the sharpness of his new jack knife, and Birdie had run to their one mirror to try out the many-colored hair ribbons she'd just received. Oren was content to sit in the baby chair and suck on a piece of molasses taffy which Ida had made the night before.

Although the little cabin was full of laughter and gaiety, Ida felt something was missing without the presence of her brothers-in-law. Wes and Owen had gotten itchy feet shortly after the Wolcott Bridge was completed and decided to go over to the White River County to find work. Ida supposed it was time they lit out on their own. It wasn't as if they were young men. Wes was thirty-one and Owen was twenty-nine, but they had been with Ida and Josiah for almost ten years.

In September, after Josiah had settled up all his expenses on the Wolcott Bridge, he started looking around for a piece of land where he could settle his growing family. It was apparent that a three-room cabin would not be adequate much longer. Birdie was openly complaining about having to share a bedroom with her younger brothers. "Ma, I hate havin' to sleep with those smelly boys. If you won't do anything about it, I will. A lady in town has a spare room, and she said I could stay there for my helping out after school. I know you need me here, but this place is just too small for the eight of us, and in a few months, it'll be nine." Ida winced with embarrassment from the pointed look Birdie directed toward her barely swollen stomach.

"How do you know, Miss Sassy Britches, that I'm going to have another baby?"

"Oh, Ma, for pity sake. I'm not a little girl any more. Don't you think I have eyes and ears? There aren't many secrets in this little place–day or night!"

Ida was glad that Birdie had sashayed out the door and didn't see her face turn crimson. She remembered feeling the same way at Birdie's age as she listened to the night-time noise from her parent's bed. And, the girl was right—she shouldn't be sharing a bed with her younger brothers. She had recently become a woman, and should have a bit more privacy.

Ida shyly broached the subject to Josiah that evening. She wasn't accustomed to discussing this sort of thing with her husband, but it had to be done. "Josiah, you need to know that Birdie is thinking about taking a boarding room in town if we don't move to a bigger house where she has more privacy. I don't know whether you've paid attention, but our daughter is quickly growing up. In fact, she is now a woman if you know what I mean. I can't bear the thought of her living away from us, Josiah. Can't you find us a bigger place?"

"It's funny that you should bring this up now, Idie. I've been thinking the very same thing. We've got all these boys to put to work soon, and I've been thinking we might try ranching again. We could find some acreage and spread out, maybe buy some stock and raise a big garden again. Timothy is bringin' $9.50 a ton now, and we could make a few dollars selling what hay we don't need. What do you think?"

"Oh, Josiah, that would be wonderful." Ida thought back a few years ago to their comfortable spread at Avon. "Are you really serious about this? I would dearly love to move my children to a nice little ranch. Promise me you'll start looking right away, so we can get settled before snow flies."

Ida's biggest mistake was allowing her husband to buy the place without her approval. Ever the cock-eyed optimist, Josiah Herwick never looked at life the way it really was, but as he wanted it to be. Early in October, he came home excitedly waving a deed in his hands. "Well, Mrs. Herwick, I've bought you a ranch!"

Ida was so thrilled she hugged Josiah. "Where is it? Tell me where it is! Who are our neighbors? Oh, I'd love to move back up to Edwards. We had such a beautiful place."

"Whoa, lady! Give me a chance to tell you. And don't get too excited, because you probably won't see it until next spring. When we were cutting ties on Milk Creek, I happened over the Divide to the Catamount area. That's just about the purtiest place you've ever seen. Lots of open fields for grazing stock, and with some cultivation it should grow tall hay. The stream is small, but runs the year round. And, in the winter time we might trail the stock down around the Grand River where it stays warmer.

"But," Ida interrupted, "what about buildings? Are there buildings on the place? Surely you didn't buy a place that has no cabin or house? And what about neighbors? Who are they, and how far away from our ranch?"

"Of course there are buildings," Josiah replied rather defensively "They just ain't in too good a shape. Peter Brunner wasn't very fussy about where he lived. There's a small cabin, but I don't think it will do for all of us. So, we'll have to get busy in the spring and build us a nice tight log place. I can probably do some of the timber cutting this winter, so we'll be all ready to go come spring thaw. As far as the neighbors are concerned, I think there's one family about five miles away, and maybe another the same distance in the other direction. We won't have to worry about the kids not having room to roam about."

As her husband hurriedly tried to convince Ida of his marvelous purchase, she sighed with resignation. Once again Josiah's rose-colored glasses had prevented him from being practical. Instead of moving to a well-established ranch, the family would be starting all over one more time. "But, I can't say I'm not partly to blame for this. Maybe Josiah wouldn't have been so all fired anxious to buy a ranch if he hadn't been encouraged. Now, all I have to do is convince Birdie to stay here until next spring," Ida told herself.

The year 1890 ended as a moderately prosperous one for the Herwick family. The Wolcott Bridge had been a springboard for Josiah who now had a reputation for being a good builder. He was getting other offers for construction work, which paid better and required less labor than some of his previous jobs. After the first of the year, Josiah spent some time up in the Castle Peak area, cutting logs, and preparing them for the haul down to Catamount. In the meantime the family settled down into the small cabin to wait out the remainder of winter. Birdie grumbled when she learned that they couldn't move until spring, but the rosy picture her father painted of the ranch kept her tolerably satisfied for the moment. However, she did put down a small pallet by the kitchen stove on which she now slept, and that seemed a reasonable compromise.

With her family gathered near her on Christmas Day, Ida was satisfied with her life, even though she knew that come spring she'd be pulling up stakes and moving again. "At least this time," she reflected, "we'll be going to our own place. Everything we do there will be for our sakes and not someone else. Thank you, Lord, for your blessings. Help me to be strong enough to take good care of my family. Amen."

∾ Republican Benjamin Harrison visited Leadville and Glenwood Springs in the spring of 1891. He got a very poor reception due to his stand on repealing the Sherman Silver Act.

∾ The first bridge was built over the Grand River at Parachute, Colorado.

∾ The White River Plateau Timberlands Reserve was created October 16, 1891, preserving 1,198,180 acres of timber and grazing land.

∾ The first National Irrigation Congress met in Salt Lake City, Utah. It was proposed that massive reservoirs be built to stabilize stream flows.

MAY 17, 1891   THE ROAD TO BURN'S HOLES AND CATAMOUNT CREEK

Josiah turned west onto Willow Creek about six miles south of the State Bridge. "I think the road's dry enough now, and it will cut off some miles we'll have to travel today. No sense in going on to the Windy Point Road if we don't have to. If it gets too rough or muddy we can always swing north and hit the Point Road again."

Ida nodded her assent as she shaded her eyes to look at the vista stretching to the west. The austere cedar and pinon-dotted hillsides were softened by shoots of new grass and plants which were pushing their heads to the bright sun. Off to the northwest she could catch a glimpse of Castle Peak from time to time. For the most part, the terrain was rolling hills, broken occasionally by grassy parks. There was a different feeling up here on the divide than in the valley. The warm sun's rays were lessened by the constant breeze blowing over the undulating landscape. The heavy scent of sage wafting through the clear air reached her nostrils and she breathed deeply of the pungent aroma.

Birdie, Wid, and Fred rode their horses beside the wagon, which was loaded with all their earthly possessions. Paul watched after little Guy and Oren in between the household goods , and Ida carried two-week-old "Tiny," who was sleeping soundly, oblivious to the rough bouncing ride she was receiving.

Ida had prevailed upon Josiah to delay their trip to Catamount until she could have the baby baptized by Reverend Winne. This was a spiritual comfort she'd never been able to indulge in before, and she would not be denied, especially since she'd again be going so far away from church services. The other children might still be considered heathens, but, by golly, she was going to have one child who'd received the blessings of the Church! Ida looked down at the tiny infant, and love flowed through her at the sight of the blond fuzzy head. She'd finally been blessed with another daughter. After six sons, it began to look like she'd never have another girl, and now here was this sweet little bundle. Tiny was a small, but perfectly formed baby, who slept and ate on schedule. She seemed content to soak up all the love that her mother and family could lavish on her. "Birdie will be gone before we know it, and this little girl will be here for her mama," Ida mused, as she hugged the wee babe to her chest.

It had been a long, hard day by the time the little group finished the fifteen mile trek to their new home. The sun was starting to set when they pulled into the wooded glen, the site of the cabin, corral, and a few out-buildings. Catamount Creek, with its spring runoff, rushed through the property just a few yards from the cabin door. "It won't be as swift or as wide in another month," Josiah said, "but there will always be enough water for our needs, and you won't have to pack it very far to the cabin. I had that in mind when I was planning where to put the cabin."

Ida smiled at her husband with approval. "He looks just like one of his boys when they're trying hard to please," she thought.

"That's wonderful, Josiah, I'll be happy for that on wash day. The spot you picked is so nice, with all these trees around it. It reminds me of some of the little glens back home in Nebraska. And it looks like there's a good-sized piece of ground between the hill and the creek which will make a good garden spot. I think we're going to be very comfortable here."

After receiving his wife's approval, Josiah hustled her to the door of the dug-out cabin. "Let's go inside, and see what you think." Ida entered the log structure and looked around at the biggest room. It contained a good-sized kitchen range and some shelves attached to the wall along one side. There was barely enough dirt floor space for their table and chairs which would seat ten people comfortably. One window facing the front of the room had a burlap covering over it. Come winter that would be replaced by canvas or deerskin.

Josiah had added a room on both sides of the main cabin, and cut openings into the heavy log walls so a person could exit to each room. The overhanging roof logs had been extended beyond the newest two rooms, providing a porch type shelter on the front of each. Toward the west he had built up an existing rock cache to make a bigger cellar and storage room for their food supplies. The entire structure was dug into the side of a small pinon and sage covered hillside, which provided a southern exposure for the structures. The head room in each room was very limited, barely allowing six-foot-four inch Josiah to stand erect.

"See, Birdella, you've now got your own room," her father said. "The other side of the wall is for the boys, and the one on the other end is Ma's and mine. What do you think?"

Birdie silently appraised the tiny little room which had been partitioned from the larger room. It looked more like a barn stall, but Josiah had built in a small bunk, which would accommodate her bed pallet, and it was private. "It's fine, Pa. Thanks for thinking of me."

The other side of the log partition also held built-in log bunks for the boys' bedrolls. No windows graced this room, but light filtered through some of the less tightly filled spaces between the logs, making the gloom less intense.

Ida and Josiah's room on the east side would hold the big double bed still packed in the wagon, plus several trunks which contained their personal possessions. In good weather the door could be left open to the over-hang shelter, and Ida could see that the morning sun would hit their room first.

Ida had to turn away from Josiah's imploring look. When was she going to have a decent home? The three room house in Wolcott, with its warped green lumber which left large gaps in the wall, looked like a castle compared to this...this...rabbit hole! Tears stung her eyes at the thought of what the coming winter would be like. With the one window covered, their lives would be spent in several months of semi-gloom. If the winter was extremely cold, everyone would have to move into the one room which held the stove, or be prepared to freeze in the cold, drafty, adjoining bedrooms.

Looking around, she realized that her family was waiting to take their cue from her. No matter how badly she felt, the children must be made to feel comfortable in their new life, and she didn't want to embarrass her husband in from of them. She shook off her despair and looked around.

"Isn't this the prettiest little park you ever saw? We'll set up a fire pit out in the middle and have picnics everyday. And you boys won't have far to haul water for wash day, will you? Yessir, by fall we'll have that little rock cellar heaping full of all sorts of good things to eat."

∾ Grover Cleveland was elected President of the United States. Silver prices dropped to eighty-seven cents an ounce.

∾ Pitkin County had an estimated population of 14,000 people in 1892. This would decline dramatically in the next few years.

∾ The Busk-Ivanhoe Tunnel was completed through the Continental Divide. It was 9,394 feet long, 15 feet wide, and 21 feet high. This tunnel was 581 feet lower than the Hagerman Tunnel, and shortened the rail distance by 6.9 miles.

∾ Construction was started on the Hotel Colorado in Glenwood Springs during August, 1892.

∾ The coal mining areas south of Glenwood Springs were producing 77,576 tons of coal for the area's coke ovens. One hundred seventy miners were employed at Spring Gulch.

∾ The gold mining community of Fulford, south of McDonald (Eagle) was gaining some prominence. Orion Dagget moved to the area where he dabbled in some mining ventures and operated a general store. It was a favorite past time for area residents to attend dances at Fulford.

SEPTEMBER, 1892   CATAMOUNT CREEK, COLORADO

Throughout 1892 the family worked diligently to improve their home and the ranch. Josiah and the two oldest boys immediately started cultivating land for hay fields, while Ida and Birdie spaded up the dirt in the designated garden plot. By the end of summer, the children as well as the crops had flourished from their healthy environment. Though tired to the bone each night, Ida thought she had never been happier. This was what she had hoped for all these years, even though they were very isolated from other ranches in the area. Even the gloomy little cabin looked more inviting, and she'd quit calling it the rabbit warren under her breath.

Wildlife was more abundant here than in other places throughout the region. Does and fawns could be observed almost every morning while they grazed in the spring fed grass close to the cabin. They also experienced, first hand, why the creek was named Catamount. It was not at all unusual for the family to find mountain lion tracks around the cabin, and there were frequent signs of deer kill in the fields. Meat had to be securely stored, so, for the rock cellar, Josiah fashioned a log door which would keep the predators out and their foodstuffs safe.

There was no post office in the district. Mail came from McCoy, fifteen miles away, whenever someone traveled to that settlement and was good enough to pick it up for the whole neighborhood. In late 1891, a letter finally reached Josiah from his brothers, Wes and Owen. The big news was that Wes had married a young woman by the name of Irene Moore, in Meeker. Wes reported that they were doing well and hoped that the two families would be able to meet some time in the future. He was working for some ranchers and trying to buy a few head of cattle for himself, which he hoped would be seed for a future herd.

In 1892, the indomitable Walter Cock started carrying the mail twice a week from McCoy to Burns, in order to get a post office designation. Mrs. Macmillen, the wife of the first school teacher in the area, had agreed to act as Postmaster without pay. Unfortunately the wheels of government turned slowly without forthcoming official approval. "Yeah," growled Josiah, "they can't get around to approving a post office for us, but President Harrison can find time to create the damned White River Reserve. You mark my words, that bill is gonna run us all out of the country, unless they loosen up the regulations. But it will take a while for them to come around to check on us, and in the meantime my livestock's going to graze wherever the grass is the greenest, and the government be damned."

Any provisions being brought into the area required the use of heavy freight wagons and at least four-horse teams. Each family made several trips each year to Wolcott to provision their households. The only times the roads were easily passable were during the winter when the ground was frozen, or during the summer and early fall.

Josiah decided to file on a piece of land adjacent to his Catamount land, thinking that he needed to acquire more property around the ranch in the event the government continued to withdraw its lands. The new land was mostly sagebrush and cedar juniper, but there would be enough graze for a few head of stock. Josiah also planned that he could cut some cedar fence posts for sale, which might give them a bit of money to get the family through the winter months.

Mr. Macmillan had started the first school in Catamount, which was only about a mile and a half west. The Herwick children were all students when the weather and road conditions permitted. Birdie, Wid, Fred, and Paul were able to attend when the mud and snow dried up and before the summer work started on the ranch. This left about a three month term for their education, but much could be crammed into young minds in a short period of time. Young Paul especially enjoyed his schooling and was often the focus of his sister and brother's teasing about being the "Teacher's Pet." He grimly endured the good-hearted badgering in order to read the books his teacher allowed him to borrow. Whenever he was not doing chores, you could be sure to find him nestled into a corner or under a tree, engrossed in devouring the latest loan from Mr. Macmillan.

Josiah had been able to buy some buttermilk calves from a rancher who wintered down in the canyon by Red Dirt. The animals were fattening up nicely on the good nourishing pasture land and would eventually become the nucleus of a nice little herd. Throughout the year, other animals had been added to their ranch life; a milk cow, some chickens, a few ducks and turkeys, several hogs, and a couple of "bummer lambs" which had to be kept behind the kitchen stove and fed by hand until they were strong enough to live outside. A big, ragged-looking dog had also been acquired to act as a watch dog over the domestic animals and sound a warning at the first sign of predators.

It was in the midst of this happy existence that Ida scared everyone with her illness. The summer of 1892 had been a busy one. Josiah and the boys were busy mowing the hay and stacking it in the fields. Ida and Birdie had been equally busy preserving, drying, canning, and storing all the abundance from the vegetable garden. Service and squaw berries were starting to turn color on the hillsides, and Birdie had found a small patch of wild raspberries which tasted so good with thick cream. By September, the hay was all in stacks, and the men of the family were preparing to start on the winter wood pile.

Ida couldn't say when the pain began. It had increased so gradually that she was able to ignore the cramping for some time, and her fatigue could be explained by all the hard work she did. Then the sharp pains began to send forth their piercing stabs into her gut, taking away her breath with the intensity. "Dear God," she fervently prayed, "don't let me get sick. There's so much yet to do, and I don't think I could stand to ride all the way to Wolcott to see a doctor." She tried to keep at her duties between the pains, which were becoming more frequent each day. Finally, one morning she doubled over the milk pail she was lifting to the kitchen table, and her family finally realized that their mother was sick.

Fred ran up the gulch yelling for Josiah, who followed him on a hard trot to the cabin. Josiah felt Ida's forehead. "My God, Ida, you're burning up. How long has this been going on, woman?"

"I don't know, Josiah. I started having some pain a few days ago, but it wasn't so bad. I thought it would finally go away. I'm sorry. I just don't know what to do."

The next few days she was in a semi-dozing, feverish state, while Josiah tried every remedy he could ever recall his mother using in cases of pain and fever. The fact that this was in her gut caused him to believe that it had something to do with her female organs, which he knew absolutely nothing about. All of the horror stories roamed through his head about women dying from these mysterious maladies. "If only Mother were here, she'd know what to do," he thought, "but she isn't, and I've got to do something. I can't get her to a doctor in time, so I've got to figure it out."

He set Birdie to boiling water, while he wiped Ida's brow. Once the water was bubbling, he wrung out hot compresses and put them on her abdomen, replacing them as soon as they started cooling. "Wid go down to the creek, and cut some willow branches–six or seven will do. Birdie, I want you to steep the bark in boiling water for about an hour. Then put some honey in it, and we'll see if we can get your mother to drink the tea. The

Indians always said that this was sure to take a fever down. Let's see if it works. It sure as hell can't hurt."

Ida drifted in and out of her trance, silently allowing Josiah's ministrations. Occasionally, a sharp pain would awaken her and she'd cry out, but the spasms seemed to be lessening, whether from the hot compresses, or willow bark tea, he didn't know. On the second day, he decided to slice fresh onions and lay them on Ida's belly before placing the hot compresses over them. Their odor also helped camouflage the other smell coming from Ida's body. The sweetish scent of putrefaction horrified him, and he prayed that Ida was strong enough to fight off this terrible infection. The children stood in silent fear as they watched their mother's silent frame in the bed. Sixteen-month-old Tiny whimpered with longing for her mama, and Birdie's loving arms did little to lessen the yearning. The boys quietly took up the farm chores without discussion, while their father kept a constant bedside vigil.

By the evening of the third day, Ida's fever was slight, and she was no longer awakened by the sharp stabbing pains. She was able to take some regular sips of hot chicken broth which Birdie had prepared, and she rested comfortably at last. Josiah poured a pan of warm water into the wash basin and shooed the children out of the room. Stripping off Ida's nightgown, laying bare her fever worn body, he gently and tenderly washed away the signs of her sickness.

As she began to recuperate, Ida was overwhelmed by the tender care she'd received from her husband. She could not recall this much attention since the first months of their marriage, and tears welled up in her eyes as she remembered his devotion. For once she was content to lie still and allow her body to heal itself, even though there was so much work to be done before winter hit. She knew the household was in capable hands. At almost fifteen years of age, Birdie was a very competent person, who kept the household functioning very efficiently, especially when it concerned whipping her brothers into action. She'd even been able to shame them into helping her with the sizable washing which had been piling up since Ida took sick. They were mortified at doing "women's work," but knew it was useless to appeal to their father who had given Birdie total authority in household matters.

The weather stretched into a lovely mild Indian summer, allowing the Herwick family to prepare for whatever winter was yet to come. As Ida regained her strength, she was able to take over the less physical tasks from Birdie. Life started to return to normal in their small part of the world.

The year ended and the growing family was thankful that there was hay in the fields, food in the cellar, and everyone was again in good health. Who could ask for anything more? Perhaps Ida, having missed that far-off glint in her husband's eyes, would have done well to be more observant.

∾ The Sherman Silver Act was repealed in November, 1893, leading to the slowdown of silver mining and depression in the mining camps of Colorado. Too much silver was being produced, and the world markets were closing. Silver fell to 61 cents per ounce. By midsummer, 90% of the Leadville work force was idle. People started hunting game to provide food for themselves. Children were sent out to collect coal along the railroad tracks. On September 14, 1893, miners agreed to a wage cut from $3.00 to $2.50 a day in any month when the silver price was less than 83 1/2 cents per ounce. People starting looking to iron ore production as a supplement to silver. Almost all of the mines were back in production by the end of 1893.

∾ The first train went through the Busk-Ivanhoe Tunnel on December 17, 1893.

MAY, 1893   WOLCOTT, COLORADO

Dr. Evens finished his exam and stepped outside so Ida could dress herself. Seated across the desk a few minutes later, the physician shook his head as he peered at her with his perennially grumpy gaze. "I can't believe that you are actually pregnant, Mrs. Herwick. My examination shows that you did, indeed, have a severely ulcerated womb. I can feel some of the scar tissue, and it's a miracle that you conceived again. It doesn't seem to be bothering this pregnancy. It looks like everything is fine for right now. But, I think it's a good idea that you will be here in Wolcott for your confinement. Let's see, how many children do you now have?"

As the doctor completed taking her medical history, Ida relaxed for the first time since walking through the door. She had been so frightened when she discovered she might be pregnant in March. After last September's horrible infection had run its course she, too, thought perhaps this would bring an end to her childbearing. When she began having the unmistakable signs of morning sickness and fatigue, there were moments of ambivalence. On one hand, she would be glad to never have another child. Seven younguns were plenty for her to take care of, and she had barely recovered all her strength from the illness. But, there was an ancient voice in her head that said it was her duty to bear all the children that God saw fit to bless her with. She struggled with this knowledge for several days. She knew that some women, who were much braver than she, chose to end their unwanted pregnancies by a variety of means, the most bizarre being the insertion of a darning needle into the womb. Even if she had been less spiritual minded, the thought of mutilating her child and possibly her body was absolutely unthinkable. But, in all honesty, she had to admit that she wouldn't be overly grieved if God decided to end this pregnancy. God didn't end the pregnancy, though, and after several weeks of alternating happiness and sorrow, she finally told Josiah that another baby would be born sometime in October. He received the news with an unaccustomed show of emotion. "My God, Ida, are you all right? I'm sorry. It's all my fault. I shouldn't have come near you. How are you feelin'? Are you havin' any pain? Well, I can tell you one thing, we're gonna move to town. I'm not takin any chances on you gettin' sick again without a doctor bein' handy."

Josiah's vehemence startled Ida, who was used to his customary nonchalance when it concerned her many pregnancies. Of course he'd never had to nurse her to health as he did last September. She was touched by his loving solicitude, and offered very little resistance to his proposed move. Although she loved the ranch and having all her family around her, the thought of being so far from medical care was pretty frightening.

If Ida could have entered Josiah's head she might have been far less impressed by his tender compassion about her condition. For truth be known, Josiah Herwick had itchy feet, and this was a very convenient reason for them to make another move.

For the past year, Josiah had been thinking about going back into the sawmill business. Every time he looked at the substantial, albeit dwindling, stands of prime timber, he saw all the financial possibilities. Eagle Valley was filling up with disillusioned miners and other pioneers who had gone to the mining camps to seek their fortunes, and then moved on to a more stable means of making a living. Other settlers were arriving who saw the fertile valley as a means to a prosperous future in ranching. Whatever the reason, these settlers all had one thing in common, they needed good lumber for their towns, farms, and ranches which were sprouting up. Before the federal government tied up all the lands in the proposed reserves, Josiah intended to make some money. If he could get someone to loan him the money to get started and find a tenant to operate the ranch, he could start cutting the timber stands between the ranch and Castle Peak. His thought was that there was a whole lot of land up there, with a ton of trees. If he could get started soon, maybe he could keep the competition out. As far as he knew, no one was doing any cutting between Castle Peak and Milk Creek. That was a good six miles in just one direction. The wagon roads would have to be improved to get the timber out, but he had built them before, and he could do it again.

By the end of April, Josiah's family had been deposited back in Wolcott. But this time, Ida had the luxury of a flimsy-built frame house, rather than a dug-out in the side of a hill. The little settlement had grown by leaps and bounds since becoming the stage route to Steamboat Springs. The streets were shin deep with horse and cow manure from all the stagecoach traffic and cattle drives into the large stockyard east of town. It was common for the stage company to own at least a hundred horses, strung out along the stage route, and a good twenty-five percent were stabled in Wolcott. As many as thirty to forty wagons left Wolcott each morning with freight for the northern regions of McCoy, Yampa, and Steamboat Springs. Some of the precious cargo included gold shipments of $10,000 to $12,000.

Ida's ears were assaulted by the raucous sounds of the town; the lead-tipped whips being cracked over the teams pulling the Concord Coaches as they careened down the hill into town, the constant bawling of the cattle in the stockyard pens, the blasphemous yells of the teamsters "pulling the ribbons" over the backs of their sweating horses, the whistle of the frequent trains on their daily runs. After several years of peace and quiet on the Catamount, the sights and smells of the town were less than pleasant, especially since their home was only two houses away from the main street.

But, if Ida was disconcerted by the dirty, smelly, noisy little town, her children were enthralled. Birdie happily sought out some of her former school chums and was more than a little pleased to observe the covert looks from young fellows she met on the street.

Wid had immediately high-tailed himself down to the livery stables and stagecoach barn to resume his goal of being a top notch stagecoach driver someday. Fred never had problems finding new and unusual challenges to his young life. His spare time was spent soaking up the ambiance of the thriving little community, and every day's adventure was entertaining, even when it involved a bloody tussle with one or two bullies whose territory he might have invaded. Paul was looking forward to resuming his school work because he had about exhausted the resources available at Catamount. Guy, Oren, and Tiny were too young to mind where they lived as long as they were well fed and loved.

Another letter from Wes Herwick reached them in June, reporting that he was the proud father of a baby boy named Clarence, born in May in Aspen. His note mentioned that he and Owen were seriously thinking about leaving Aspen for work further down the Roaring Fork Valley. Plummeting silver prices were throwing the mining town into a panic, and the handwriting was on the wall. People were leaving in droves, and teamster work had almost come to a standstill. Wes reported that the coal mines, such as Sunlight, were still working steadily and he thought he and Owen would have less trouble finding jobs there. He promised to write again as soon as they were settled somewhere.

Josiah was able to rustle up some money to cover the cost of buying sawmill equipment, and he was in the mountains cutting timber most of the summer, when he wasn't in town trying to secure lumber contracts from various builders. He took Wid, Fred and Paul with him, thereby lightening Ida's work load at home. Between her and Birdie, the little ones were easy to care for, and she found there was actually time for them to do some limited visiting with the other ladies of the town and to sew some badly needed clothes. Church services were happily resumed and she took part in the activities associated with the church society. She looked forward to the sermon and hymn singing each week. It was the spiritual boost she needed to cope with her family life and all its challenges.

Josiah had just moved the sawmill to a lower elevation on Milk Creek when another baby girl was born on October 14, 1893. "It looks like you're getting the hang of having little girls now," he teased Ida. "Maybe you're just lookin' to even up the number of boys and girls! She's a pretty little thing, isn't she? What's this one gonna be called?"

"I think maybe I'll call her Mary, after my mother. How 'bout Mary Margaret? How does that sound?"

"Sounds just dandy. As long as you're both okay, I really don't care what she's called. Now, get some rest. Birdie has everything under control. I've got to get back up to the sawmill with the supplies, or the men will be going hungry pretty soon. I'll see you in a few weeks." Plopping a swift peck on her cheek, Josiah left Ida and his newest child.

~ The Populist Party held office in 1894. It had been formed largely because of the push to maintain free and unlimited coinage of silver. Governor Davis Waite, an Aspen lawyer, supported a number of reforms, including women's suffrage. His two-year tenure was marked by all types of controversy with the legislature, labor, constituents, and elected officials.

~ J.B. Hurlburt and Milton Billiter went to "Peach Day" at Grand Junction in September, 1894. While they were gone, forty armed and masked men met at DeBeque, Colorado, and rode to the mountain between DeBeque and Parachute, where 2,000 head of sheep were grazing. The presumed cattlemen tried to drive the sheep over the cliff, but the animals refused to jump. The men then clubbed them to death, or bunched them up until many suffocated. One of the sheepherders was wounded in the hip, but a doctor with the group of butchers treated the wound and allowed the herder to ride away.

AUGUST, 1894   WOLCOTT, COLORADO

The heat rising from the fiery cook stove, the flies congregating on the recently pitted apricots, and the children running through the kitchen yelling at the top of their lungs caused Ida to sigh as she went about her work. Not that these events were unusual, but today she seemed to have less tolerance for the dirt and hubbub.

"Guy, Oren, Tiny–you children settle down, or I'll make you lie down for a nap with your baby sister. You've been noisy all day, and it's time for you to play quietly. Do you hear me?"

"Yes Ma'm," the children dutifully responded, before charging around the corner of the house.

"I wanna be the cowboy for a while," Oren complained as he resisted falling to the ground when Guy tried to "shoot" him. "You be the Indian so I can shoot you."

"Me too, me too," echoed Tiny as she struggled to catch up with her brothers.

Ida had worked for the past several days putting the house to rights and preparing for an afternoon tea she was hosting for Reverend Winne and some of the church ladies. She'd decided to make some fresh apricot jam from the bruised fruit picked up from a peddler passing through. She wished she had a fancy teapot and dainty cups to serve her guests, but there wasn't money for such luxuries.

The money had been tight this year, not that Josiah wasn't working hard on the sawmill, but it seemed to go out faster than it came in. He'd had to hire some extra help to get orders out, and that cut down his profit. He was always complaining about how much food that hungry bunch of men and boys could consume in a day's time. Ida chuckled to herself and thought it served him right. In all the years she'd been struggling to feed their sprouting family, she could recall few times that Josiah expressed any appreciation for her ability to produce three meals each day. Maybe he'd be more sensitive to her cooking in the future, but somehow she doubted that.

Even though Josiah didn't take much interest in the household duties and chores, Ida had always been able to count on Birdie, and now she sorely missed her daughter since she had found work helping in other women's homes. The girl, at almost seventeen, acted more like a confidante than a daughter. Birdie was a beautiful, willful, stubborn young lady who generally got her own way through the force of her personality. But she could also be extremely loyal, dedicated, and loving to her parents and siblings. Through the many years of being alone with her children, Ida had gradually accepted Birdie as the friend she had always yearned for but was seldom blessed with. The girl's quick wit and take-charge ways amazed Ida, while intimidating her just a little bit. Even Josiah steered clear of heated debates that usually led to angry, foot-stomping tantrums, but nevertheless, he admired his stronghearted daughter.

One Sunday the Jonathan Ashlocks, who were living at the ranch on Catamount, came to the Herwick's home for dinner while they were in Wolcott buying supplies. Their twenty-three year old son, Norman, had accompanied them on the trip and joined his parents at the Herwick's home. A blind man could have seen the mutual attraction between Birdie and Norman, who did little else but gaze at each other. "Even though I don't want to face it," thought Ida, "I'll be losing her very soon. She's a beauty, and if young Ashlock doesn't get her, some other man will." In a country where the men outnumbered the marriageable women more than two to one, even homely spinsters were finding themselves with many suitors. "But, it's going to take a mighty powerful man to tame that girl. I hope she holds that temper 'til she gets a ring on her finger!"

Ida contrasted her own life with that of her daughter's who was almost two years beyond the age Ida had been when she married. Sometimes she could hardly believe that such a spitfire could spring from her and Josiah. Ida would never have thought to question things the way Birdie did. She wondered if she had failed in raising her in some way. Perhaps some would say she had spared the rod too much. But for all her outspoken ways, Birdie was a good girl. Ida sometimes tried to imagine what it would be like to actually demand her way once in a while. But she just didn't have that in her. She was a product of upbringing and habit. It simply never occurred to her that she could be so selfish as to consider herself first.

The summer was a wet one, the rains helping to make a lush garden in which Ida's vegetables grew to mammoth proportions. It was less favorable to Josiah, who was often bogged down in heavy black mud while trying to bring the cut lumber down from the sawmill. By Thanksgiving, he had managed to fill all his contracts and was taking a short break before going back to the mountains.

Josiah also wanted to keep an eye on the Catamount place because he had bought a small band of sheep and taken them onto the grazing land south of the ranch. Not too many ranchers even knew the fifty head of sheep were there, but several men had made some pretty pointed remarks about his being a traitor to the cattlemen's cause. While there had been no open threats, he wanted to be sure that no harm came to either his animals or the people living there. The newspapers had been filled with the news of the dastardly massacre of two thousand head of sheep owned by their old friend, J.B. Hurlburt of Parachute. When told of the news, Ida thought back six years to the dear, kind folks who had offered her family shelter their first night in Parachute, and she said a prayer for their well being as she wiped tears from her eyes.

The boys came down for the winter session at the newly built schoolhouse. Wid was openly rebellious about attending. He argued that he should be allowed to find a job because he was almost full grown, and he'd been doing a man's work for the past two years. Josiah finally gave in and allowed the boy to do what he'd been longing to do for years—get a job with the stage company. A good share of the time he was nothing more than a glorified stable boy, mucking out the stalls and feeding the horses, but, once in a while, he was allowed to ride "shot-gun" on the stage route north to Steamboat Springs and back. On these four-day trips, he eagerly learned everything he could about what it took to be a good "Jehu." He watched in admiration while the driver put his horses through their paces, holding all three pairs of reins in his left hand so his right hand was free to flick the whip over the backs of the racing animals. Wid always shook his head at the deceptively smooth training and management of the teams, and he vowed that someday he'd be one of the best teamsters around.

Birdie would not be going back to school either, so that left Fred, Paul and Guy to start the fall session. This was Guy's first year, and he took it all very seriously. Each day when he came home from class, he repeated his lessons to his little brother, Oren, who held him in high esteem for knowing how to spell his name. The brothers, so near in age, were very close and Oren missed his playmate. But, within a few weeks he had accepted the fact that he'd have to stay home with sister, Tiny, for one more year, and then he, too, could escape to that magic world of school.

The church was planning a big Thanksgiving celebration as a way of giving thanks for an abundant year, in spite of the silver decline. A big pot luck dinner would be held following the services. Everyone agreed that it had been divine guidance for them to come to this fertile valley. Because it would be on a Thursday instead of Sunday, an itinerant photographer was supposed to be there to take pictures of all the families coming in for the celebration. For once Ida put her foot down, and insisted that all the children accompany her to both the service and lunch afterward. Wid and Fred grumbled about having to get all "spiffed up" in Sunday clothes, but they sensed that this was very important to their mother so were reluctant to raise much of a fuss. However, Ida wasn't so fortunate with her husband. Josiah begged off with the excuse that he had to ride up to Catamount to make sure the sheep were moved down around the river before the first snow hit. Ida knew it was useless to argue with him when he had his mind made up, but she couldn't help being resentful that he was unwilling to wait one more day before leaving. "Oh, well, when did Josiah Herwick ever do anything he didn't want to do?" she mumbled under her breath. "I should be used to that by now. At least the children will all be here."

She hadn't told any one her secret. For several months she had been putting a little money away for a special occasion, and she intended that having a family portrait done would be it. Of all the things she could think of, having a picture of her young family would be the most precious. As she dressed the younger children, and then herself, she took special care that they all looked very presentable. She hoped the photographer would make the pictures before the food was served or her boys would be a mess.

When the service was over, and the congregation filed out, Ida spotted the photographer's wagon by the side of the building opposite the food preparation. "Come here children. I've got a little surprise for you," she said as she hustled them over to the short line of people waiting their turn.

"I've managed to save a few cents here and there, and I think I have enough for us to get our picture made. Isn't that exciting?"

The children weren't given enough notice for them to put up much resistance. Before they could blink an eye, the photographer was positioning them into a semi-rigid pose while he prepared his wet plates for exposure. "Okydoke, folks, now just look at me, and stand very still. Little boy stop wiggling, or you'll blur the picture. One, two, three, and it's done!" Ida was pleased that in years to come she would have a picture to remind her of how the children looked at this time. And she remembered the little boy in a grave a few miles away who hadn't lived long enough to have his picture taken. "Life is short and we don't know what God will give us tomorrow, but at least we will have a memory of this day. I do wish I had a picture of your father, though," she told her children as they moved on to the celebration.

ல The townsite of Castle (later to be called Eagle) was purchased by A.A. McDonald from B. Clark Wheeler in 1895 and was renamed McDonald. He also sponsored a direct road over the Castle Range to Burns in order to attract people to his town rather than to Wolcott.

ல Copper-bearing quartzite was discovered in the vicinity of Red Gorge Canyon, about eight miles east of McCoy. Reports indicated that assays were running 40 percent. Eastern speculators started investing in the mining claims.

ல Leadville had a banner year, despite the concerns from the previous year. The mines posted an annual production of over nine million dollars. The Cloud City Miners Union, local #83, was formed.

ல The townsite of Fulford was filed at Eagle County Courthouse on December 18, 1895, by Orion Daggatt. About one hundred people were living there at that time, and 25 buildings had been constructed. Although the mines had been operating for years, this was the first filing on a townsite.

ல In Garfield County the Antlers Land and Reservoir was formed with $100,000 capitol. The Harvey Gap Dam broke, washing out fields below the structure.

APRIL, 1895 WOLCOTT, COLORADO

"There, by God, this ought to put those damned commissioners on notice that I don't intend to take this sitting down. Someone's gonna pay for my stock, or I'll know the reason why. That black-hearted bunch of cattlemen think they own this range. Fifty head of sheep, on my own property, shouldn't be much of a threat but those sneaky bastards are so scared of letting even one animal on the range, they'll do anything to keep them off, including getting rid of my small flock. I wonder how the hell they managed to get rid of them without anyone hearing something? Read this, Ida, and tell me what you think."

As Josiah continued to rant and rave, Ida took the piece of paper from his hands and read:

Catamount Creek
Wolcott P.O.
April 12, 1895
To: Honorable Board of County Commissioners of Eagle County

Gentlemen:
I have reason to believe that there is a plot to kill or run off and scatter and destroy my flock of sheep that is running on the range at my ranch on Cata-mount Creek, and I ask that you render to me such protection for any stock as I am entitled to under the law.

Yours Truly,
J.L. Herwick

"What makes you think the county commissioners are responsible for someone running the sheep off, Josiah? They didn't have anything to do with it, did they? I don't understand what you think they can do about it. We're not even sure what happened to the animals."

"By God, woman, they can pay me damages for those five sheep that're missin'. Maybe this will force them to take some action on all this foolishness that's been going on. A man doesn't stand a chance any more. If the hard winters and predators don't get the stock, then his God damned cowardly neighbors will. You'd think they'd have the decency to at least warn me to get rid of the sheep, for Christ's sake."

As Ida watched her angry husband, she knew it was useless to try to calm him. He'd rage and yell for a while, then quiet down and listen to reason. Not that Ida didn't sympathize with him. The loss of five sheep meant a loss of at least $50-100, and that was a substantial part of their income.

The culprits had apparently been watching everyone's coming and going at the ranch. Josiah had ridden up every two weeks during the winter, except when storms made the trip impossible. John Ashlock reported that the sheep were doing pretty well down in the creek bottom, with a little supplemental feed. He hadn't seen anyone nosing around the ranch and, on Josiah's last trip, John mentioned that they had probably been concerned about nothing.

Those words had a hollow ring when John rode into Wolcott to tell Josiah that five head of ewes were missing from one day's feeding to the next. He'd searched up and down the creek, thinking that they had gotten through the fence but couldn't find a break anywhere. A storm that night had successfully covered their tracks, as well as that of the presumed thieves, so he couldn't even say which direction they might have been taken. He looked for blood or signs of a struggle, but he was unsuccessful with that as well. It was a mystery how the sheep could have disappeared so completely without a trace.

Josiah didn't have any doubts about what happened to those ewes, and he was hell bent on making someone pay. If it couldn't be those misbegotten ranchers, then, by God, he'd sue the county. If the commissioners weren't so afraid of alienating the ranch owners, they'd have gotten the sheriff on these periodic sheep disappearances long before now. So, that very day, he posted his letter to the county seat in Red Cliff.

"Now, Josiah, don't get your hopes up that they'll do anything about this," warned Ida. "You can't even prove that the sheep were stolen or killed. You said so yourself. I can't imagine that those commissioners are going to do anything about it, especially when it comes to paying you for the ewes."

Ida's prophecies were proven true when the May meeting of the Eagle County Commissioners failed to mention Josiah's letter in their minutes. It was as if they had never received it, and Josiah was doubly incensed that he had been ignored. From that day on, he began to lose interest in the ranch and his hope of becoming a big rancher in Burn's Hole.

But if the sheep affair was a sad loss, another event which occurred on its heels, helped to line the family coffers. The copper mining in the area east of McCoy was spurring interest in all the placer claims of that area. Before long, Josiah and his partners were approached by Henry Johnson and Solon Ackley in regard to selling the Florence and Coleridge Placer Claims west of McCoy. It had seemed to be a good investment when he filed on these claims in 1890, even though Josiah was not a mining man. But a bonafide hustler never says no to a possible opportunity, so the initial work had been done, and the yearly assessments were completed, although Josiah had no intentions of actually mining the property. The offer from Ackley and Johnson seemed to be divine reimbursement for the loss of his sheep. He was astounded when he found out they were offering $2,000 for the Florence and Coleridge claims, plus $500 for another eighty acres he also co-owned adjacent to the claims. That meant, as a quarter interest holder, the Herwick family would be over $800 richer, and Josiah was a happy man.

"Idie, you've always wanted your own home, well by God you're going to have it," Josiah exclaimed as he waved the check in front of her face. "We'll buy a lot right here in Wolcott and I'll build you a nice place. We've got enough lumber cut and planed for most of it, and maybe I can trade a little of next summer's lumber for seasoned wood around town. I should be able to get you all moved in before the boys and I head for the hills. The rest of the money will go back into the sawmill equipment. I've got a feeling this is gonna be a good year!"

When the mud started drying up, Ida noticed that Norman Ashlock seemed to be making more frequent trips into Wolcott from the Catamount Creek Ranch. He never failed to stop by the Herwick house to pay his respects and to give Josiah a report on the ranch, if Josiah was home. But Ida could tell he was far more interested in her daughter than the transparent reports he concocted in order to stop by their place. Norman's eyes followed Birdie wherever she moved, and she seemed more than a little pleased by his attention. At twenty-four years of age, Norman acted much more mature than the local town boys. He had piercing dark eyes that could convey his thoughts without a word, especially when he was angry. Ida had heard stories about his short fuse, matched only by her daughter's temper, and wondered what in the world those two young people saw in each other. "It's a question of who gets burned first," Ida decided, and vowed to try to talk to her headstrong daughter about the dangers of getting involved with such a volatile young man.

But, Birdie had made up her mind. The darkly handsome Norman had captured her heart, and she wouldn't be swayed from her course. It was exciting being around him, with his penetrating glances. She sensed a power, almost a danger, brooding just under his surface, and she was fascinated by the challenge of capturing this man for her own. At seventeen years of age, Birdie was a mature young woman who was ready to become a wife. She had always been a surrogate mother to her brothers and sisters, as well as a confidante to her mother and, consequently, much older than her years. The feelings stirring inside her would not be denied. It was simply time for her to find a man of her own. She had dreamt about the moment when she could give herself fully to a husband, and started practicing her considerable wiles on Norman, who didn't stand a chance of escaping the tender trap of matrimony!

There was only one problem regarding marriage about which Birdie had considerable doubts. After helping to raise her siblings for most of her young life, she absolutely did not want to have children right away. The close quarters of their past living arrangements left no doubt about procreation in Birdie's mind. She knew she would be following in her mother's footsteps, having one baby after another, unless she could find out how to stop it. Surely there was something that could be done to prevent her from getting pregnant, and she intended to find someone who could give her that information. But it wouldn't do to share this information with her mother, who would likely be horrified at Birdie's temerity.

After some searching, she found her way to the cabin of "Negro Rose," the nice black lady who had tried to help Birdie's mother so long ago when she was pregnant with baby Collins. She instinctively knew that this woman was wise in the ways of women and their bodies. Surely, if any one knew the sought after secrets, it would be Miss Rose.

The elderly woman didn't show any surprise when she answered the door of her cabin. "Why, Miss Birdie, come on in. My you've grown into a fine young lady. I bet you got lots of beaus swarmin' round you, just like bees buzzin' 'round honey. Come, come sit down. I was jest bilin' up some sasserfrass tea and I'll pour another cup. Nothing like sasserfrass to clean the winter's bad humors out. Just a drop of honey to sweeten it up some. Hmmmm, now doesn't that taste good?"

Birdie sat across from the woman and made polite talk about the town and its inhabitants. She believed that Miss Rose probably knew more about the citizens of Wolcott than did anyone else. After years of tending to the needs of so many people, she had become a fixture and heard all sorts of things that would never have been said around their friends or relatives. Birdie had discovered this for herself from her limited work for other people. They tended to share their secrets and gossip with her as if she was a confidante. Rose had a fine sense of humor and made Birdie laugh about her perceptive comments regarding some of the leading citizens. Birdie settled back and almost forgot the intent of her visit until Rose looked at her with a penetrating gaze and said, "Well, Miss Birdie, this has been a pleasant chat, but 'ol Rose's got to hitch her fanny over to Miz Carey's, and that lady don't like to be kept waiting. I 'spect you might have another reason for comin' to see me?"

Now that the moment had arrived, Birdie almost lost her courage. But she took a deep breath and said, "I might be married soon, and I don't want to have lots of babies. I thought maybe you might know ways of keeping from getting that way."

"Well, now, I thought it might be somethin' like that. That's a big worry for women. Look at your mama. She's had one youngun after another. Yeah, I can see where you'd want to wait a bit for a baby, but it's hard to do when you're lovin that man and wantin' to do man and woman things with him. Hmmm, Hmmmm. Some of us weren't equipped for making babies, but you never know whether that's true 'til it's too late, and then it's harder to get rid of. The good Lord's never blessed me with a chil' but I hear 'bout things that other ladies try to keep from gettin' that way. I think the best one might be to use somethin' to keep the man's seed from going inside you. I hear tell that ladies of the night flush it out after they've been with a man, but I still think a sponge soaked in vinegar works better than anything. Do you know how to do it?"

At Birdie's shake of her head, the elderly lady clearly and explicitly explained how the procedure should be carried out. Upon leaving her house a short time later, Birdie clutched a small sponge in the pocket of her skirt, while thanking Miss Rose profusely for her honest advice. "Now, I don't have to put Mr. Ashlock off any longer," she said to herself, as she started for home with a sly smile on her face.

The romance gained momentum very rapidly, and finally resulted in the marriage of Birdie and Norman on Wednesday, July 24, 1895, at the home of the Justice of Peace, I.G. McMillen in Wolcott. Ida had unsuccessfully pleaded with Birdie to wait until the minister arrived so he could marry them. "Ma, it isn't important to me or Norman to have a preacher," Birdie replied. "Norman's coming down for supplies, and we'll just say the words so I can go back up to the ranch with him. John and Hannah Buchholz have offered to be our witnesses, and we'll be on our way as soon as the ceremony's over. We figured we might camp out one night on the way, and then move into the lean-to Norman's built onto our old cabin. I think I'll enjoy being back up at the ranch. I always liked it there."

Ida knew it was useless to argue with Birdie, despite her reservations about the impending marriage. On one of Josiah's brief trips from the sawmill, he had given approval to the marriage and informed Ida she should be grateful that their daughter wanted to marry a fine young man, like Norman. "Just look around at some of these ne'er-do-wells bumming around town," he said. "Birdie and their children will always be taken care of. I think she's a lucky girl to land such a man."

"The Ashlocks are good people, and we've known them for a long time and had business dealings with them. I know that Birdie could do much worse. Norman seems to be a tough young man who'll always manage to make a living for his family. It's just that, when I look at those young people, all I see is two brush fires who threaten to burn each other out. I just pray that the good Lord will protect them and give them the patience they'll need in order to make this marriage work," said Ida.

For several nights following Birdie's departure, Ida lay awake long after the children were bedded down and asleep. The feelings scampering around inside her were hard to describe, but she supposed the closest she could come would be to say that she felt as if she had lost a significant part of herself. As the hot tears slid down her face, Ida knew that her daughter and friend had left forever. She would see Birdie often, but the old relationship would not be there. In its place would be a new woman—someone she didn't yet know. And she grieved the loss of a very special relationship.

Josiah and the three oldest boys were at the sawmill all summer, leaving to Ida the care of the home and children in Wolcott. She found herself enjoying the warm languid days with her young family. It was unusual for her to not be pregnant, and the freedom was almost heady. The mornings were spent on household chores, when everyone pitched in to complete their tasks. The afternoons were saved for jaunts along the Eagle River, walking, fishing, or just taking off their shoes and dabbling toes into the icy water. Ida tied a light rope around little Mary's middle and the other end to a tree along the water, in case the toddling two year old decided to take a dip into the rushing stream. Guy and Oren became adept fishermen, and their day's products oftimes graced the supper table. Tiny flitted from flower to flower, picking the very best of the lot for her mama who taught her to make a little floral crown for her beautiful blond head.

Ida discovered a new dimension in her relationship with the children. In the past she would have left much of the child care to Birdie while she tended to other chores. Now she was with her little family all the time and found it to be quite rewarding. Guy, Oren, Tiny and Mary displayed personalities that she had never seen before, and Ida realized she was getting to know these children as she had not been able to do with the older ones. Most nights she slept soundly from the day's exercise, and contentedly from the peace she was blessed with. Life seemed to be a very pleasant experience.

Occasionally she and the children would accompany Josiah or Wid back to Milk Creek for a few days of camping when the men returned from a supply trip. The two little boys loved these outings, as extensions of their favorite afternoons on the Eagle River, but Ida had to be constantly vigilant because of the dangerous machinery all around the camp. She was usually worn out after several days, and very willing to be taken back down to Wolcott where the children could run about with less risk to their lives. She knew that Josiah would prefer her being at the camp full time, but she side-stepped the issue by saying that no one was tending to her garden down in town. "What will we eat next winter if I don't preserve all the produce?" Josiah grudgingly gave in for the time being, but Ida knew that the subject would be broached again, if not this summer, then the next.

Reports from Birdie, Norman, and the Ashlock family indicated that everyone was well and happy. Several times, during Ida's sojourns to Milk Creek, Birdie had ridden over the divide to visit. She reported that everything was fine on the ranch. The remaining sheep had produced a good lamb crop in the spring, and were fattening up on the far pastures of the place. No more were found missing, and everyone still wondered how in the world five sheep could disappear without a trace.

Birdie told her father that John Ashlock was interested in buying the ranch, if Josiah ever decided to sell. Ida could tell that this was a definite possibility from the look in her husband's eye. He was still so mad about the sheep that she suspected he'd sell just to get rid of the memory. Josiah might be able to ranch, but this was not his first priority. He preferred the sawmill, but mostly he liked the excitement of making his 'deals.' "I don't suppose he'll ever change," Ida thought with some resignation, "but I guess I knew that when I married him."

Josiah did sell the Catamount Ranch to John Ashlock in December, and barely made it back from recording the deed in Red Cliff before the first blizzard of the winter hit. The house was full once again, and Ida thought longingly of her brief summer respite. Wid and Fred were down at the stage barn most days, and Josiah frequently traveled around the valley hustling lumber deals for next summer. Paul, Guy, and Oren were once again in school, leaving Tiny and Mary home with their mama during the day. The chores were never-ending, and Ida thought about Birdie with longing. Josiah loved having his boys, but he never stopped to think about how much care those boys took. Tiny was starting to be of some help in small ways. She was good with her sister and she minded well. Ida was thankful for any blessing God gave her.

Another by-product of Josiah's returning home from Milk Creek was made evident by Christmas, 1895. The on-set of early morning queasiness signaled that another little Herwick would be born next summer. "Well, at least that takes care of my having to move up to Milk Creek for the summer," Ida thought wryly, "but I didn't count on having to pay such a high price."

∾ Although December, 1895, was very warm (the temperature rose to 65 degrees on December 12th) the Leadville Ice Palace was opened on January 1, 1896. There were skating exhibitions, rock drilling contests, ice sculpture, merchant displays, costume contests, and toboggan rides. Additional ice was shipped in by rail. The Palace closed March 28, 1896 due to an early spring.

∾ On February 18, 1896, at 11:27 A.M. the Vulcan Coal Mine at Newcastle, in Garfield County, exploded killing forty-nine miners.

∾ On June 28, 1896, all Leadville miners making less than $3.00 a day went on strike, a total of 968 men in thirteen mines. The mine owners closed all the mines putting another 2,300 men out of work by June 23. By July, the Cloud City Miner's Union had 2,600 members. On September 20, 1896, a giant stick of dynamite exploded inside the defense compound of the Coronado Mine, followed by others. The official death toll was six men. On September 25 the first trainload of militia arrived.

∾ The town of McDonald sold for $210.42 of back taxes and became the town of Eagle. Mr. McDonald struck out for the Red Cliff District to try his luck at mining.

JULY 7, 1896   WOLCOTT, COLORADO

"Another bouncing baby boy, Mrs. Herwick," said Dr. Greene as he placed the bloody, squalling infant on her newly emptied belly. "Miss Rose, will you come get this baby cleaned up while I take care of its mama?"

"Lordy, Lordy, would you look at that dark hair! I never thought I'd ever see a Herwick baby with anythin' but yaller hair. Maybe this little boy's gonna take after his mama. Here, here let ol' Rose get you all wiped off so's you can be loved. I was thinkin' that girl of yourn would be havin' a youngun any time now, Miss Ida, and here you are, beatin' her to it. Your ninth baby, and sixth son, if I'm 'memberin' rightly."

"No, Miss Rose, my tenth child and seventh son," Ida murmured wearily, remembering the tiny grave at Edwards at she dropped off to sleep. The baby cuddled by her side would be called Albert Bryan.

∾ On January 31, 1897, the Colorado legislature ordered an investigation of the Leadville Miners Strike. The strike officially ended on March 9, but the downtown mines would not open for two years because of the flooding caused when the pumps were shut off.

∾ The need for lumber and timber was still critical. In March 1897, woodcutters were at Holy Cross City. Wood sold for $1.00 a cord, and the average cutter could produce 4 to 5 cords each day. The old forests were becoming decimated.

∾ The Colorado Fuel and Iron Company re-opened the coal mine at Sunshine (later called Sunlight). This mine would operate until 1904.

SEPTEMBER 8, 1897   MILK CREEK SAWMILL, EAGLE COUNTY

In later years, Ida tried to remember if this day started out being any different than all the others in her life. Was there some premonition or sign that her world would be turned upside down before the next sunrise? She was always haunted by questions which defied answers. One that loomed the largest was, "If I had been in Wolcott, near a doctor, would this horrible thing have happened?"

True to Ida's prediction, Josiah had started to gently coerce her to close the house for the summer and move up to the sawmill with him and the boys. "You can have as good a garden up there, as you do down here. There's a nice little stream of water runnin' through the campsite and the boys and I will get the ground dug up for you. The corn and tomatoes might not do too well, because of the shorter growing season, but the potatoes and cabbage will grow as big as houses in that good mountain soil. What do you say, Idie, would you give it a try? We get lonesome and it would be great to have you up there every day."

"Oh yes, they get lonesome," Ida thought. "They're lonesome for my cooking and cleaning and laundering, and all the other things I do for them. Otherwise they'd be content to live like boar hogs up on their mountaintop." But as the departure time neared, she found herself wavering in her determination not to spend the summer at Milk Creek. Finally she gave in to the demands of Josiah and the boys and started packing up the household goods they'd need for their summer camp.

Despite her reluctance, Ida discovered that she mostly enjoyed the cool, crisp nights and the balmy, sun-filled days punctuated by afternoon mountain showers which seemed to arrive promptly between two and three o'clock. The children grew brown as nuts from their carefree outdoors existence and developed voracious appetites. That fact may have led to the tragedy which followed.

On Sunday, Wid had gone to Wolcott for supplies and returned Monday night with some fresh produce brought in from the Lower Grand Valley where orchardists were shipping fruit and vegetables to all parts of the state. The children fell onto the plums, peaches, and pears with alacrity, eating until their tummies were round and swollen. Ida couldn't blame them; the sweet fruit was a rare delicacy, and one to be enjoyed for the short period available. She, too, overindulged, and paid the price with a slight stomach ache from all the unaccustomed produce.

The next morning, all the children had summer complaints, which didn't surprise Ida in the least. But, by midday, they had regained their appetites and were impatiently waiting for their dinner to be served; all except one. Paul was still sick; in fact he got progressively worse. By mid afternoon the vomiting and diarrhea became almost constant, and his fever rose dramatically. Ida was kept busy wringing out cool compresses to bathe his feverish body when he wasn't up and heading for the bushes. By evening he had become so feverish and lethargic that he could no longer rise to attend to his bodily needs, and Ida had to bathe him constantly in order to keep him clean. She administered measured doses of paregoric, only to have the liquid erupt from his lips before it could do its magic.

Guy summoned Josiah, Wid, and Fred from the cutting area. They arrived to stand silently around Paul's feverish form, feeling very helpless to combat this virulent illness which did not respond to any available care. It was apparent that Paul was far too sick to be taken to medical services in the valley. After a hurried discussion, Wid mounted the fastest horse and started down the trail toward Wolcott in the gathering dusk, hoping to transport a doctor back to the camp before morning.

Ida kept a constant vigil by her son's bed, while Josiah tended to the needs of the younger children. Little Al stood by his mama's skirts, watching her ministrations, not understanding what was happening but knowing it was very serious. He finally was lured away to eat some mush and be bedded down with his brothers and sisters. Then the parents sat by their son's side while the illness raged within him, until the last brief shudder erupted from his young, slender body. And then he was gone.

Ida and Josiah tried to comfort each other, but it was with a sense of unreality. This horrible thing wasn't happening. Paul couldn't be dead— their little scholar, the boy that was so vitally alive twenty-four hours ago. The young man who was enjoying the sweet taste of the ripe fruit with such gusto must still be with them. How could this be? Their movements were automatic as they prepared the little body for removal to its final resting place. Then Ida sat awaiting the arrival of the doctor, while Josiah gathered up the smoothest boards he could find to build a casket.

Wid arrived with Dr. Greene just as the sun was rising. After a cursory exam, and a brief conversation with the parents, he shook his head. "I'm sorry, folks, it doesn't look like I could have done anything, even if I had been right here when your boy got sick. There are some things we can't treat, and this kind of dysentery is one of them. Hard telling how he happened to be the one to get it, and not the others, but to be on the safe side, I'd boil the drinking water if I was you. I'll look at the other children to see if they have any signs before I start back to town. The little ones are usually hit the hardest, but you never can tell."

Later that morning, the family was seen wending their way down the mountain trail with Paul's body. Josiah had thought to bury his son on Milk Creek, but Ida was adamant. "He's going to rest with his brother and Grandma Herwick," she insisted. "I want him to be where I can visit his grave when I've a mind to, and I can't do that on this damned mountain."

Josiah's surprise by his wife's profanity caused him to readily acquiesce to her wishes. He gathered up a few items along with the small children, harnessed the team to the wagon, and started southeast toward Wolcott. By late afternoon the little group of mourners had arrived at the Edwards cemetery where Josiah, Wid, and Fred speedily dug the grave next to the small one of little baby Collins.

Ida sat by the box which held her son's body, reluctant to contribute one more child to the barren confines of the graveyard. Her disordered thoughts carried her back to the other times she had visited this final ground, and she remembered that she had then believed she would never feel worse pain when the final good-bye had been said; first to Susannah and then to her baby, Collins.

"I was wrong," she thought as the hastily built rough coffin was lowered into the deep hole. "My God, how can I stand it? Why, why, did you take my son? He was such a good boy; so smart and obedient. Have I sinned, Lord, that you would take this innocent soul from me? Have I been a poor mother? Has Josiah been a bad father? Just tell me why. Help me to accept your will."

Josiah stepped to her side. "Do you want to say a few words from the Bible, Idie?" he gently asked. His pain and sorrow were evident.

Ida stepped to the edge of the grave. She hugged the Bible close to her breast as if it would give her comfort from this horrible agony that was piercing her soul. She tried to speak, but no words came. Clearing her throat and shaking off the sense of despair, she opened Paul's tattered brown Bible.

> *The Lord is my shepherd, I shall not want.*
> *He maketh me to lie down in green pastures;*
> *he leadeth me beside the still waters...*

"Oh, God, please take this little boy to your care, and let him walk through your fields of green with the other angels in heaven. For surely he is an innocent soul, my Paul. A good boy, maybe too good to live. Not like the other children, who are more able to stand up for themselves..."

> *Yea, thought I walk through the valley of the shadow of death*
> *I will fear no evil for thou art with me...*

"Take good care of this child, Lord, until I can again see his face in Heaven."

> *thy rod and thy staff they comfort me...*

"Bless us, Heavenly Father, help us to get through this terrible time. Josiah's suffering and he can't show it as well. Give him comfort, Sweet Jesus..."

> *I will dwell in the house of the Lord forever.*

"Help me to make it through this life, so I can be with You and my children again some day."

The prayer over, Ida turned her back while Josiah and the boys shoveled soil into the hole. She couldn't bear to hear the sound of dirt hitting the wooden box, and she started down the hill to the Eagle River. Tears formed channels down the light dust on her face as she resisted the urge to look backward at the barren heap of brown dirt. The wagon and its occupants caught up with her as she reached the bottom of the hill, and the grave was out of sight. Wearily climbing over the wheel, she sat silently clutching her son's Bible on the way back to her home in Wolcott.

Ida Herwick, 1902.   Josiah L. Herwick, 1902.

Catamount Creek cabin presumed to have housed the Herwick family in 1891.

Susan and Joe Herwick, taken 1906.

Grant Oyler circa 1900.

Wesley Herwick seated with sons,
Clarence and Fred circa 1911.

Laura Herwick and
Mary Herwick Duplice.

Battlement Mesa Bible study, 1915 — Ida second row center with children, Tiny, Mary, Susan, Joe and other class members.

Guy and Laura Herwick, Chris Deere, unknown man, Susan Herwick at Cottonwood Camp, 1917.

Birdella Ashlock with children Henry and Ruth circa 1912.

Ida Herwick and granddaughter, Olive Duplice circa 1918.

Taken March 11, 1919 after Ida's funeral. Left to right: Oren Herwick, Wid Herwick, Fred Herwick, Joe Herwick, Josiah Herwick, Guy Herwick, Al Herwick.

part four

1898-1902

- The "Sisters of Humility" started the first hospital in Glenwood Springs in 1898.

- The first "Strawberry Day" in Glenwood Springs was held in June, 1898. Both the Denver and the Rio Grande and Colorado Midland Railroads ran special excursion trains to the event.

- There were numerous bears and lions bothering stock during July and August, 1898.

- The dry weather created severe forest fires around the Eagle Valley and Homestake. Seven bridges burned between Red Cliff and Gold Park the week of August 27, 1898.

- Chief Colorow was found hunting off the Utah reservation. Black troops were sent to escort him back.

- The Peachblow Quarry on the Fryingpan River was furnishing red sandstone building blocks to local and national outlets. In just one shipment 3,000 carloads were sold to a Chicago buyer.

- The Midland Railroad decided to utilize the old railbed through the Hagerman Tunnel between Leadville and the Fryingpan River Country rather than the lower Busk tunnel because they believed they could maintain the higher route for a lesser cost.

FEBRUARY 23, 1898 WOLCOTT, COLORADO

"Hey, Ma, you're a grandma!" Fred burst through the door with an envelope in his hand.

"I stopped at the post office on my way home for dinner, and the stage was just in from McCoy. Birdie sent us a letter about the baby bein' born a week ago today, on the sixteenth. Sounds like everything's okay. The little fella just missed being born on your birthday."

While Fred sat down to eat his noon meal, Ida quickly read the letter:

February 20, 1898

Dear Folks,
This will be just a note to tell you that the baby arrived on February 16 early in the morning. He is doing very well, and we have named him Henry Richard. He is a healthy baby and has a good appetite. Mrs. Ashlock has been taking good care of me, and I am doing as well as can be expected. I hope you will be able to see the baby in the next few months when the weather gets better.

Your daughter,
Birdella
Burns, Colorado

Ida felt a twinge of guilt for not being with her daughter for Birdie's first delivery. But she shook her head and knew there was little she could do about that. The trip over to Burn's Hole would be terrible this time of the year, and she had little Al and Mary to think of, not to mention what she'd do about the rest of the family. Josiah, Fred, Guy, and Oren could probably fend for themselves, but Tiny, at seven years of age, was too young to be left on her own. She was in school and was enjoying it so much that Ida didn't want her to miss any days.

"No," she decided, "as much as I would have liked to be with her, Birdie surely understands that it is impossible. Besides, it sounds like Mrs. Ashlock is doing a fine job of taking care of her."

The thought of being a grandmother didn't seem quite real, especially when her own youngest was less than two years old. "Where did the time go?" she wondered. "Twenty-two years Josiah and I have been married. Somedays it seems like only yesterday, and then, on other days, it feels like an eternity. There's been a whole bunch of pain and sorrow wrapped up in our years together, and I don't suppose it's over yet. I wonder how many more children I'll carry. Here I am, just turned thirty-seven and you'd think the good Lord would stop blessing me with any more babies. It doesn't seem proper, somehow, for a woman as old as I am to be having younguns." The unspoken, more honest, thought may have been that it was unseemly to still be having babies after her daughter started her family. For some reason, it just didn't seem proper.

Ida's musings took a back seat to all the activity that went on in the Herwick household that spring. Josiah sold off part of his lots in Wolcott to the Eagle River Mercantile and Forwarding Company, and promptly bought some land on the northwest side of the river down by Eagle. Although still making deals for cut lumber from his sawmill, he branched out by leasing the Matthews Ranch on Brush Creek, where he planned to grow hay and grain, as well as on the river front property in Eagle. He hired a man to irrigate, and went back and forth between Brush Creek, Milk Creek, Eagle and Wolcott all summer.

Wid had finally realized his dream of having his own stage run between Wolcott and Steamboat Springs, so he was home just a few days each week. Josiah took Fred with him all the time and occasionally included Guy and Oren. This left Ida with Tiny, Mary, and Al, which seemed almost no family at all! She enjoyed her time with the young children, and made friends with other women who also had small ones. Even the less than welcome proof in April of another pregnancy, did little to diminish Ida's well-being.

In late May, the newspapers started advertising the first "Strawberry Day" in Glenwood Springs. The much heralded affair was to be held Saturday, June 18, in the downtown area. Special excursion trains would be running from Leadville, Aspen, and Grand Junction so folks in the outlying areas could take part in the festivities.

Ida mentioned the festivities to her friend, Lila Warren, who also was excited by the idea of spending the day in Glenwood Springs. The more they discussed it, the more excited they became. Before they could change their minds, they bought the special rate train tickets; $1.25 for the adults, and $.75 per child. Then they spent the next several weeks anticipating the big day, what they'd need to take, and what they'd do once they arrived. This was a big step in emancipation from the usual wife and mother roles, and it felt positively heady to be making plans without their husbands.

Early on the morning of June 18, Ida roused the children to get them dressed in their Sunday best apparel. Tiny and Mary both wore white organdy dresses with big pink bows. Twenty-two-month-old Al was dressed in little knickers and high topped shoes which made him squirm from their unaccustomed stiffness. Ida chose a light shirtwaist for herself because the day promised to be a warm one. She took a small carpetbag full of items which might be needed by three children on a day's excursion trip and herded her little brood out the door.

Train #15 pulled into the Wolcott Station at eight o'clock, and the Herwicks and Warrens became part of the jousling crowd who were eager to get on board. Between Ida's three and Lila Warren's four children, it took some finagling to find seats in close proximity to each other. But the little group was finally seated and eagerly watched the landscape zip by as the train headed west to the great adventure, through the scenic Canyon of the Grand River into Glenwood Springs.

Two hours later, the group stepped down from their packed railroad cars to merge with an even greater crowd which was heading for Grand Avenue where the parade participants were lining up. Ida and Lila held the youngest children and linked hands with the older ones while they moved along with the human tide. All seven little people looked at the scene with big-eyed wonder. They had never been in such a large town with so many people, and were daunted by the sight.

"There must be over two thousand people here," Ida said, impressed herself. Looking at her friend Lila, she could tell that the awe was mutual.

The parade had started its progression down the Avenue. Once it had passed by, the crowd started milling around. Some families were pulling out baskets of food from their wagons and heading for a shady place to eat their lunch.

Ida and Lila realized they should find a place to have a bite to eat before going over to the hall where the strawberries and cream were being served. They shoved the seven children into a crowded cafe and ordered pieces of fried chicken for each, along with some soft rolls and butter. Although none had mentioned being hungry, everyone ate the food with gusto and announced that they were ready for their dessert. So, once again, they joined the crowd, and before long arrived at the "Strawberry" building. Seats had been taken out of the hall and replaced with long tables. The mothers nudged their way to a table that held enough seats for all of them. They plopped the children down to await the ladies who were serving the luscious desserts. The mothers were kept busy cleaning off the faces, hands, and clothes of the seven young-sters who relished the ripe sweetness of the berries swimming in the smooth, thick cream accompanied by all types of cakes with frothy frostings. Their little tummies were stuffed by the time Ida and Lila moved them from the hall and walked across the Grand River Bridge to the lawn surrounding the nata-torium where hundreds of people were cavorting in the mineral hot springs.

Other mothers had also found shady places for their little ones to rest and take time out from all the exciting activities. It gave the women a chance to rest from their child-tending activities and to visit with each other. Ida knew that if the older boys were with her they would have been begging to go into the mammoth pool, but, thankfully, the children were too young and too tired to even consider the possibility.

Ida looked at the bathers and wondered what it would be like to sink into the warm caress of the mineral water, which was said to have such healing properties. As she laid back upon the grassy hillside, she decided that she'd be happy to just dabble her hot feet in a cool stream at that mo-ment. However, propriety forbade it, so she'd just rest her eyes for a few minutes and enjoy the quiet moment before they were up and off to the next event.

When the mothers and children boarded the #16 eastbound train that evening at six o'clock, they all looked quite rumpled and soiled but very satisfied with their day's outing. The train had barely left the station before the children's heads were nodding with fatigue. "It's been a big day for all of us," Ida mused, as her head rested on the seat back. Soon everyone was snoozing away on their two-hour journey back home.

Ida had cause to remember the Strawberry Day trip with ambivalence, because she soon became quite ill. Although she couldn't say that the excursion had anything to do with it, Ida often wondered if her pregnancy had suffered because of the trip.

After the big day, Ida felt more tired but blamed it on the unaccustomed activity, her growing family, and the warm weather. After a few days of taking it easy, she expected be back to normal, but she wasn't better in two weeks; in fact, she realized that she felt even worse. She was puffy and swollen at the end of the day, and the mild headaches had become increasingly more severe. Occasionally she experienced a dizziness and was fearful of passing out. Finally, after a month, she convinced herself to go see her friend, Dr. Greene, if only to reassure herself that she and the unborn baby were really all right.

After the examination was over, and she was seated across from him at the big desk, the physician's piercing eyes bore into Ida. "I'm sorry you didn't come to me sooner, Mrs. Herwick. I think you have a rather severe kidney infection which we need to get cleared up right away, before it harms you and the baby. The medical routine is not complicated, but it will require complete bedrest and a proper diet for a while. Where's your husband working now? Will he be able to assist you with the children and the household, or should we look for someone to stay with you?"

"Goodness, Dr. Greene, you make this sound so serious. I'm just a little tired with this one but, of course, I'm not as young either. Surely I can do whatever I need to do without going to bed! I don't know where Josiah and the boys are right now. Somewhere between Brush Creek and Milk Creek, but I expect them home day after tomorrow, so we can talk it over then, and let you know."

"Very well, Mrs. Herwick, but I want to impress upon you how serious your condition is. If we don't get it under control, your life as well as that of the baby's could be in danger. I have no wish to frighten you, but I know that you've always kept going on even when you are as sick as a dog. I'm telling you that isn't possible now. You simply have to follow my orders or you and that baby won't make it."

For once, Ida really listened to the doctor. When Josiah came home, he agreed that they should get a lady to take care of the household and children, so Ida could have the bedrest prescribed by Dr. Greene. It was mid-July and he could not stay home with her because he had several lumber orders to get out. The hay on Brush Creek and the Eagle River was also ready to be cut, and he couldn't let it go. So, he talked to Dr. Greene, who recommended a recently widowed lady who needed the work and hadn't any responsibilities at her house to keep her from staying until September, when the baby was due. Josiah came home with Mrs. Nelson in tow that same day, and with her firmly ensconced in the house, he gathered up the boys and headed back to the sawmill.

Mrs. Nelson was a warm, loving lady, who needed someone to look after. Her husband had died in a horse accident several months before, leaving her with little resources. Her family was in the north, and she had no children, so she was a gift from Heaven for Ida and the children, who soon came to enjoy her company, as well as her help. She kept the household humming smoothly and took good care of Ida. Her custards and soft foods were easy to digest, and she made special teas of comfrey, sassafras, mint, and other natural diuretics which would help Ida eliminate the fluids which threatened to overwhelm her heart and kidneys. Despite some guilt at being the cause of all the extra expense and attention, Ida enjoyed the ministrations of her new friend.

Dr. Greene visited at least every other day, to check Ida's urine for impurities and to check the amount of fluids she was still retaining. Each day Ida waited hopefully for a positive sign from the doctor, who only shook his head. "It's too soon to tell, Mrs. Herwick. We'll just have to wait and see what happens. I know you're a praying woman, so have faith that everything will be all right." But, once outside the room, he would shake his head at Mrs. Nelson, indicating that no significant improvement had been made. "I don't want to worry her yet, but I haven't heard the baby's heartbeat for several days. I'm not sure the baby is alive, but I want to wait a little longer before I discuss the possibility with Mrs. Herwick."

He needn't have worried about Ida. She already knew something was dreadfully wrong. Her beseeching looks implored the doctor to say that she was just imagining that the baby wasn't moving. She lay rubbing her hands over her swollen belly hour after hour, as if by some maternal command she could force the child to stir within its embryonic nest. But to no avail.

Ida awakened early one morning to relieve herself of the ever-present urge to rid her body of the excess fluid. As she crawled back into bed, the first sharp jab hit her, and she quietly waited for the next one to occur before rousing Mrs. Nelson.

"Lord, Lord, be with me and this child," she prayed. "It's too early for the baby to be born. Don't let it suffer for anything I might have done or not done. This is your child, and I humbly ask you to protect us both–now and in the hours to come. 'Yea, though I walk through the valley of shadow death, thou art with me.' Please be with us, Heavenly Father. Amen."

Four hours later, Ida lay in an exhausted, grieving silence while the tiny, limp body was wrapped in a clean cloth and handed to Mrs. Nelson. As he worked over Ida, Dr. Greene, with some emotion, assured her that the infant's death could not have been avoided. "I'm sorry, Mrs. Herwick. I wish I could tell you exactly what went wrong but I can't. The baby just wasn't formed the way a baby should be, probably right from the first. I doubt that your condition had anything to do with its death. But it might have been God's way of relieving you of this unfortunate child. Even if it had been born alive, it couldn't have lived for very long. As difficult as it may be, I think you'll eventually come to see that it was for the best. I'm going to find someone to ride up to the sawmill and bring your husband back. The least the man can do is be with you."

"I want to see her," Ida pleaded. "You did say it was a little girl, didn't you?"

"I'd really advise you not to do that. It's best that you not remember the child this way, Ida."

"I'm sorry, Doctor, but I've got to see her. She's my baby and I've carried her all these months. I've got a right to say good-bye."

Mrs. Nelson, tears running downs her cheeks, entered the room with the clean little bundle and placed it in Ida's arms. "It's just a little angel, now, Missus Ida. The good Lord was kind and took her to his arms."

Ida unwrapped the flannel blanket to expose the twisted little form that should have been her baby. A painful moan escaped her lips as she bent to kiss the tiny round head, but her eyes were hot and dry. No tears threatened to escape as she lovingly tucked the blanket around the body and gently handed it back to Mrs. Nelson. She closed her eyes, trying to shut out the sight of the tiny crippled infant and the gut-wrenching agony that was churning within her.

"These God-damned lusty husbands should have to bear a few of the babies they make so easily," Ida heard the doctor say in the next room. "Maybe if they had to go through just a little bit of the pain they force on their wives, they wouldn't be so quick to act like stud horses every chance they get. I think I'm going to have a talk with Josiah Herwick very soon."

Ida never knew whether the good doctor did have his planned conversation with Josiah, but her husband was very attentive for the rest of the year. He insisted that Mrs. Nelson stay on to care for Ida and the family until he was sure Ida could assume all of her household duties. He also made sure he spent several nights at home each week, which was a nice gesture, but added more work for Ida, what with having to feed four extra mouths. But she didn't complain because the unusual attentiveness was rather pleasant. It was nice to know that someone cared about her well-being.

The fall of 1898 saw another sign of Ida's change of status by her husband. In the past, Josiah had generally conducted his business-social affairs isolated from Ida, who was either raising children or birthing them. It wasn't done by design as much as by mutual understanding of their respective roles. Si Herwick was most happy when he was in the limelight, and Ida was most comfortable out of it. This changed, however, in October when Josiah persuaded her to join him in becoming members of the Woodmen of the World, and Women of Woodcraft. The fraternal organization had become very popular with citizens of the Eagle River Valley, who had even constructed a "Woodmen Hall" in Eagle. Josiah welcomed the rituals and feeling of belonging that the organization brought and was soon immersed in its work.

Ida, despite being flattered by her husband's renewed interest, was a more reluctant participant in the organization. Her natural shyness made her suffer when in the company of strangers, so she acted somewhat reserved. The thought of chatting with more educated ladies brought terror to her heart, but Josiah wasn't to be put off.

"Oh, come on, Idie, once you try it, you'll enjoy gettin' out with other couples. They're planning on having some socials and dances, and I think it's high time you and I took part in some of the activities. It'll be good for the business, too. Will you go with me?"

Ida, as usual, gave in to her persistent husband's demands. Their first trip was to the Eagle W.O.W Lodge. To Ida's surprise, she was met by some friendly wives who took her under their wing and proceeded to explain the rituals and rules of the organization. Despite her shyness, Ida found herself relaxing in the company of these ladies. She found herself understanding the information and was able to ask appropriate questions about her responsibilities. The wives clearly accepted her as one of them, and she responded to their kindness. That night, on their way back to Wolcott, Josiah was full of conversation about the Woodmen of the World, the business contacts he'd made, and how they might take part in the future of the Lodge. His preoccupation caused him to ignore Ida's silence, which was fine with her because she could replay the evening in her own mind and savor the feeling of belonging. "Sometimes Josiah does know what's best for me," she thought.

Although Ida was enjoying her participation in the W.O.W. Lodge that fall, she left her husband's other interest strictly alone. Josiah had an abiding concern in politics and was a dyed-in-the-wool Republican. He loved nothing better than to engage in heated debates about the affairs of the country, especially now that the "damned Democrats" were out of power. Ida had learned to tune out her husband's political rantings and ravings as she went about her daily business. At Josiah's insistence, she had registered as a Republican, and dutifully went to the polls on the last election but her real interests were much closer to her home. So, Ida didn't pay much attention when he started attending the Republican Committee meetings in Eagle County. Si Herwick believed in expediency, and his comings and goings were usually by design, so Ida understood that this latest maneuver was probably motivated by more than just love of the political process.

Josiah had decided to take a trip to Basalt to drum up lumber contracts for some of the current building construction going on over there. He returned several days later to news about the catastrophe which had befallen the town of Minturn, Colorado, and its some 400 residents, on the previous Saturday night. A fire of enormous proportion had burned down the post office and seven other buildings, the biggest part of Minturn's business district. Josiah lost no time in getting to the victims of the fire to offer his services for lumber. His efforts were even acknowledged in the *Eagle County Times*, which reported, "Mr. Si Herwick, the hustling sawmill man of Eagle, was in Minturn Monday negotiating lumber. There will be considerable building at Minturn soon replacing the houses destroyed by the recent conflagration." Ida was very proud to see her husband's name in print, and she thanked God for giving her such a hard-working man.

The fall weather had been very mild until late November, and even then there were few storms which left little snow. Everyone, while enjoying the temperate weather, watched the skies for the winter to begin. Josiah was occupied in getting as much lumber as possible out of the hills before the storms finally did hit. Ida was enjoying her health and her family, as well as Josiah's continuing care and attention. He had even urged her to get a medical examination for her own piece of mind, as well as to apply for life insurance through the Women of Woodcraft.

"It's a good opportunity for both of us to get some cheap insurance, Mother," he said. "We'll never get anything cheaper than $1.15 per thousand. I'm gonna take out a couple of thousand, and I think you ought to do the same. We're not gettin' any younger, and if somethin' happened to either one of us, the children would have a little bit to pay for their keep."

As usual, the mention of her children's welfare was all the motivation Ida needed to go see Dr. Greene. "Well, well, Mrs. Herwick, I must say it's a pleasant surprise to see you looking so fit. What brings you to see me?"

Ida ducked her head at the doctor's inquisitive gaze. "It isn't what you're probably thinking, Dr. Greene. For once I'm not here because I'm expecting. I want a medical exam for the W.O.W. life insurance policy. Can you do that for me?"

The good doctor hid his smile, thinking that the little talk he'd had with Si Herwick must have paid off. "I'll be glad to oblige you, Mrs. Herwick. Let me take a look at the medical form and see what we have to do. It asks about your family's health history. As I recall your father and mother are both dead, is that right?"

"Yes, Ma died from childbed fever in 1873, and I got word in 1885 that Pa died from gastritis. He always did have a bad stomach. It was too expensive for me to go back to Nebraska, and Mother Herwick was getting worse. I figured that Pa would know I had my family to take care of. But my two brothers and one sister are doing well. Emer is in Indiana. He went back there with some of my mother's kin when Pa died. Grant's now in Denver. He was fourteen when Pa passed away. I keep hoping to get over there to see him some of these days. And Ella is planning on coming out for a visit, maybe this year. I haven't seen her since she was a baby. Ida was chattering about her family, and she couldn't seem to stop. Seldom asked about them, she realized there was a yearning for her own kin. She'd been a part of the Herwick family for so long that she sometimes forgot about her own roots.

Dr. Greene completed the exam and gave Ida the good news. "I'm pleased to say that you are the picture of health, Mrs. Herwick. There's no sign of the kidney problems you had a few months ago, and you look very fit. In fact, I don't believe I've ever seen you in better shape. Life must be treating you kindly, and I hope it lasts."

Dr. Greene was quite perceptive. She, indeed, was feeling very well. Her lifestyle these days seemed so much less stressful than past years. Al was out of his baby stage, and although she still had dawn to dusk chores to complete, the daily burdens seemed more manageable. Perhaps her own attitude had something to do with the change, or perhaps it was just a matter of growing maturity. Ida found herself accepting, without internal agonizing, many of the events that had caused frustration in the past. Whole days went by without feeling overwhelmed by her responsibilities.

Perhaps most gratifying was how Josiah behaved toward her. Since the baby's death, he continued to display more tenderness and consideration than he had for years. Ida couldn't deny that this change was very pleasant. She suddenly felt elevated to a higher plane in her husband's estimation. Even his familiar salutation of "Idie" had been replaced by the more reverent term of "Mother." She also realized that he was not taking advantage of their marriage bed. He pointedly made mention of nightly exhaustion and rolled over to his side after a rather quick peck on her cheek.

Ida had grown to accept the fact that warmth and physical love exacted a high price from her, with the inevitable pregnancies, illness, and perhaps death of her babies. But this new behavior initially concerned her. Perhaps he no longer loved her, or maybe he found her too old and unattractive. She found this hard to believe in view of the fact that he was so loving and considerate. One morning as she was pondering the situation over a cup of coffee, a recollection of Dr. Greene's voice came to mind. "I wonder if that's what's happening," she wondered. "Could it be that Dr. Greene warned Josiah about my getting pregnant so soon? I'll bet he did. It makes sense considering Josiah's attitude toward me."

All of a sudden Ida's concerns fell away as she finally understood why her husband was staying celibate. "It isn't because Josiah doesn't love or want me; he's doing this for my protection. The knowledge of his marital sacrifice caused her to overflow with love for this man, and she settled into a placid interlude, feeling quite cherished and secure. Her new sense of confidence permitted her to enjoy the social life that she and Josiah were beginning to have in the W.O.W. and her church. For the first time, Ida felt that she could manage life on life's terms.

The warm dry autumn was pleasant, and people discovered they had several months longer to prepare for the wintry blasts which would surely be hitting any day. Periodic storms rolled in through the end of the year, but the snow melted almost as quickly as it fell. Josiah was able to harvest all his crops and honor the lumber contracts with time to spare. Ida's root cellar was bursting with all the sparkling glass jars of fruits and vegetables, sacks of potatoes, carrots buried in sand, not to mention a few good cured hams which Josiah had traded for some fence posts. Aromatic scent of sauerkraut wafted from the kitchen pantry. Guy and Oren had been diligently chopping up the big logs in the wood pile and stacking the cords close to the door so they would be handy when winter set in.

Christmas was a noisy, happy holiday. Birdie, Norman, and little Henry arrived the day before amid hugs and laughter. At eight months, the baby was a happy healthy child, who only cried for food or clean diapers. The small Herwick home was filled to the rafters with twelve bodies, but Ida didn't mind. As she gazed around the groaning Christmas table there was a pang of grief for the ones not there; Mother Herwick, Paul, baby Collins, and the crippled girl baby. "I suppose so much happiness has to be countered with an equal share of pain," Ida reflected. "I wonder if one ever totally lets go of the grief. But, what am I doing? I should be concentrating on what I have, instead of what has gone. Come here, little boy, let your Grandma give you some potatoes and gravy. Maybe you'd like to suck on a piece of meat. My, oh my, you've already got teeth, and I can see you know how to use them!" Ida pulled back her finger to show two little bite marks on it. "With that kind of appetite, I'll bet you're going to grow up to be a big strong man, like your daddy and grandpa."

The weather continued its dry spell until after Christmas, which allowed Birdie and her little family to get home to Burns without any problems. As everyone returned to their jobs or to school, Ida was left with a feeling of momentary emptiness, she shook it off by busily resuming her daily activities. All in all, 1898 had been a busy year filled with events and emotions. "The Lord gives and the Lord takes away," thought Ida. "My poor little twisted baby girl was taken from me, but then Birdie was given a fine healthy baby boy, my first grandchild. Perhaps that's the way life will always be—you give some, and you get some. If we didn't have the pain, maybe we'd not appreciate the joy. Help me to be strong, Heavenly Father, for whatever you choose to give me in the future. Keep my family safe and sound."

∾ *The beginning of 1899 saw the worst winter to hit the Colorado mountain valleys since 1884. On January 16, fourteen inches of snow fell in twenty-four hours. By January 31, there were fifty-eight inches of snow at Leadville. The Midland Railroad sent out crews to clear the Hagerman Tunnel only to have the snow shed collapse. A trainload of cattle slowly froze to death on the 11,000 foot mountain top. Other trains also became derailed or stranded in the immobilizing drifts. Between January 15 and March 28, a total of 187 inches of snow fell at Leadville*

∾ *Horace Tabor, the famous Silver King of Leadville, died of appendicitis on April 10, 1899, at the Windsor Hotel in Denver, Colorado. His death bed instructions caused the beautiful Baby Doe Tabor to live the rest of her life as a virtually penniless recluse on their mining property.*

∾ *Sister Superior Mary Agnes of the Sisters Of Mary purchased the St. James Hotel at Eighth and Cooper in Glenwood Springs and created the "St. Joseph Sanitarium and Hotel." The good Sister made a naive but fatal mistake when buying a building which was in the midst of the Red Light District. Despite her best efforts, the facility failed to attract patients and went broke in three years.*

FEBRUARY 1, 1899 WOLCOTT, COLORADO

"Damnation, will this never stop?" Pulling trousers over his heavy long handle underwear, Josiah moved to the window, which afforded very little view except the constant falling of white flakes. "I've lost track of when we last saw the sun. I didn't hear Number Fifteen go by this morning, so I'm bettin' the train's still stranded somewhere between here and Leadville. If it doesn't let up pretty soon, the higher communities are gonna be shut down completely. They were talkin' up at the store yesterday about how we might have to form a rescue party if the rotary plows can't push their way through."

"Surely the snow will stop soon. I just pray that all those people up there are all right," said Ida, sipping a cup of early morning coffee.

Josiah's predictions became reality about mid-morning when Fred came sailing through the door, snow flying from his heavy coat in small icy clumps. "Better get ready, Pa. There's a bunch of men heading up to Rock Creek, around Beldon Siding. It looks like the rotary can't punch through the drifts, and we'll have to do some hand shovelin'. We'll work on this side, and another bunch will be diggin from Red Cliff. One way or the other we have to get to the train crew before they run out of fuel. I talked to Wid, and he said that the off-duty teamsters will haul us as far as the horses can go, and then we'll have to go the rest of the way on snowshoes. Hurry up and get dressed, cause everyone's leaving in an hour." Fred pulled on his gloves and cap and headed back into the swirling white landscape.

For the next four days, Ida anxiously awaited news from the rescue party. She kept the children inside, except for allowing Guy and Oren daily trips to the depot for word about any progress in extricating the train. Around noon on the fifth day, Josiah and his sons came trooping home, snow encrusted and very fatigued. They reported a successful mission, having been able to rescue the train crew and bring them out of the canyon to Minturn in the nick of time. The rotary plows were still hammering away at the drifts, which were higher than the locomotive in places. A relief crew continued the hand shoveling on both sides and were expected to break through in another day, if the storm let up. Red Cliff had been snowed in for almost three weeks, and the citizens were getting dangerously low on supplies and coal. When the rails were cleared on the western side, supplies could be brought in from Grand Junction or Glenwood Springs. It was hard to say when the railroad would be cleared toward Leadville.

The country remained a giant snow-encrusted land through the end of March. Ida's days were taken up with endless chores of keeping house for her men-folk and small children, who restlessly prowled the house, getting on each other's nerves.

"Please let it end soon," she prayed, "before I go out of my mind." When she couldn't stand the close confinement any longer, she'd don her heaviest clothing and make an excuse to go check on a friend, only to find similar home circumstances. Everyone was suffering from cabin fever.

When the weather started clearing up in April, everyone emerged from the snow-covered houses like groundhogs leaving their burrows after a long hibernation. The warmth of sunshine on Ida's face was a delicious sensation, even though the weather remained cooler than normal on into June. The knee-deep muck in the streets of Wolcott failed to dim her enthusiasm for the coming spring. As soon as she could, Ida stripped beds and washed the winter grime from sheets and blankets. The springtime ritual was a welcome occurrence in every household, especially when one crawled into a clean-smelling bed for the first time in several months. The "rites of spring" also cleared the emotional cobwebs which had accumulated throughout a winter spent in close quarters with eight other people. Everyone, including Ida, could find a bit of privacy in which to relish the silence of their thoughts. It was a wonderful feeling.

Wid was now a regular driver on the stage route to Steamboat Springs, while Josiah and Fred were gearing to up to resume the sawmill and ranching operations. The children were again in school after their snowy hiatus. Tiny loved the daily experience, especially arithmetic, in which she excelled. Guy and Oren, on the other hand, were much better spellers and were called upon to help their sister with her words each night after supper.

In June, Josiah sold off a parcel of land on Rube Creek to Pierce, Reef, and Co. and used the money to purchase four lots at Third and Howard Streets in Eagle. Some weeks later, he invited Ida to go for a buggy ride to see the property. Ida questioned why he was so eager to show off vacant lots in the fairly new town, but considering his changed attitude about making her a more active participant in his affairs, she willingly accompanied him. It was a beautiful day, and she was glad for an excuse to escape the never-ending household tasks for a little while.

As the high-stepping team of bays pulled into the embryonic hamlet of Eagle, Ida looked around at the landscape. The town center had been laid out on the high south bank of the Eagle River, across from their property on the north side. Just a little more than a hundred citizens called it their home, but the surrounding ranch country, as well as the Fulford mining district to the south-east, was helping to create a hub of commerce. The town boasted a general store, hotel, and post office as well as a livery stable, and newspaper, *The Eagle County Examiner*. The Woodman Hall and Dr. Greene's new building were surrounded by a few new homes to the south and east. Although the population was still smaller than Wolcott, Ida looked at the little settlement with approval. Its location on the high river bank gave the town better drainage than Wolcott had, so the muddy morass was less of a problem. Little clumps of trees dotted the landscape, and the few home owners had been busily setting out seedlings, which would give wonderful shade in a few more years. The routine hustle and bustle of Wolcott, with its congestion of freight wagons and stage coaches, was absent in Eagle. There was an aura of quiet, peaceful living which appealed to Ida. "You know, Josiah," she said, "I think I'd enjoy living in this little town."

The buggy and its occupants had reached the southeast end of the business district and Josiah pulled up the reins. They stopped at their lots on Howard Street. On the corner lot, a house was under construction. "Let's get out and take look, Mother," Josiah said as he held out his hand to Ida. "You can tell me how good a carpenter you think your son is."

With a bemused look, Ida followed her husband into the dim interior. They entered a large living room, which was joined to an equally large dining room connected by a double doorway. Leading off the dining room was the door to the kitchen, still under construction, but promising a respectable amount of space. A short interior hallway led to a spacious back bedroom and a staircase to the second story. Emerging on the upper landing, Ida could see two doors on one side, and one on the other, all leading into well proportioned bedrooms, with deep set gable windows letting in the midday light. "My, oh my! Are you telling me that our son is building this house?" exclaimed Ida. "Why, it's really wonderful, Josiah. Gracious, any woman would be glad to live in a place like this. So light and cheerful. And it's got a good sized space for a nice yard and garden plot. Well, are you going to tell me what this is all about? Why have you and Fred been keeping his carpenter skills a surprise, and what are you going to do with this lovely house once it's finished?"

"I guess it's stretching things to say that Fred is building the house, but he's certainly learning a lot by working along side the carpenter, and I think he'll be able to build one on his own before long. We thought we'd keep this as a nice surprise for you, Mother. He and I started talking about it last winter, and when I got a deal on the lots, it seemed a good time for us to branch out to house building, what with the sawmill and everything. So, tell me, do you still think you'd like to live in Eagle? How long do you suppose it will take you to get used to all these rooms?"

Slowly it dawned on Ida what her husband was saying. A look of confusion was replaced by amazement. "Are you trying to tell me... no, you can't be saying...it can't be true...this is our house?"

"It's all yours." Josiah wrapped his long arms around Ida and laughed with delight at his well kept secret. He then cleared his throat and spoke gruffly, "I don't tell you very often, but I do love you, and I know I haven't made your life very easy. Maybe this house will make up for all the cabins and dugouts you've had to live in for the past twenty-some years. I hope you'll be happy here, Mother. You've been a good wife." Pulling away from her embrace, Josiah turned his face away, embarrassed by this unusual display of emotion. "Come along now, we've got to inspect the rest of the place, and you need to put in your order for the kitchen cupboards. We want this to be to your specifications!"

Wiping her eyes, Ida followed her husband down the steep staircase.

She thought her heart would burst with love and appreciation. Imagine Josiah and Fred keeping this a secret for so long, just to please her. To a woman unaccustomed to regular displays of tenderness and consideration, this was so alien that she didn't know quite how to respond. A part of her was feeling very cherished, but another part wanted to turn away from this astounding event and to kindly reject the offer. It was almost as if she was afraid that she would somehow not live up to the expectation of the givers— that she was not worthy of this extraordinary gift. She mutely walked around the building in a dazed state, trying to reconcile all these new feelings boiling up inside.

"Hey there, Ma." Fred's voice reverberated throughout the empty structure. "Guess we surprised you, didn't we?"

Ida composed herself and stuffed down her ambivalent feelings. "Oh, son, I can hardly believe this is happening. And to think that you've been building it with your own two hands. I can't get over it. It's just wonderful."

"Well, then you'd better come with me and tell me where you want the kitchen cupboards built. We want this kitchen to be just right when you cook our first family dinner in it." Josiah led her to the kitchen.

The weeks flew by until the house was finished and the Herwick family was ready to make their move down river ten miles. Ida had been constantly busy ordering material for curtains and deciding what furnishings needed to be purchased for the new, greatly expanded, living space. She had also decided to plant her garden at the new house because they would be moved in by harvest time. So once a week, she hitched up the buggy and drove down to nurture and weed the tiny green shoots poking their heads above ground. The trips also gave her an opportunity to check on the progress of the house completion and to stand in the bare rooms while she dreamt of how they would look when equipped with furnishings. Her energy was fueled by enthusiasm, and she happily worked from sun-up to sun-down, while her family became exhausted by all the chores she could think of for them to do.

The only ugly blot on the summer months of 1899 was the letter from Wes and Rena Herwick, at the coal camp of Sunlight, telling them of the death of their baby boy, Charles Edgar. Ida cried as she read the harsh words. There seemed to be no gentle words to describe it. Passing away. Went to sleep. Slipped away. Euphemisms meant to lessen the pain of the word really had no comfort . Death was death, and there weren't any words to make it better. Ida cried for Rena as she was crying for her own little baby who should have been almost a year old but instead was lying in a small barren grave. She immediately sat down to pen a note of condolence only to find that her brain was unable to bring up the words of comfort that she wanted to convey. "It's hard to say the things so close to one's heart," Ida wrote. "I wish I could let you know how I feel, but the words just won't come. I hope you know how sad I am, because this letter sounds so cold." Ida signed the letter with her love and addressed it for the post.

The Herwick family was firmly ensconced in their beautiful new home by the time the first snow storm of the season arrived in October, making their summer season a very short one. The blizzard dumped six feet of snow in the Deep Creek region of the Flat tops, stranding ranchers and hunters in that area. Birdie wrote from Burn's Hole about the early storm and how they had all been caught unawares. But she hastened to add that the Ashlocks were all fine now that the fall weather had resumed.

The move to the new home had also heralded another change in the marital life of Josiah and Ida. In late November she was forced to admit that she was once again carrying a child. When told the news, Josiah was overwhelmed by guilt. "My God I'm so sorry, Ida. I never meant for it to happen. Just a few times. What's a man to do? You get right in to see Dr. Greene and find out if you're okay. I sure hate to hear what he'll say about me letting this happen to you again."

Ida found herself suppressing her own feelings of frustration and anger to comfort her husband. " Hush, Josiah. We didn't do anything to be ashamed of. That's part of being married, and I'm not going to feel guilty because the good Lord saw fit to bless us with another child. It'll be all right, you wait and see."

Despite her words of encouragement to Josiah, she realized that she was making excuses for not making an appointment with Dr. Greene. Once again, she was embarrassed to be dealing with this particular problem at her age.

During the fall of 1899, possibly because he was bored from not being able to do his fall work due of the bad weather, Josiah made a bid for the Republican Party's designation as Sheriff of Eagle County. Unfortunately there were members who strongly supported Mack Fleck, the Silver Teller Republican candidate, and they were successful in swaying the rest of the committee. Josiah grumbled and cussed for several days about loyalty of the "Party", and he even threatened to change parties. Ida knew that it was an idle threat because her husband would rather be dead than be a Democrat. Sure enough, he gradually got over his disappointment and threw himself into the matter of getting the business ready for the winter which was fast approaching.

Josiah's contacts told him that Leadville was desperate for lumber and mine timbers but, thus far, he hadn't been able to find a means of transportation during the winter months which would be cost effective. To complicate matters, a new mill was being erected at Red Cliff, and he knew they would undoubtedly get the first chance at any contracts. So, he concentrated on getting some contracts to re-build the parts of Gilman which had burned earlier in the year, and, he authorized Fred to start another house on the adjacent lot, hoping to make a tidy little profit from its sale.

Despite her advancing pregnancy, Ida was in the height of her glory, arranging and rearranging furniture, adding brightly colored quilts and rag rugs to each bedroom, and stocking the abundant cupboards in her bright, light kitchen. She still had to haul water from outdoors, but the water barrel, supplied by the water route man, was much closer to the door than a ditch or stream. Her garden had done well, and the new pantry was filled with the results. The boys had started on another wood pile during the dry days of fall, and everything seemed to be ready and waiting for the next blast of winter.

Looking down the big dining room table on Christmas Day, Ida believed that her life could not be more perfect. All her children, including Birdie's family, were seated around her and Josiah—happy, healthy people, of whom she was so proud. The Christmas feast seemed to cook itself in her commodious new kitchen, and the table threatened to bend from the weight of it all. While the wind howled around the eaves and light smatterings of snow began to blow against the window panes, the Herwicks bowed their heads in gratitude for all the blessings which had been bestowed upon them during the past year. Ida added a private prayer that God would forgive her for her initial reluctance to carry this unborn child. "Please don't make my baby suffer for any of my earlier thoughts. Make it healthy, dear Lord, just make it healthy."

∾ In January, 1900, Eagle County advertised for bids on a proposed bridge over the Colorado River at Dotsero. Josiah Herwick was one of the bidders, with a price of $1,000 for a wooden bridge. He lost out to the Pueblo Bridge Company with their proposal for a steel structure. The bridge was completed on August 2, 1900. Theodore Von Rosenburg was the engineer.

∾ The first movie was shown in Glenwood Springs in 1900. The picture was projected upon a white canvas sheet suspended on the north wall of the First National Bank Building. It only ran for a few minutes before the film caught fire.

∾ The sugar beet industry was advertising the benefits of farm living in the Grand River Valley near Grand Junction.

FEBRUARY 15, 1900   EAGLE, COLORADO

"Hey, Pa, you got your name in the paper," hooted Fred while he read the newly arrived *Fulford Blade*. "It says here that J.L. Herwick went hunting mountain lions on Tuesday without a saddle, and you're now eating your meals standing up!"

"Damn fool editor," grumbled Josiah as he gingerly rose from the dinner table. "You'd think he could find enough important news without having to report on my sore backside."

"Well, Pa, you've got to admit it was a stu——— ,uh, foolish thing to do." Fred stopped short of calling his father stupid, while trying hard not to laugh out loud. Josiah's discomfort made the situation even more hilarious.

"By God, I bet you would have done the same thing if a lion was staring you in the face," Josiah bellowed. "I wasn't gonna give him any lead time by stopping to saddle up. I just didn't figure on having to track him so long. He was a wily son of a gun."

"But, Papa, you didn't kill him!" chimed in Mary.

"Well, no one can say I didn't try," growled Josiah as he stomped from the house. On the other side of the door he could hear noises that sounded suspiciously like muffled laughter. It was difficult to determine which was more injured, Josiah's back side or his pride.

Several storms had dumped considerable snow in the mountains, causing the deer and elk to migrate to the lower valleys, bringing the mountain lion (or catamount as some people called them) to follow the game. Josiah had been scouting for good stands of timber toward the Fulford area and had decided to warm up at a cow camp near there. He unsaddled the horse and placed the saddle over an old barrel lying in the lean-to shelter while giving the animal some grain. He had just finished building up a fire in the cook stove near noon, when he heard the horse's distressed snorting. Heading around the corner of the cabin, Josiah came almost face to face with a big lion who was sizing up the frightened gelding. The lithe, graceful cat bounded up the hillside and was away in a flash. Acting mostly on instinct, Josiah grabbed his rifle from the saddle scabbard, jumped atop the horse and, using just the halter rope, galloped off in what he thought would be a short pursuit of this potential trophy. He'd show Jake Borah that someone else could also kill the elusive mountain lion. In his mind's eye, he already had the hide tanned and stretched on the living room wall.

But the lion was a worthy adversary. Mile after mile it traveled, with Josiah trailing behind at least a quarter of a mile. Just as the early winter sun was preparing to sink into a gloriously colored sleep, the animal seemed to disappear into thin air. Josiah circled around the last tracks, trying to explain how the cat could have leaped such a long distance onto adjacent rocks. But that was the only explanation unless he was willing to believe that the animal had supernatural powers as some old timers professed. Discouraged, cold, and very uncomfortable, Josiah headed his horse back to the cabin. The next day, with his butt barely touching the saddle, he rode into Fulford and stopped at Orion Daggett's store. While telling Orion about his adventure, he glanced up to see the weasel-shaped face of the *Blade* editor, who made haste to include Josiah in the day's news. "Snoopy bastard," he thought. "Too bad I need to stay on the good side of him and his damned paper. Otherwise I'd teach him not to spy on folks' conversations."

Although the good natured ribbing ceased several days after the paper's expose, Josiah's pride suffered again when, by the end of the winter season, Jake Borah had killed a total of five mountain lions.

The moderate winter of 1900 was transformed into an early spring. By March 10, the newspapers all were reporting that sleighs had been replaced by wagons. By mid March, the *Eagle County Times* reported that crops were being sown. Fred's house construction, Josiah's sawmill, and Ida's pregnancy were all making steady progress.

Ida had been welcomed into the Methodist congregation at Eagle and did her part in the usual volunteer work surrounding the operation of a community church. Although the Eagle population was only 124, many residents were parishioners and had been successful in raising enough money to build a beautiful church, which was to be dedicated on June 28. Ida and the other ladies were busy making curtains, altar cloths, and other miscellaneous accouterments. Although her advancing condition would soon make public appearances improper, she enjoyed the prospect of vicariously experiencing the dedication events.

With Guy, Oren, Tiny, and Mary in school each weekday, Ida explored the silent spaces of her mind. Al, almost four years old, was a quiet child who amused himself for hours on end, permitting Ida to go about her chores in a reflective manner. This was an unaccustomed gift to a woman who'd always been pulled along by the demands of her large family. At first, her musings revolved around daily life, what she needed to do next, concern for her children's croupy coughs, and other miscellany that successfully barricaded her within the small confines of mother and wifehood. But, gradually, as she was gliding steaming hot irons over stiffly starched material or kneading the bubbles out of her marvelous sour dough, other thoughts would come racing across her mind, unbidden and provocative. Portions of Reverend Gordon's sermons, childish questions, articles extracted from the newspaper, conversations overheard at social gatherings, all combined to help her discern, consider, discard, keep, accept, or reject. This was new. Until now, Ida's existence had been spent in survival mode, going through life one day at a time, struggling to maintain throughout all of life's challenges. Thinking about these ideas was like learning a foreign language, but she gradually came to realize that her advancing maturity had also given her the ability to see things more clearly and to have opinions on issues that she'd previously ignored. Eagle County was in the midst of a growth period. Its people and events were exciting and Ida felt a significant part of the whole fabric. Whether at home, at W.O.W., or at church, Ida's new confidence was demonstrated on a daily basis. Life was very good.

The Woodmen of the World and their female counterparts were all excited about the district conference to be held in Denver for four days in June. A large delegation, including Josiah, was traveling from the Eagle River Valley. Ida sadly prepared his suits for the trip. The baby was due around the last of June, and it was too risky to travel that distance, not to mention the impropriety of being seen in public. Her newfound independent self chafed at the restriction but acknowledged there was little she could do about it except to promise herself that someday soon she would go to Denver—maybe just to see Grant and his new wife who were expecting their first baby in August. She thought, with longing, of the many years since she had seen this younger brother, who was so little when she left Nebraska. "Yes, indeed," she decided, "some day soon I'm going to Denver to see my brother."

Josiah had only been home for a week when Ida awoke on the morning of June 27 with the tell-tale signs of impending labor. Before eight o'clock, Dr. Greene had been brought to the house to check on the baby's progress into the world. He reported that Ida's pulse was extremely rapid, and he was also concerned about her blood pressure being elevated. "Let's hope this little fellow gets here in a hurry, Si. Otherwise both your wife and the child are going to be in danger. I might have to do a cesarean operation if nothing else works, but let's wait and see how they do for another hour or so."

The children were hastily sent to neighbors for the duration of labor, and then Josiah and Fred went to the new construction next door to await word from the doctor or midwife. Although the men did some minor carpentry work on the house, Fred could tell that his father's mind was in the bedroom next door. The old man was clearly worried, and Fred suddenly felt the same fear that his mother might not pull through this time. "My God," he thought, "what would it be like for us without Ma? "Just entertaining the notion was too frightening to consider. Ida had always been the constant in her family's lives. Her death would be like a death for all of them. "Surely a loving God would not tear such a good woman from her family." It was as much a prayer as a thought. But the young man knew that goodness had nothing to do with death. This young country was full of orphans born to righteous and loving women. Fred shivered as he acknowledged the possibility.

When later trying to recall the circumstances of that day, Ida could only bring to mind small bits of memory. She knew that she was floating in an agony filled haze induced by the labor pains and soaring vital signs. In the distance, she could hear Dr. Greene issuing commands to the midwife, finally followed by the sound of a baby crying. Only it really wasn't crying. It sounded more like a tiny kitten mewing. "My baby," Ida murmured. "Is my baby all right?" But the words were never uttered because she was being pulled into a whirling vortex of light and sound, and finally into the warm, dark, comforting silence.

Four days later, Ida opened her eyes to the late afternoon sunlight filtering through the tree beside her bedroom window. A figure by her bed moved to lay a hand upon her arm. "Hello there, Mrs. Herwick. You've had us all worried, but now you're going to be just fine. Don't worry if you can't focus your eyes just yet. You've had a serious infection, and it will take some time for all the poison to leave your body. In the meantime, just lie back and get some rest. I'll tell your family that you can have short visits tomorrow, if you feel up to it."

As she listened to the voice of beloved Dr. Greene, Ida knew that he had saved her one more time. She wanted to ask about the baby, but the doctor had left the room and she was so very tired. Her eyes shut and she was carried back to the place of safety, where there was no pain, no demands. And she slept.

This time it was Ida who made the news. The *Eagle County Blade* reported, "Mrs. J.L. Herwick is out of danger and fast recovering." Ida had been bedridden for sixteen days before Dr. Greene would allow her to be up and moving around. During that time, she rested and lay caressing the downy head of her infant daughter, who had been named Helen. The baby had a perfectly formed body, which helped to off set the memory of the other tiny being with such a twisted shape. Her skin was like the soft pink petals of a newly budded rose. But there was a problem inside.

Ida listened while the doctor tried to explain that some children seemed to be born with undeveloped parts, and that it took some time for the natural process of organ development to occur. In this case, the child's body was not thriving, although they tried desperately to feed milk formulas which would offer the highest nutrition. Ida's milk had dried up as a result of the illness, which caused her no end of grief, because she believed that the baby would get well if she could nurse her. So, day after day, the two lay together while Ida dozed and prayed for the life of this tiny innocent being.

For the remainder of the summer all events seemed to take a back seat to the spiritual struggle going on between Ida and the grim specter of death. Birdie had arrived from Burns shortly after Helen's birth and stayed to run the household while Ida was recuperating. She soon had the family operating on a firm schedule, which startled the younger children, who'd not had the advantage of knowing their sister as well as the older siblings had.

In August, the Ashlocks moved to Wolcott. Norman went to work at the sawmill, enabling Birdie to make frequent trips to Eagle so she could check on the Herwick household. Josiah had hired a lady to come in on a daily basis, but Birdie needed to keep some control over the family unit. Her presence was like a breath of fresh, if brisk, air which always made Ida feel better. If only she could take some of her eldest daughter's strength for her youngest babe.

Despite the baby's grave condition, family activity continued. In late summer, Josiah moved the sawmill onto a fine stand of timber about four miles west of Minturn. This necessitated his being gone several days each week, which Ida barely noticed. She was far too preoccupied to notice her husband's familiar absences. Her days were spent coaxing droplets of milk into the tiny shell pink mouth, praying all the while that this nourishment would be the magic elixir to heal the sick little body. But Ida was forced to admit that the baby was not growing despite her efforts and prayers. Little Helen was barely larger than she was at birth. Ida could not admit to herself, however, that the child was growing weaker. Each day she eagerly looked for any sign of progress. "Look here," she'd call to the family, "I think our little girl is moving about more today. And, she sucked on her bottle harder this morning."

Her husband and children would enter into the conspiracy by assuring Ida that they, too, saw improvement—as much for their comfort as for Ida's.

When he was home, Josiah could be found in the bedroom staring down at the tiny form in her crib–not touching, not talking, just looking, as if he could somehow forever memorize the small, perfect features of this child.

News of the birth of her nephew, Albert, in Denver, penetrated Ida's preoccupation long enough for her to pen a congratulatory note to Grant and Helen Oyler. She briefly remembered her promise to travel to Denver for a visit with her brother and his family. Was that only two months ago? It seemed like a lifetime.

EAGLE COUNTY TIMES, SATURDAY SEPTEMBER 22, 1900
Word comes from Eagle of the death last night of the infant daughter of Mr. And Mrs. J.L. Herwick at only three months of age. The child was very delicate from its birth. The burial will take place Sunday at Edwards.

The train screeched to a stop at the Edwards Cemetery long enough to allow the group of people to alight from the baggage car with the small wooden box. The party started down the hill toward the cemetery; Ida, Josiah, Wid, Fred (carrying the tiny casket), Guy, Oren, Sarah, Mary, and

Al. They were met by many of their friends, and the Norman Ashlocks who had come by wagon from Wolcott.

"How many times have I stood on this plot of ground?" Ida numbly questioned. "Is it three times? No, no, it's four counting Mother Herwick. How many more, dear God? How many more loved ones will I have to leave in this damned barren ground? Each one has taken a part of my heart with them, until I sometimes can scarcely believe there's anything left of me. Why do you take the innocent and leave the sinful? Mother was old, and I could accept it was her time, but my babies, my Paul. Why did you have to take them? If you have to take someone, Lord, take me. I don't think I could stand to put one more child in the ground."

The brief services concluded and their friends gathered around Josiah and Ida. She smiled politely and accepted the words of comfort, knowing that these people offered the only thing they could; love, support, understanding. There were few in the assembled group who had not also lost a loved one, including a child. But Ida also knew that other's compassion did little to lessen the searing band of grief burning within her at that moment. Looking across to her husband, she could see that he, too, was struggling with the need to be polite and the urge to run. Finally, as the line of mourners reached its end, he took her arm and gently guided her to Birdie and Norman's wagon. They would all be going to Wolcott to await the next train going back to Eagle. Ida sat in silence during the entire trip, her dry eyes staring straight forward, her mouth set in a grim line. "Never again, God. Do you hear me? I don't ever want to lay another body in this ground. If you need to take a soul, then let it be me." At one time the pain of her grief had been sharp and piercing. Now it was just a dull, familiar ache. "Perhaps this is nature's way of protecting us from feeling so much that we want to go mad. Four children, God. You've taken four of my children. Why? Why let me go on having babies if you mean to take them away. What have I done to be punished like this?" No divine voice answered her questions as she sat in stony silence. Indeed, that explanation never came.

Ida's internal flames of grief seemed to be echoed by the forest fires raging throughout the region that fall. The first storm of the season, on October 12, quenched the timber destruction, and Ida appeared to be finally putting the baby's death behind her as she resumed her daily duties. Only she knew how often the tears flowed when no one was around, and how empty her arms felt now that they had no tiny, helpless infant to cuddle. Life goes on, but not before small chunks of oneself are left behind as payment for the pleasure of living.

Josiah, in typical fashion, threw himself into his work and politics. He was made chairman of the Eagle County Republican Party and stumped around the area building up enthusiasm for the coming election. Unfortunately, his party lost some offices to the Teller Silver Republican candidates, but Josiah didn't seem to be discouraged by the local Republican defeat.

ᗧ Vice President Theodore Roosevelt spent ten days, from January 11, 1901, hunting mountain lions in the Meeker area.

ᗧ President William McKinley visited the Western Colorado in June, 1901. "Teddy" Roosevelt became President on September 14, 1901 after the assassination of McKinley.

ᗧ Cardiff, Colorado, namesake of the famous English city, was a bustling town of 250 people. The coke output was constant from 240 ovens which usually smothered the town with their smoke. Most of the citizens were employed in the coke production. The blazing ovens were an awesome sight after dark, and it was a routine pastime for citizens of Glenwood Springs to drive out to view the glowing spectacle.

ᗧ Upriver, at Redstone, Colorado, John Osgood had developed a model town for the employees of his coal and coke operation. The settlement boasted 500 residents living in 150 neat frame cottages or boarding in the nicely furnished Elk Mountain Lodge. A schoolhouse, club house, library, and theater complimented the other amenities of Redstone.

ᗧ The Glenwood Post reported, "Parachute, Colorado is the center of unusual interest because of the report of rich discoveries of both oil and asphalt."

DECEMBER 25, 1901   EAGLE, COLORADO

The long dining room table was not large enough to accommodate all the assembled family and guests for Christmas dinner, so a smaller table had been set up at the end of the room for the younger children. Guy, the oldest at age thirteen, had been given the task of keeping order at the table, a task which sorely tested his patience. He believed that he was too old to be sitting with the little brats, let alone taking care of them, and he was not reluctant to pinch ears or give swift kicks under the table to anyone getting too rowdy. The socks, hung up for Santa Claus, had been full of nuts and candies that morning and a good share of the goodies had already been devoured. Still the children waited impatiently for the arrival of the turkey, dressing, and other holiday foods which were sending forth such wondrous smells from the kitchen.

The adult table was crowded, too. Besides the Ashlocks, the Herwicks were joined by elderly Lou Albright, Irish Bill Fisher, who was a sawmill hand, and Andy MacNeil, a teamster who hauled the sawmill products to their final destination. Andy, a huge black man, looked a bit uncomfortable in the confines of a family home. Since leaving his family home in Mississippi, the young man had never known anything other than boarding-houses and rough construction camps until he arrived in Wolcott. He had signed on with Josiah to haul the lumber and he boarded with the Ashlocks.

Ida and Birdie emerged from the kitchen with platters and bowls of steaming food, and the family grew quiet while Jonathan Ashlock, the eldest, said grace. As she settled into her chair, Ida looked around the two tables and her heart was full of thanks for a plentiful and prosperous year. The sawmill continued to bring in a small but steady income for their family. Norman was working there, and had taken over much of the daily management, which allowed Josiah to help Wid and Fred who were now farming. The wheat crop had been good, and they had gotten a good price for it. There truly was much to be thankful for.

A movement in Ida's belly caused her to smile at one more blessing. Another child was growing under her heart, and she knew it was God's gift to her for little Helen who had been dead now for over a year. The baby was due sometime in May, and she hungered for the little bundle which would be placed in her arms. Even though she was forty years old, this pregnancy had thus far been uneventful. There had been no sickness or fatigue, which plagued so many of her pregnancies, and Ida took this as a good omen. She eagerly looked forward to the delivery some five months away. In the meantime, she could cuddle her newest grandchild, Ruth Ashlock, Birdie's baby, who was just two months old. "A woman's arm is shaped just right for a round little bundle like this," she cooed as she and the baby sat in the midst of the noise and confusion of the day. The baby's brown eyes seemed to stare into her grandmother's face, as if searching for some inner answer. "You're very young to be so serious, little one. There'll be plenty of time for you to be an old sober chops. How 'bout giving your Grandma a smile?"

part five

1902-1919

∾ During 1902, President Theodore Roosevelt withdrew 68,160 acres of ranching and grazing land from the White River Reserve in an attempt to appease the radical opposition of hunters, ranchers, and timbermen of the area.

∾ In May, 1902, the last section of the "Taylor State Road" through the Glenwood Canyon of the Grand River was completed, although newspaper reports admitted a great deal of work still needed to be done. This portion was the most difficult of the entire route which stretched from Denver to Grand Junction. The total cost of the entire road was $60,000, half of which was spent in the canyon. Dynamite drillers had to be let down on ropes over the steep precipices which towered 2,000 feet in places. One man was overheard to say that there wasn't a bushel of dirt in the whole twenty miles. Upon the road's completion, tourists soon crowded into the canyon with buggies, bicycles, and other conveyances to view the magnificent formations of nature. A restaurant and dance pavilion were established at the old Captain H.T. Sales place on Cascade Creek

JANUARY, 1902   EAGLE, COLORADO

Ida's complacency of 1901 was soon interrupted. Although the Herwick family was making a decent living as a result of their hard work, Josiah, in his on-going drive to better himself, bought more land than he could afford. Despite trying to juggle their resources by "robbing Peter to pay Paul," it became apparent, in January, that he would have to turn back one of the riverfront properties on the north side of the Eagle River. This bothered him a great deal, and it was probably no coincidence that he started looking for greener pastures.

Other friends had moved west to the Glenwood Springs area, including their friends Bill and Laura Livingston. The Livingston's Hyde Mill, serving all of the Roaring Fork Valley, was a thriving enterprise. The towns of east Garfield County were burgeoning with the coal and coke industry as well as the ranching and farming which complemented the growing tourism business. This region had all sorts of interesting possibilities, and Josiah, looking through his rose-colored glasses, decided this was the place to be.

Ida knew she should be accustomed to these periodic upheavals, but she never quite adjusted to her husband's need for new horizons. In February and March, Josiah made trips to Glenwood Springs, ostensibly to buy horses, but the whole family knew he was scouting new deals and opportunities. Each time he came home with effusive enthusiasm for everything from the weather to the job opportunities. In mid April he returned with news that he had found some property adjacent to the Hyde Mill which could be bought for a song. Elizabeth Pierce was hoping to get rid of the 320 acres laying between the Rio Grande tracks and the Roaring Fork River, and he thought he could make a very good deal on this property.

Ida never quite knew how her husband managed to accomplish his "deals," but accomplish them he did. Before she had time to adjust to the possibilities of moving to Glenwood Springs, she was there. There was a shabby house located on the property down by the Roaring Fork, and this was the home to which he brought his family. Ida's time was getting near, and he wanted her to be all settled in so she wouldn't over-do. Although Ida seriously doubted the sincerity of Josiah's intentions, she couldn't argue that this would certainly be a better time to move.

The move from Eagle to Glenwood Springs seemed to break the circle of family that had remained around Josiah and Ida throughout their married lives. Birdie, Norman, and Wid remained in Wolcott and managed the family property and sawmill until they could be sold. The house and property in Eagle were rented out until a buyer could be found. Although Fred moved with his family, he soon found a job on a ranch down by Silt which included his room and board. That left Guy, Oren, Tiny, Mary, and Al at home with their parents.

A late snow had frosted the mountains around Glenwood Springs on the morning of May 24, 1902. Looking east from her bedroom window, Ida could see the summit of Mount Sopris, glistening with its newest layer of white. She sleepily wondered if the new peas and lettuce would be frosted that night. The snow was unseasonable for even this high altitude. At that moment, the door opened, admitting a woman holding a small blanket-wrapped bundle which gave forth urgent cries. "Well, well, Mrs. Herwick, we have a very hungry little girl here. She wants some breakfast."

Ida made room for the baby and watched as the infant took hold of her swollen breast. "My, you really have an appetite," she laughed as the baby vigorously pulled at the nipple. Ida's concern about having another sickly child melted in the clear and convincing evidence of this infant's health. "Thank you, God, for this perfect little creature."

That evening the family gathered in the bedroom to discuss a name for their newest member. Ida had been watching the baby's facial expressions all day, and she fancied that the little wrinkled face looked remarkably like someone she had known and loved so much. "I think it's about time that someone is named after their Grandmother Herwick," she said. "I swear that she has Mother's eyes and mouth. It's just something about the way she sort of scrunches up her face. I remember Mother doing that when she was really concentrating on a task. I'd like to call her Susan for Mother, and Ella for my sister. How does that sound?"

Everyone agreed it was a good name, especially being a namesake for a grandmother who none had personally known but whose memory had been kept alive by their mother. Josiah, as usual, was content with any name that Ida liked. "Maybe we'll finally get that sister of yours to come for a visit if she knows she has a baby named after her," he laughed.

Ida felt a tug in her chest at the mention of her sister, Ella. Where had the years gone? Ella was now twenty-nine years old, and Ida had not seen her since leaving Nebraska. Although they corresponded at regular intervals, it wasn't the same as seeing her in person. Ida knew that she'd never get back East, and all she could do was hope that Ella would come see her.

"Well, we'll see if it works," she replied.

If the Herwicks had lost some of their immediate family by moving to Glenwood Springs, they renewed their acquaintance with others. Wes and Rena Herwick were living at Cardiff, just a short distance from Josiah and Ida's new place. Ida was pleased to meet Rena and to have another woman friend. Wes's children, Clarence, Fred, and Mary fit in well with Ida's younger children, and many summer days were spent at the Roaring Fork place where the children played and the two mothers worked together canning, sewing, and carrying out other household tasks. Ida once again felt a sense of fulfillment in having a female confidante and friend.

Wes had been helping Josiah with the ranch chores whenever he had time. When Josiah decided to divide the acreage, Wes asked if he could buy some of the land, so Josiah sold eighty acres to Wes, and another eighty acres to Juliett Taylor, while retaining 160 acres for himself. There were no structures on Wes's property, so his family continued to live in Cardiff while he farmed the bottom land, and helped Josiah run some cattle on the parts not under cultivation. But Ida's house became a gathering place for everyone There was always a great deal of mutual meal preparation and chores taking place. The river bottom was a green oasis from the summer heat, and the family often ate meals outside beside the swiftly flowing Roaring Fork whenever the voracious evening mosquitoes could be smudged away.

The sale of the riverfront parcels and the four lots in Eagle allowed Josiah a little breathing room from his self-imposed obligations. He paid off the note on the cattle which were purchased in July and stocked up on supplies for the winter. One day while he and Ida were in town settling up their affairs and doing business at the Court House, Ida spied signs advertising a newly arrived photographer. She had yearned for a portrait of her husband all these years and, in a moment of impulse, suggested that they get their pictures taken. Josiah's initial response was negative. "Why in the world would I want to spend good money having a picture taken of my ugly mug? It's not like we don't see each other every day."

"Because it's something for us to have in the years to come," Ida replied, not being able to tell him the real reason. To a person accustomed to the pain of saying good-bye to loved ones, any graphic memory is welcome. She often sought the picture of the children and her, taken in 1894. She would look lovingly at the picture of young Paul, the only thing with which she had to remember him. This was her way of keeping the memory of his handsome face from fading in her heart, and she had been so grateful for that picture. "Please, Josiah, it isn't all that much money, and besides we're all dressed up; we shouldn't let it go to waste." She said no more, but her dark eyes appealed to him He finally gave in to her whim.

"I still think it's a crazy idea, but if you've really got your heart set on it, I guess it can't hurt."

Although Josiah didn't want to spend his hard-earned money on portraits, he did take a flight of fancy by applying for a Homestead Act Relinquishment of eighty acres in the Ruedi area. He defended his actions by saying that the Forest Reserve was all around the property, and that it should have considerable value as the only private piece of ground. Ida just shook her head as she smiled at the lame excuse. If anyone could make a silk purse out of a sow's ear, it would be Josiah Herwick.

ᴄ❧ Carrie Nation visited Glenwood Springs April 11, 1903. It was Election Day so the bars were closed, but her hatchet was firmly tucked into the belt of her dress as she alighted from the train.

ᴄ❧ Dr. W.F. Berry, just graduated from the Mayo Brothers Medical School, arrived in Glenwood Springs and established a small hospital.

ᴄ❧ A "County Poor Farm" was established September, 1903 in Glenwood Springs, and a pest house was also erected in the gulch some distance from the main building. Bedbug powder was purchased by the barrel full.

ᴄ❧ John Cleveland Osgood built his famous "Cleveholm" mansion at Redstone, Colorado.

JUNE 13, 1903   GLENWOOD SPRINGS, COLORADO

"Pa's gettin ready to leave you if you don't get out here," yelled Guy. He, Oren, and Al were almost jumping up and down in their impatience to get to town. It was Strawberry Day, and there was a wealth of wonderful things to see and do. Ida, Tiny, and Mary were gathering up the picnic food, swim wear, and other miscellaneous items which would be needed during the day-long event. Little Susan sat in the midst of the chaos, sucking her thumb and wondering what all the fuss was about. Finally, everyone was packed into the buggy, and they took off at a crisp trot toward all the festivities.

They had barely gotten settled on Grand Avenue when the parade started. Afterwards, they strolled through the booths lining the street and listened to the vendors hawking their goods.

Guy and Oren had been saving their hard-earned money from the mill for something special, and they paid close attention to the dazzling array of possibilities. Jack knives, pocket watches, cowboy boots and hats, colored neckerchiefs and lariats all beckoned for the boys' precious dollars.

Ida, the girls, and Al trailed behind the boys, while Josiah was content to engage in street corner conversations with his friends. Tiny and Mary ooohed and aaahed over the pretty ribbons and hair decorations which one vendor offered. After purchasing a few yards of ribbon for the girls, Ida caught up with Oren and Guy who were looking at a sparkling display of watches. There were all types, ranging from a purely utilitarian plain silver instrument, to the most ornate railroad watch imaginable. As the boys examined the assortment, Ida spied a small display of women's watches. One in particular caught her attention. It rested on a bed of red velvet, its case a gleaming gold. The domed engraved cover opened to display the face with roman numerals. A delicate gold bow tie pin was attached to the case so ladies could fasten it to their bodice. She picked it up and ran her fingers over the delicate floral engraving and looked longingly at the price tag. Oren watched the expression on her face. "Why don't you buy it, Ma?"

Ida shook her head. Ten dollars was just too much to spend on foolishness like that. The children all wanted to go on the carnival rides, and the money would be better spent there.

She suggested they go to the carnival on the next street before it became too crowded. As they started off in that direction, Oren said that he would catch up with them shortly. He left so abruptly, Ida didn't have time to question him, but she shrugged and knew that nothing would keep him away from the carnival for too long. The day was filled with exciting activities including the ferris wheel rides, high dive acts, moving pictures, free swims at the pool, baseball games, and finally the afternoon concert where everyone rested before the evening's activities. Toward supper time Josiah and Ida started gathering up their family, despite long and loud protests from the children.

"You seem to forget that we've got animals to tend to," Josiah replied. "Old Bossy will be bellerin' her head off 'cause we're late with the milkin. I think you've had enough fun for one day. Get aboard."

Their horse and buggy joined many others who were also headed for home. The sun had gone down over Red Mountain, creating a pleasant coolness which was refreshing after the warmth of the day. The children quickly settled down and happily recounted all the details of their exciting experience. The five miles were covered quickly in a happy state.

Later that evening, after the chores had been done and the remains of the day's picnic had been eaten, Ida put Susan to bed and went out on the porch to listen to the sounds of the evening. It was there that Oren, with his hands behind his back, found her. As she inquisitively looked up, he held out his hands which contained a velvet-covered box. "I thought you might like this," he timidly said as he set the box in her hand. "You looked like you really wanted it this morning."

Ida opened the lid to reveal a small gold watch. The very watch she was admiring at the festival! "Oren, I can't believe it! You must have spent all your money on this. You dear, dear boy. I don't know what to say." She rubbed the engraving while a myriad of thoughts and feelings rushed through her mind. Having so rarely received gifts, she didn't know how to respond gracefully. Looking into her son's eyes she could see eagerness for her to tell him his gift was appreciated. "Son, this is the most wonderful gift I have ever received." She pinned the watch to her bodice. "My, doesn't that look downright elegant?" Reaching up, she kissed his cheek. "Thank you so much, I'll cherish this for the rest of my life." Tears clouded her eyes, and she was glad the darkness hid them, if not the quiver in her voice. "Now, you'd better get to bed, or you won't want to get up in the morning."

As Josiah was getting ready for bed, he heard voices coming from the front porch. As he made his way through the darkened house, he could make out the outline of his wife sitting there, and she was crying. Tears had always undone Josiah, and he hesitated in the dark, wondering what to do. Part of him wanted to go comfort Ida for whatever painful moment she was experiencing. But another part wanted to escape as fast as he could from the onslaught of tears. As he quietly retreated to the bedroom, Josiah reasoned that if Ida wanted him to know what she was crying about, she'd tell him in due time.

- On May 21, 1904, President Theodore Roosevelt withdrew another 159,400 acres from the Forest Reserve. He also won reelection in November, 1904.

- On June 7, 1904, shortly after 1:15 A.M., the Grand Valley Train Robbery occurred. A posse was formed the next morning, tracking the outlaws to East Divide Creek where Harvey Logan (alias, Kid Curry) was shot. He killed himself before he could be captured.

- The Moffat Railroad line, with its tracks running over Rollins Pass, was completed to Hot Sulphur Springs on November 11, 1904.

- On October 1, 1904, the name of Parachute, Colorado was officially changed to Grand Valley.

- In December, 1904, the Rifle Reveille estimated that 22,800 head of cattle and 1,000 horses had been shipped from Rifle. In addition 50,000 baskets of apples, 20,000 boxes of plums, 5,000 pounds of honey, and 60 cars of potatoes were among the prodigious amount of produce shipments.

JANUARY, 1904   GLENWOOD SPRINGS, COLORADO

The western part of Garfield County was rapidly growing with farming, ranching, and oil development. More people were flocking to the area each day, and Wes Herwick was one of them. Early in 1904, he found an ideal acreage in south Rifle which would allow him to cultivate a larger piece of ground than the Roaring Fork property, which was better suited to stock grazing. He sold the old land to his brother-in-law, Will Moore, and moved Rena and the children twenty-eight miles down valley before the birth of their daughter Susie in May.

Ida sorely missed her sister-in-law and the shared times of work and play. It seemed that she was destined to find female confidantes only to soon lose them. But Tiny and Mary were getting old enough to be good company for her, and she was able to occasionally see Birdie who was still in the Eagle River Valley. The house by the Roaring Fork was still full of people in the evening, but the boys were traveling farther away to get work and she knew that they would likely be leaving before long.

Fred didn't like farming nearly as much as he liked being with people. His early inquisitiveness and gift of gab had not left him, and he had been able to find several jobs in a mercantile store in Glenwood Springs. He was a popular young man who loved the girls, and they seemed to love him. He never wanted for invitations to parties and other social events. "He's definitely his father's son," thought Ida as she watched him getting ready for another evening party. "He's in the height of his glory when he's able to dazzle people with his wit and sense of humor, although I'd be happy if he didn't tease his sisters so."

When they weren't helping out on the home place, Guy and Oren worked at the Hyde Mill, or at other odd jobs in the Glenwood Springs area. The boys, still in their mid teens, were growing tall like their father. Ida always felt a surge of pride when she saw them together. With only sixteen months difference in their ages, they were more like twins, and where one was, the other could usually be found.

Eight-year-old Al was a quiet boy who seldom caused any problems. He reminded Ida of Paul, and she resisted the urge to protect him more than she did the others. The fact that he was more like his dead brother didn't mean that he was also destined for tragedy, or so she tried to convince herself.

Susan, as the youngest of this big boisterous family, was slightly spoiled from all the attention she received from her brothers and sisters. "Well, that's going to change," thought Ida as she was watching her family around the supper table one night "I wonder how she'll accept the new baby." At forty-three years of age, Ida had really believed that her childbearing days might be over. There had been some signs that her body was undergoing its natural change. After thirteen children, Ida did not yearn to have more babies. Where had the years gone? Then, the all too familiar signs of pregnancy assured her that she wasn't as old as she thought!

The end of 1904 saw a gathering of all the Herwick clan at Ida's home for the holidays. Wes, Rena, their four children, and Owen had arrived from Rifle. Birdie, Norman, Henry and Ruth Ashlock traveled from Wolcott. Wid rode up from Divide Creek where he was working on a ranch. Christmas Day fell on Sunday that year, and Ida yearned to go to church services in the morning. With wall-to-wall company, she knew it would be impossible, and resigned herself to a few early moments of prayer before the small children woke to open their presents. She loved each and every one of her immediate and extended family, even though the noise and confusion could be overwhelming at times. There was no doubt that the Herwicks were a loud, teasing, boisterous family!

∾ On April 15, 1905, President Teddy Roosevelt arrived in New Castle for a three week bear hunt on Divide Creek. On April 22, 1905, he attended Sunday services at the Little Blue School at Raven. People from all around the area attended the services to hear the President's speech. The Hotel Colorado's maids reportedly stitched together a little bear doll for the President, while he was staying there, which became the first "Teddy Bear."

∾ On August 5, 1904, a Silt news item reported that the ferry would soon be in operation.

∾ The Holy Cross Forest Reserve was created August 27, 1905, which included parts of the Roaring Fork Valley. The first supervisor was Skip Husted.

∾ Rifle, Colorado, was incorporated in 1905 and citizens started to clean up the town. It had become a "Saturday Night Town" where the cowpokes came to drink and fight. A double homicide had occurred the previous year. The new railroad grade had created a stinking swamp north of the tracks which contributed to the ever-increasing cases of typhoid and diphtheria. By the end of the year, a marshall had been hired, and a water and sewage system installed.

∾ At Marble, Colorado, a road was cut on the west side of Yule Canyon and the quarry started operations. Two pack trains of forty burros each hauled the marble down the steep mountain and then hauled coal back up to the quarry.

JUNE 30, 1905   GLENWOOD SPRINGS, COLORADO

"Hello Mother, are you still awake?" The smell of tobacco smoke and a faint odor of alcohol wafted in as Si quietly entered the bedroom where Ida was nursing four-day-old Josiah Lafayette Herwick. Si stuck his big finger out, and the baby curled his tiny fingers around it. "How's my namesake doin' tonight?"

"He certainly seems to have a good appetite," Ida replied, wrinkling her nose at the odor of smoke and alcohol. "If he keeps eating like this he'll be huge before his first birthday. What time is it? Midnight? The dinner must have been a success."

"It sure was. There must have been three hundred people there. The hall was packed, the food was okay, and some of the speeches were pretty good. And, I think we succeeded in getting a lot more W.O.W. members for the organization. Twenty-eight applications were filled out tonight."

Ida could see that Josiah was still wound up from all the evening's activities. She wished she could learn to enjoy people as much as Josiah did. She knew that even her children were more outgoing than she was. Although Ida occasionally accompanied Josiah to the Woodmen of the World affairs, she had never gotten over her early shyness. Maturity had allowed her to socialize more easily, but it was still a chore to be in big groups. She was admittedly a home-body, and she was happy to let Josiah do all the talking for both of them. Hearing about it second-hand was good enough for her.

"Some fellers came up from the Antlers area, and they tell me that things are really booming down there–at least the places gettin' water are doin' good. It seems three farmers down there took first place for their fruits and vegetables at the World's Fair in St. Louis. 'Course the real problem is gettin' water to their land. They need to enlarge Harvey Gap Dam so it will hold more water, and if they do that, all of Cactus Valley will soon be settled. One of the guys was telling me that someone should start up a ditch construction company in that area."

"And are you thinking that someone should be you?" Ida asked.

"Well, no. Not necessarily. I was just sayin' how important gettin' those ditches dug is to getting the rest of this area settled. Someone will come in and get it going."

Ida heard his answer, but she still got that knot in her stomach every time Josiah started talking about a new business.

The summer was a long, miserably hot one, and Josiah worked hard to cultivate and cut the acres of alfalfa and tend the stock, only to have a poor crop. It didn't look as if they would get much cash this year, and Ida was thankful for the supplemental money the boys were able to bring in.

In early September, Josiah was approached by a real estate agent who had a prospective buyer for the property. When Josiah discovered that he could make as much as two thousand dollars on the deal, his excitement couldn't be contained. "I think this is the answer to our prayers, Mother," he exclaimed. "It'd take a long time to clear two thousand dollars on a cash crop. We could find you a house in town, and then I can put some money into good horses and go back into the sawmill business. I bet it will pay more than grubbing for a living on this damned rocky hillside."

"Maybe this sale is the answer to your prayers, Josiah Herwick, but it isn't to mine," Ida retorted. "This is a nice place, and I've just about got the house and garden the way I want them. We're not doing so bad here. The children have lots of room to stretch, and now you want to uproot us all over again. I hate the idea of living in town, do you hear me?" Ida tried to sound authoritative, but she knew it would do no good.

And Josiah heard, but he didn't pay much attention to his wife's desires. By the end of October, the Roaring Fork property had been sold to Anna Bellem, and the Herwick family moved to Palmer Avenue in Glenwood Springs. The house was located in a newly built area on the side of Lookout Mountain. Because of the steep slope, the front of the house was built up with a rock foundation which necessitated a set of stairs leading to the street. To Ida, a person who didn't like heights, the house seemed about ready to fall into the street any minute. It took her several months to be comfortable with being perched on a hillside. She also had to watch her irrigation water carefully, or else the house would become flooded from the higher back yard garden. But, it was a nicely built structure with adequate room for her family, even if it lacked the cool serenity of the riverfront house.

Tiny and Mary were thrilled to be in town where there was always something exciting to do. The Methodist Church was just a few blocks from their house, and Ida thought that was the most redeeming feature of the new residence. She and the younger children were regulars at church, something they hadn't consistently done since moving to Glenwood Springs.

Birdie and Norman had moved to Meredith, Colorado, on the Frying Pan River where Norman had been appointed one of the rangers at the newly established Holy Cross Forest Reserve. This was a good job, and Ida was relieved that her son-on-law was such a good provider. She just wished that Birdie was a more compliant wife. Ida had been horrified many times by the arguments she witnessed between the two young people who weren't bashful about exchanging words any time or any place that they disagreed with each other. Ida could not conceive of ever conducting herself in that manner and regularly chastised her daughter for the hot-headed displays of temper.

"Well, Ma, if you think I'm going to be a quiet, meek little wife, you've got another thing coming. I've watched Pa walk over you all my life, and I don't intend to let Norman get away with that nonsense. I'm sorry if it upsets you, but you'd best get used to it, because I'm not going to change, and I doubt that he will either." The truth in Birdie's words stung Ida, but she quietly swallowed them knowing it was too late for her to change, too.

The end of 1905 brought bad news from her brother, Grant, in Denver. They had corresponded periodically through the years but had not been able to visit in person. Now Grant was notifying her that his wife, Helen, had died unexpectedly. She was expecting their second child, and no one suspected that there might a serious health problem. One noon hour Grant came home for lunch from his dairy delivery route and found her dead. The cause of death was an apparent heart attack, leaving behind Grant, and their five-year-old son, Albert.

Grant's letter was rather disjointed as it outlined the details of Helen's death and subsequent funeral. Ida, from her experience of having to say good-bye to loved ones, knew that he must be devastated. To lose a wife and unborn child would be a terrible burden of grief. She immediately wrote, extending an invitation for him and his boy to visit Glenwood Springs. Grant declined, saying that he had a good job with the dairy, and he thought he'd better stay in Denver.

Ida felt relieved to learn that his sister-in-law, Margaret Brown, was helping him to care for the boy while he worked, but that didn't ease the guilt she felt at not being able to be with her brother at his time of deepest grief, a time she knew so well. She vowed that she would keep in close contact with Grant and continue to urge him to move closer so she could be of more help.

∞ On January 1, 1906, a new law went into effect. The Federal Government would henceforth be charging twenty to thirty-five cents per head for the regular stock grazing season and from thirty-five to fifty cents per head for the entire season. Chaos erupted within the ranching communities. Teddy Roosevelt, once revered by citizens of western Colorado, became the focus of their anger. It would be almost a decade before the ranchers decided to accept the federal law.

∞ The San Francisco earthquake struck on April 18, 1906. Refugee trains passed through the towns of Grand Junction and Glenwood Springs. Citizens of these areas turned out to feed the unfortunate passengers.

∞ High waters of the Grand River took out several bridges west of Glenwood Springs in June, 1906. Witnesses reported that a man, driving a heavy wagon, was swept away with one of the bridges. He was able to rescue himself and one of the horses but couldn't save the other horse or the wagon.

∞ By November 3, 1906, a standard gauge railroad was extended from Placita to the town of Marble, which expedited transportation of the huge marble pieces.

∞ On November 22, 1906, six enginemen were injured in a head-on collision of two Colorado Midland Engines at Hell Gate, three and a half miles west of Ivanhoe on the Frying Pan River. Although badly shaken up, none of the passengers was injured.

JANUARY, 1906 GLENWOOD SPRINGS, COLORADO

Fred Herwick was in love! As Ida watched him slicking down his hair and patting bay rum on a freshly shaved face, she barely contained a chuckle. Her twenty-four year old son was certainly bitten by the love bug, and it wasn't difficult to understand why. The object of his affection had bowled everyone over with her wit and sophistication.

Madeline Florin had entered the Herwick's lives during the holiday season just past, when she and Fred had met at a mutual friend's party. Fred had asked for permission to invite her for Christmas dinner because she was new to the area and had no family. When Ida readily gave her approval, she had no idea that the lady in question would end up stealing their hearts.

Miss Florin, a dark haired, dark eyed beauty from Salt Lake City, had recently been hired as a reporter for the Aspen newspaper. It was pure coincidence, or perhaps fate, that caused her to be at the Glenwood Springs party. Fred Herwick took one look at this lovely, intelligent, scintillating woman, and became hopelessly enamored. Most of the Herwick family also fell under the mesmerizing spell of the young lady. Although cosmopolitan and well educated, Madeline took special care to make everyone feel very comfortable in her presence. She insisted on helping with the after-dinner cleanup, and paid extra attention to Tiny and Mary, who were enraptured by her looks and personality. The other family members were equally fascinated by Madeline's vivacious, outgoing behavior, but sister Birdie wasn't about to give her approval so quickly. "Well, la de da! We have a silk purse in the middle of a bunch of sow's ears! What in the name of heaven does my brother see in her, apart from the obvious? And what does she want from him?"

"There's no need to be vulgar, Birdella. I think she's as smitten with Fred as he seems to be with her, and I don't know why she shouldn't be. He's a big handsome man with a gift for liking people. I think they make a handsome couple. Your brother won't be content clerking all his life. He's got ambitions, and maybe she can help him achieve them, "Ida said.

Now, as she watched her son's toilette, Ida spied a small box in his vest pocket.

"Is that box what I think it is, son?"

Fred ducked his head in embarrassment. "Yeah, Ma, it is. I thought I'd keep my plans to myself until I find out if Maddy says yes. I guess I didn't want anyone to know if I got turned down. If you were a bettin' woman, how would you bet?"

As she gazed at her big, handsome son, Ida felt a rush of love for him. He might be twenty-four years old, but he was really just an over-grown boy. "I think she'd be a fool to turn you down, son, but of course I'm just a bit prejudiced!" she laughed. "I hope she does accept your proposal. I like her, and she'll be very welcome in our family."

What Ida couldn't share with her son was the small nagging voice deep within that questioned why a worldly woman, such as Madeline, would want to marry a young man who had never been beyond the confines of two or three counties. But she quieted the voice by assuring herself that love is blind, and perhaps Madeline was attracted by the same good qualities in Fred that his mother saw.

Whatever Madeline's reason, she did accept Fred's proposal and the couple hurried to the Herwick home to tell Ida the good news. "We're not sure when the ceremony will be, but I want you to be there, Mrs. Herwick. It will mean a great deal to Fred and me."

"Please, Madeline, call me Ida or Mother or even Ma like Fred does! You're almost family. I'd love to come to your wedding, and I'm sure the others will also want to be there."

"No, I mean we want you to stand up with us. Fred and I agree that it will have so much more meaning if you are part of the ceremony. I can't think of anyone I'd more like to have, except for my best friend, Caroline Norman, whom I've asked to be the other witness. Say that you'll be there with us, please?"

Ida was taken back by the request. She'd never considered this! Her first response was to say no, but she looked at her son's face and she couldn't find it in her heart to refuse. "Well, I suppose I could do that, if you really want me to. But isn't there someone else more your age that you'd like to ask?"

"No one more important than you Ma. Please, just say you'll do it."

On February 5, 1906, Fred and Madeline were married at the Episcopal Rectory, and Ida stood up with them, barely able to control the burst of pride she felt.

As the family gathered around the young couple that evening, there was an air of celebration. Although Fred was the second to marry, the family hadn't had the opportunity to celebrate Birdie's wedding, so this seemed like the first one. They were impressed, not only with the ceremony itself, but more with their newest family member who seemed to add a glowing presence to their rather commonplace existence.

Fred and Madeline were leaving for the new little town of Silt, where Fred hoped to become a real estate tycoon, or at least a successful salesman. All of the area between New Castle and Rifle was opening up to farming and the former stage stop of Ferguson was turning into a shopping center for the area residents. A few hurriedly built houses had been erected at the town site and Fred and his bride moved into one of these. Fred hired on at the small general store, and Madeline did some reporting for the Glenwood Springs and Rifle newspapers. Between them they made enough money to exist, and they managed to put away a few dollars to buy some land. Madeline made it perfectly clear that she was willing to live in this bare little town for the time being, but she didn't plan on living there long. Fred's ambition was exceeded only by his wife's.

Josiah kept busy doing any number of construction jobs in the area that year. There wasn't any shortage for a person who had horses and knew how to work them. From his sawmill work, to re-building washed out bridges and digging ditch extensions, he did it all. It looked as if his decision to leave the farming to someone else had been a good one. The family had a small amount of cash, and life began to look more promising.

Wes and Rena were also prospering in the Rifle area. The land which

Wes had chosen proved to be excellent, and his fields promised to yield incredible crops.

Owen, who was a died-in-the-wool bachelor, continued living with Wes and Rena. He had discovered a talent for carpentry and stayed busy building structures all over the vicinity. Ida didn't think he'd ever choose to live on his own.

Wid had found a ranch job down on Divide Creek and was gone most of the time. At twenty-seven years of age, Ida thought he should be looking for a wife, but he hadn't shown much inclination. She hoped he wouldn't turn out like his Uncle Owen."

Garfield County and most of its residents prospered in 1906. Industry was all around them, from the newly opened Yule Marble Quarry southeast of Carbondale, to the coal mining around Sunlight and New Castle and on to the rapidly developing agricultural community around Rifle and Grand Valley. The newly developed areas clamored for more lumber and building materials. Josiah had Ida buy more horses and equipment to expand his sawmill and construction operations. He'd received the final homestead patent in August and decided to harvest all the timber growing on the eighty acres of homestead land in the Ruedi area. Sleds would be needed to get the logs out during the winter months. In two deals, Ida bought three horses, two sleds, two wagons, and an assortment of log and rough chains.

Ida was never sure why, but occasionally Josiah insisted she put the chattel mortgages in her name. He had also deeded forty of the homestead acres to her in May for a paper price of $400.00. She suspected that his frequent wheelings and dealings required that some assets be placed where they wouldn't be subject to foreclosure proceedings, but her husband was short on conversation where it concerned his business deals. She had learned long ago to accept the fact that J. L. Herwick raced the ragged edge of disaster yet always seemed to come out smelling like a rose.

In November, Ida signed three promissory notes for their house in Glenwood Spring. She'd never considered doing such a thing for herself, and it was very frightening to know she was responsible for $750.00, but she gritted her teeth and signed the papers. Josiah Herwick would always make sure he had the best horses and equipment, and he managed to pay for them. Why shouldn't she have her own home?

~ A smallpox epidemic hit the citizens of Grand Valley during the winter of 1907. Dr. Fred Miller worked day and night tending to his patients and giving shots to anyone who hadn't already taken the vaccine.

~ On January 8, 1907, the Grand Junction Daily Sentinel reported that Rio Blanco ranchers were continuing their fight against predators. In the previous six months they had killed fifteen wolves, one hundred thirty-eight coyotes, and two mountain lions. Ranchers throughout the western slope looked forward to the day when all predators would be totally eradicated.

~ The Colorado Legislature voted in 1907 to change the name of the "Grand River" to the Colorado. It was not, however, officially approved by Congress until 1921.

~ Another $100,000 was raised to (re)build and enlarge the Harvey Gap Reservoir using Japanese labor. The availability of irrigation allowed the previously dry, cactus covered land to bloom with hay, fruit, and vegetable crops.

JULY, 1907 GLENWOOD SPRINGS, COLORADO

"Mother, what's the matter? You look like you've seen a ghost?"

Tiny entered the bedroom to stand beside Ida while she read the letter. "What does the letter say?"

Ida ran her hand over her eyes as if she was trying wipe away the disturbing news.

"It's from your Uncle Grant's sister-in-law. She says that Grant has been acting strange ever since his wife died a little over a year ago. The folks at the Windsor Creamery contacted Mrs. Brown recently to tell her that they will have to replace him on his milk route. It seems that he forgets where he is, and they'll find him hours later in some part of Denver where he shouldn't be. It doesn't happen every day, but it's often enough for them to be concerned. Mrs. Brown says that she has been taking care of little Albert, and she wants to know if I can come get Grant because she can't take care of both him and his son."

A shiver went through Tiny's slender body. "How are you gonna take care of a crazy man, Mother? What can you do?"

"I honestly don't know. I'll have to talk to your father, and I suppose I'd better make some plans to go to Denver to see if it's as bad as Mrs. Brown says. Do you think you can manage for a few days without me?"

"Of course, Mother. Mary and I can see to things while you're gone. Don't worry about us, we'll do just fine."

Two days later Ida boarded the train for Denver, hoping against hope that Mrs. Brown had exaggerated the situation, and that it had been resolved by the time she got there.

When Ida returned to Glenwood Springs a week later, it was evident that the problem had not been settled. Alighting from the train, she motioned for a thin man to follow her. As he hesitantly came down the train steps, it was easy to see that Grant Oyler was Ida's brother. They shared the same strong jawline, rather wide mouth, and deep set eyes, although Grant's hair was lighter than Ida's. He seemed confused, and Ida gently urged him on with a firm hand on his back. "Come and meet your nieces and nephews, Grant. It looks like they all came down to greet us. Children, this is your Uncle Grant. He's come to live with us for a while, until he's feeling better. Isn't that right, Grant?"

Grant responded with a vague shake of his head, while his eyes scanned all the sights and sounds of the railroad station. At Ida's prompting, he picked up several valises and followed his sister and her children up the street, eyes darting left and right as they walked the three blocks to the Herwick residence, his obedience rather childlike—his unnatural silence daunting.

Life soon settled into a routine which often centered around Grant and his peculiarities. Guy and Oren were working with their father wherever the work led them, so Tiny, Mary, and Al were drafted to look out for their uncle and make sure he didn't wander away from home. But, despite their best efforts, there were times when Grant seemed to disappear into thin air, only to be found sitting on someone's doorstep three blocks away. The Glenwood Springs Marshall soon became a familiar visitor as he returned the errant man to his rightful residence. Each absence was frightening because the Herwick home was only three blocks from the Grand River and the railroad tracks, both potentially dangerous for a demented person.

Ida was terribly embarrassed by her brother's behavior. Although she knew he could not control his actions, it seemed somehow shameful for him to act so crazy. After each escape, Ida would tighten security measures, much to the children's dismay. A good portion of the day was spent doing chores while keeping one eye on their uncle.

The infrequent periods of freedom were sweet, indeed, when Grant's young caretakers were able to enjoy the summer activities without constantly watching their adult ward.

When she became so desperate about Grant's condition, Ida sought solace from Reverend DuBois, minister of the Methodist Church. The man of the cloth assured Ida that she should continue offering prayers for Grant's salvation. Her brother was obviously suffering because of some past sin which needed to be expiated by God. Ida squirmed when she heard that, wondering if the minister could read her mind.

She remembered the conversation she'd had with Grant's doctor before leaving Denver. He had candidly told her that Grant's deteriorating condition could well be caused from having syphilis years ago. The physical symptoms were certainly congruent with this disease. She had adamantly refuted the possibility, although there was a gap of many years, in which Ida knew nothing about Grant's lifestyle or behavior. But the very thought of her flesh and blood having such a morally corrupt illness was more than she could fathom.

Dr. Berry, on the other hand, was much more down to earth with his advice.

"Hogwash," he exclaimed when told of the minister's conversation. "Your brother is suffering from an illness that isn't of his choosing. We don't understand a lot about dementia, but we do know that it has many causes. Sometimes it runs in families, and sometimes it's caused by the long term use of alcohol, or when a person has had syphilis for a number of years. Others become demented because of an injury to the brain. So don't pay attention to that old Bible thumper. You don't need to feel guilty about anything."

Ida vacillated between the two philosophies, depending on the extent of Grant's illness on any given day. But, just to be on the safe side, Ida continued the daily prayer routine for her brother, as well as her scheduled vigilance. "Give me the strength to see this through, dear Lord," she prayed.

Josiah didn't fuss about Ida taking care of Grant, but she could tell that her husband thought he would be better off in an institution. "I think you've got enough to do without having to watch him like a hawk, Mother, but if that's what you want to do, I guess I understand. I'm gonna be watchin' to see that you don't get worn down from all the extra work and worry. Your first concern is your family."

A small core of resentment was ignited in the depths of Ida, but she kept her thoughts private. "First concern, indeed. Who does Josiah think tended to his mother and his brothers all those years? Who was taking care of my own family while I was watching after the Herwicks? Well, no one's going to stop me from taking care of my brother. He needs me, and I'm not going to put him in any insane asylum!"

The warm, sun-soaked summer advanced, carrying the Herwick household along through the hot days of canning and preserving, to the clear, cool evenings. Ida's favorite time of the day was after she put Susan and Joe to bed and could then relax on the front porch which faced Red Mountain. The perennial evening breeze softened the last vestiges of the day's heat, while Ida, Grant, and the older children rested and watched the first lights of the evening blink on. The hillside house was high enough to afford a partial view of the town in the places where there were no trees. Glenwood Springs looked like a twinkling jewel, which never failed to soothe Ida, no matter the tempest of the day. Somehow all the problems seemed less when you were being bathed in a lovely flower-scented breeze, and you could make believe that tomorrow would be better.

Occasionally during the summer, Wid would come in on Saturday night from Divide Creek and join the family in their evening ritual. They would exchange news about his work on the Acorn ranch and the activities of the family. Ida enjoyed these peaceful times with her son.

One Saturday night in late August, everyone had gone in to bed except Wid and Ida. She sensed that he wanted to talk. It had been so long since she and her eldest son afforded themselves the luxury of a private visit. She waited for him to speak.

"Ma, I've got something I need to talk to you about. I guess you'd say it's a problem, and I don't know what to do about it. You see there's this woman, a young girl, really. She's just turned eighteen, and she lives with her aunt and uncle on the ranch next to Acorn's. The old man's name is William Grigor and he's the meanest son of a b...uh...gun in ten counties. Jenny–that's her name, Jenny Stewart–works like a dog for that family, and he won't even let her off the place to go to church or a dance or anything. The only time she's been allowed to leave on her own is when she was going to school. Aw, Ma, you should see her. She's the prettiest little thing, even though she's too skinny. I don't think she gets enough to eat. And you ought to hear her talk–a Scottish burr as thick as molasses! I have to listen close, else I can't understand what she's saying. She was born in Scotland, and Old Man Grigor brought her over here when she was eleven. He promised to send her back to see her mother, but now he's reneged on the deal, and Jenny is stuck there with no place to go. She has no money, and they keep a close eye on her, especially if anyone comes to visit. I've not been able to talk to her alone, but the neighbors all talk about the poor little thing, and how hard the Grigors are on her."

The night deepened as the time went by. Ida felt chilled by the cool breeze, but she didn't stir as her son poured out his heart regarding this young Scotswoman. "I stopped to see Fred and Madeline on my way home this evening, and Fred said he'd back me if I wanted to get Jenny off the place. I don't want any trouble, Ma, but it might have to come to that if I can't figure any other way. The old man's son, John, is my age and he seems like a decent sort, but I don't know whether he'd fight if we went to get Jenny. I think the old man rules the roost."

Ida's heart went out to her son. She'd been concerned that he was still a bachelor at age twenty-eight. Apparently all he needed was to find the right girl. "Are you telling me that you want to marry this girl, Wid?"

"I do if she'll have me, Ma, but how can I tell her when I never get a chance to see her alone?"

Ida said, "Birdie and Norman are supposed to come for a visit tomorrow, and maybe your father, too. Why don't we sleep on it and talk with them. Maybe we can figure something out. You know we're behind you, son. If this is the girl for you, God will clear the way for your being together. Now, let's get some sleep."

All the family congregated the next day, and the house bulged with everyone home. Fred and Madeline also drove up from Silt, knowing that Wid would likely need their support. Throughout the day, Ida observed him in deep conversation, first with his father, and then his sister and brother-in-law. When everyone departed to their various destinations, a clear plan had not been created, but Wid knew that he could count on his family's support.

With the coming of September, Ida had new problems. Tiny, Mary, and Al were back in school during the day, making it necessary for Ida to watch over Susan, Joe, and Grant by herself, in addition to doing all the regular household tasks. Whenever possible, she had the three helping her with chores so that she could keep an eye on all of them at one time. She had trained Susan to "snitch" on her Uncle Grant if he tried to make detours from the outhouse or other outside buildings. It wasn't uncommon to hear her shrill little voice yelling, "Ma, he's getting loose," as Grant disappeared around the corner of the house. Then Ida would have to drop what she was doing and run to intercept her brother before he got too far away. Occasionally he'd get past Susan and then the neighbors would be alerted while Ida and the two children combed the streets.

Several times he was found on the school grounds, which embarrassed the older children no end when they had to lead him home. It must have been divine intervention that kept Grant from being hurt on his periodic forays onto the streets of Glenwood Springs because he was always returned in good physical condition, if a bit confused.

Even with the girls doing after-school chores, Ida often felt so tired by bedtime that she ached all over. To complicate matters, Grant had started occasionally sneaking out during the night. Of all his absences, this was the most frightening to Ida, and she grew accustomed to sleeping fitfully, awakening at the slightest sound. The stress and lack of rest began to take its toll on Ida and the children. It was plain that a better plan of security would have to be devised if they were going to survive.

As September rolled into October, Ida heard bits of information about her son Wid and his quest for the hand of the fair Jenny Stewart. Fred was the usual carrier of news, loving the fact that he was in the midst of this exciting intrigue. He reported that Wid had enlisted the aide of a lady named Elizabeth, living in Rifle, who was a frequent visitor at the Grigor ranch and was sympathetic with Jenny's plight. Elizabeth had agreed to carry notes back and forth between the two lovers, which soon calmed Wid's fears that Jenny wouldn't want anything to do with him. The first secreted notes contained promises to each of the other's love and fidelity, allowing stage two plans for the rescue operation to begin.

THURSDAY, OCTOBER 31, 1907   GLENWOOD SPRINGS, COLORADO
It was nearing the supper hour, and Ida had just started to prepare a pan of biscuits for the oven when she heard Joe and Susan yelling at the front of the house. Automatically looking about to see where Grant was, Ida spotted him sitting by the corner window and breathed a sigh of relief. Through the door trouped Birdie and Norman. Behind them followed Fred and Madeline, laughing uproariously.

Everyone gathered around them and Ida, almost yelling over the noise, said, "What in the world are you all doing here on a week night? It must be something important. Oh my God, it isn't your father, is it?"

"Now, Ma, calm down. Would we be laughing if something was wrong with Pa? Actually we're here to introduce you to someone special." With that Fred stepped from in front of the doorway. "Let me introduce you to Mr. and Mrs. William Herwick!"

Ida was looking right into a lovely face with bluish-gray eyes, framed with a crown of beautiful light auburn hair. The eyes begged Ida to accept her–to love her. Ida's heart went out to this pretty little lass whom her son loved so very much. Enfolding her into an embrace, Ida said, "Welcome, my dear Jenny, to our family. I hope you'll enjoy being part of us." Across the embrace Ida's eyes met her son's and she could see the relief at her approval of his new wife. "Now, for pity sakes, tell me how this all happened. It looks like you've been keeping secrets from me!"

As Ida and the rest of the family sat down, the rowdy group gave them a full report of the entire courtship adventure. The letter passing arrangement had been very successful, and if the Grigor's wondered about the frequency of Elizabeth's visits, they didn't seem suspicious of her motives. On the last day she had been successful in getting them to allow Jenny to accompany her back to Rifle with the promise that Jenny would be back by milking time. Once out of sight of the ranch, Wid, Fred, and Norman rode up. Wid reached down and swooped Jenny onto his horse, telling Elizabeth, "Now you can report back to old man Grigor that this little gal has been kidnapped and will become my bride before the day is out. Tell him that you couldn't fend off three husky gents like us, and you had no choice but to let her go. That ought to clear you with the old goat! Thanks and God bless you for all your help. Come see us at Ruedi." Laughing and yelling the trio spurred their horses into a gallop, little Jenny Stewart clinging to the back of her soon-to-be husband.

After leaving Rifle, the "kidnappers" rode to Silt, where Madeline and Birdie awaited their return. Piling into Fred's two-seated buggy, the group hurried on to the Garfield County Courthouse in Glenwood Springs. The group arrived just before the office closed for the noon hour, and Fred's gift of gab persuaded the clerk to take a few minutes to issue the marriage license.

At this point in the story, Birdie and Madeline took over the telling, "Jenny had to have a wedding dress. The men were afraid that they'd been followed, so they accompanied us to the mercantile company thinking that no one would follow them there. We got Jenny a lovely dress suitable for a wedding, plus another change of clothes. Oh, Mother, it was so exciting!"

"I can see that. Now tell me the rest," said Ida, relishing every word Birdie said.

"Everyone was getting hungry, but Wid wouldn't allow us to stop for lunch until the marriage ceremony was over. He didn't want to take a chance that Jenny would somehow be plucked from his grasp before they were legally married. So we went to the Methodist Rectory and found Reverend DuBois and pleaded with him to perform the ceremony posthaste. He was afraid to ask why the hurry. I don't think he wanted to know the answer," Birdie laughed at the recollection. "The Reverend was so intimidated by these three big men, I think he would have done anything they asked! As soon as the ceremony was over, we finally got to eat lunch at the Hotel Glenwood."

"Anyone watching us probably thought we were drunk," Madeline added.

"Well, I guess in a sense you were. Kidnapping one's bride can be a heady business," Ida said.

"Well, that's the whole story, Ma. Gosh, it's five o'clock. We have to catch the train. We left Ruth and Henry with a neighbor just in case there was any retaliation from the Grigors," said Birdie.

"Wid, where are you and Jenny going to be staying?" asked Ida.

"Birdie and Norman have offered to let us stay on with them while I try to get on with the Forest Reserve. And then we'll try to find a place of our own," replied Wid.

Fred and Madeline accepted Ida's invitation to spend the night and get an early start the next morning, since they wouldn't make the twenty miles to Silt before dark set in. Ida always enjoyed having her daughter-in-law spend time with them. Madeline brought such light to their lives.

The day seemed to come to a hilarious but poignant end when little Joe was found crying in his bed because he didn't get to go out and see the Halloween "Spooks" his sisters had promised but forgotten in the excitement of the wedding news. "There, there, little Joe," consoled his sister, Tiny. "We'll get up real early tomorrow and go see all the outhouses that got tipped over last night. That'll be more fun than watching for ghosts." This temporarily mollified the little boy, who still sniffed as he dropped into a deep, dream filled sleep.

∾ The Ford Motor Company produced the first "Model T" cars in 1908. Fifteen million cars were eventually produced.

∾ James Doyle, a lucky miner from Cripple Creek, Colorado, came to Grand Valley (now Parachute) to observe the potential for possible oil shale development. He began to lobby the government for the first geological survey. President Teddy Roosevelt was also warning of an impending oil shortage.

∾ Dr. Berry built the Glenwood Sanitarium at 512 10th Street, Glenwood Springs. In 1908 five hundred physicians, including the famous Mayo Brothers, attended a convention held at Glenwood Springs. Demonstration surgeries were conducted for the benefit of the student nurses and physicians.

∾ On October 15, 1908, snow started falling on the Government Road between Rifle and Meeker. Within twenty-four hours thirty-six inches laid on the ground, and did not leave the surrounding hillsides until the following May, 1909.

∾ The Moffat Railroad reached Steamboat Springs, Colorado, on December 16, 1908. Its advent spelled the gradual decline of Wolcott, Colorado, which had been the primary shipping and freighting locale for the North Park area. Although livestock continued to be shipped from the immediate area around Wolcott, the hey day of the Concord Coaches and horse drawn freight wagons was over.

MARCH, 1908   GLENWOOD SPRINGS, COLORADO

"I've tried to stay out of this business about your brother's care, but I'm putting my foot down right here and now. You can't go on like this any longer. Look at you, woman. You're exhausted. No matter how badly you want to, it isn't possible for you to take care of Grant any longer. He needs to be in an institution, and if you won't do it, I damned sure will!"

Ida had to wearily acknowledge that her husband was right. She knew that a decision must soon be made to take Grant back to the mental institution in Denver, but she kept putting it off, thinking that tomorrow would be better. Grant's sleeping habits were completely turned around, and he usually prowled around the house at night, causing Ida to sleep with one ear open at all times. She didn't have the luxury of sleeping late in the mornings, what with getting the children up and off to school, not to mention the other myriad household chores to be done every day. Her sleep time had been cut to very short cat naps during the day and night. When she looked in the mirror, she saw the image of a haggard, thin woman who had dark circles under her eyes. No mistake about it, she looked pretty exhausted.

"No, Josiah, he's my brother, and I'll take care of the arrangements. I've already talked to Dr. Berry, and he's contacted the insane asylum in Denver. They'll take him as soon as I can get him over there, but I do so hate the idea of putting him away. I just wish there was some way of keeping him here."

"Well, there isn't. You have enough to do with your own family without havin' to take care of him, too. I'm gonna be home for a few days, and I'll either stay with the kids, or take Grant to Denver, if it's too hard for you to do it. Take your pick. What's it gonna be?"

Ida wanted to yell at him that Grant *was* her family. She'd abandoned him years ago to become Josiah's wife, and now she had to abandon Grant all over again because of her children. Reason told her that this needed to be done, but the long established voice of guilt told her that she had once more failed her sisterly duties. "He's my brother, and I'll do what needs to be done. He doesn't know me half the time, and he certainly won't know you. It will be less of a strain for him if I'm the one to take him. Are you sure you can manage here for a few days?"

"Yeah, I've got some business to take care of in town. I think maybe we should look for new territory for the sawmill. I hear tell there's a timber allotment comin' up for bid in the Coffee Pot area, and I think I might be able to get it for a good price. Now that I've got the second steam engine, we should be able to set up a good-sized operation. I figure on Guy and Oren helping me, and maybe Wid, too, if he hasn't yet gotten on with the Forest Reserve. We should be able to get in and cut a batch of timber before fall. That'll carry us through to next spring. So, you go on to Denver and get your business taken care of. I'll tend to things here."

The train trip home from Denver was a long, tear filled time for Ida. All she could see was her brother's vacant stare when she told him good-bye at the State Hospital. He had sunk into the neverland of profound dementia, effectively alienating himself from any type of human communication. The hospital doctors assured her that Grant's condition could not improve; in fact he would continue to deteriorate at a steady pace. Ida knew, when she kissed his forehead, that she might never again see him alive, and the thought was profoundly sorrowful. It seemed she had never had the opportunity to become re-acquainted with her family. Pa was gone and Grant almost gone. In the back of her mind she had always made nebulous plans for bringing the family together one more time, and she had to accept the fact that it probably wouldn't happen. It just didn't seem fair.

The end came for Grant shortly after his arrival at the hospital. Ida was notified of his death on May 14, 1908. When the letter arrived, Ida went to her bedroom and closed the door, leaving her family to talk among themselves in a subdued and hushed atmosphere. When she finally emerged several hours later, her red, tear-stained eyes were the only signs of inner sorrow. In her hand were two stamped and addressed envelopes. Beckoning to Al, she placed them in his hands. "Son, would you take these to the post office so they'll go out on the evening train? I need to let your Uncle Emer and Aunt Ella know about Grant. Then, when you come back, we'll see about whipping up some oatmeal cookies before supper time. Doesn't that sound good?"

Ida continued to feel the deep pangs of grief, but she never mentioned it. The family gradually forgot her sorrow in their busy summertime activities.

The biggest news for both Tiny and Mary was that Fred's wife, Madeline, had sweet-talked her husband into buying one of the new pianos at the local Colorado Music Company. The girls, already awe-struck by their glamorous sister-in-law, were doubly impressed by the fact that she was an accomplished pianist. They had accompanied Fred and Madeline to the store on the day of purchase and reverently ran their hands across the smooth, polished wood surface of the massive instrument. To the girls delight, Madeline had plopped down on the seat and played a lively tune before signing the chattel mortgage which made her the owner of the beautiful piece. She promised both Tiny and Mary that they could visit her often, and she would give them some basic lessons. This was all the encouragement they needed, and one or the other of them accompanied Fred or Madeline home to Silt every time they made a trip into Glenwood Springs.

Josiah, Guy and Oren had moved the sawmill to the Coffee Pot Springs area northwest of Gypsum. They planned on spending the bulk of the summer harvesting as much timber as possible. Ida and the five youngest were left to take care of the house and garden in Glenwood Springs and to enjoy the warm, slow days without too much pressure. Ida slept and ate well, recovering some of the good health she'd enjoyed before the ordeal with her brother Grant. Mornings were reserved for gardening and household chores, but the afternoons were spent in a variety of activities, including dips in the hot springs pool, visiting friends, even traveling to Meredith on the train to see the newest grandchild, Stanley Herwick who was born August 8, 1908.

Wid and Jenny were clearly happy with their married life and chuckled that their first child didn't wait much past the required nine month period to make his entrance into the world. Wid was working at various jobs in the Meredith area, including the two sawmills on Miller Creek. He still had hopes of getting on with the Forest Reserve, but there had been no appointment thus far.

Ida was pleased to see her oldest son so happy, and equally concerned about her eldest daughter's marriage. Birdie and Norman had never had a tranquil marital life, but it appeared the relationship was further deteriorating. Norman had a full time job with the Forest Service, which brought in a steady paycheck every month. Birdie, Henry and Ruth were taken care of and had a life which might make other women envious. It wasn't for economic reasons that the Ashlocks fought; it was the case of two stubborn people who refused to admit they could ever be wrong. No matter what the topic, Birdie and Norman seemed to be on opposing sides. Ida's visit was very brief, owing to the constant bickering which neither person seemed reluctant to make public. As Ida and her children returned to Glenwood Springs, she said a prayer for all her loved ones at Meredith.

Fall hadn't yet touched the air one morning in September when Ida was doing the regular Friday baking. Her arms were immersed in bread dough almost up to the elbows when she looked up and saw Guy and Oren standing in the doorway. The look on their faces caused Ida's heart to skip a beat. "Wh—, what's the matter, boys? Where's your father? Oh, dear God, something's happened to him. Tell me what happened. Where is he? Is he alive?"

Both young men stepped up to take hold of their mother. "Pa's had an accident at the sawmill and he's hurt bad, but he's still alive. Doc Berry is taking a look at him right now."

They barely finished the sentence before Ida was running out the door, down the steep steps to the street, rushing to Dr. Berry's Sanitarium, just a block away. She burst through the door and was directed to the exam room where Josiah was being care for. At the sight of her tall, strong husband, with his bloody, pain-wracked face, Ida's knees threatened to buckle. In all of their thirty-two years of marriage, his presence had been a constant. No matter the economic problems, no matter the sorrow and grief, Si Herwick had always towered over her, lending his size and strength to her own. Now, here he lay. The giant had been felled.

Ida gripped the door jamb and took a deep breath. She stepped to the table where Dr. Berry was working on Josiah and looked into her husband's eyes. She saw a reflection of her own fear and confusion, mingled with the physical pain of his injuries. At age fifty-two, being hurt or sick was an unknown experience for him. He was forced to confront his mortality head on, and Ida could see that it terrified him. She moved to take her husband's free hand as her eyes darted over his battered body.

Dr. Berry finished his exam and, looking up from his patient, acknowledged Ida's presence. "Your husband doesn't look it, but he's a pretty lucky man, Mrs. Herwick. The log hit him square in the chest, and I think every one of his ribs are cracked or broken, but I don't think there are any serious internal injuries, aside from a lot of swelling. We'll have to just wait and observe for twenty-four hours to see what develops. If he had to be hit, it was better on his front than his back. He's probably got a concussion, too, but the log just glanced off his head instead of hitting full force. He's going to have a giant-sized headache for a few days, and he'll need to stay flat for quite a while. I want to keep him here overnight, and then, if he shows improvement, we can move him over to your house. It isn't as if he'll be very far from here."

Ida refused to leave her husband's side for the next twenty-four hours, wanting to be there if Josiah needed any comfort or attention. Dr. Berry had given him a dose of laudanum to ease the pain and allow him to rest. As she sat by her sleeping husband, Ida prayed as she had not prayed for a long time. "It's so frightening, God, to see this big strapping fellow brought down. He's never been sick a day in his life, and I don't know how to handle him being hurt. What's going to happen to us if he doesn't get well? The children and I depend on him, Lord. How're we going to get by without him working? I know I get impatient with him and his schemes, but I do love Josiah so much. Please, please, please take care of him and make him well."

Ida closed her eyes and thought back to Josiah taking such good care of her when she got sick at Catamount Creek. She remembered his night time vigil with her while young Paul struggled with life and lost. She remembered him holding her when the babies died. "He's been a rock to me, Lord, and now I'm asking you to be a rock for Josiah. I can't heal my husband, but I'll be your hands, and I'll do whatever your divine guidance tells me to do. Just make him well, dear God. Just make him well."

The following weeks were a trial for all the Herwicks. Josiah showed slow improvement even though he was a rather poor patient, as most people are who have not previously been ill. He was in a good deal of pain, and it required the use of opiates to ease the discomfort. Ida and the children were captive caretakers for most of the convalescent period which lingered into the fall. Josiah's prolonged presence was unusual. He was seldom at home more than several days in a row, and everyone heaved a sigh of relief when Josiah was again on his feet and able to think about winter employment.

The accident had brought the timber cutting to a crashing halt, but Providence had decreed it to happen late in the season, allowing the Herwicks to harvest most of the allotment Josiah had paid for. The sale of the sawed lumber and cut timber had helped to sustain the family during Josiah's recovery, but money, never in great abundance, became their biggest concern. Oren and Guy both brought home their pay from whatever jobs they could find, but it was barely enough to support the entire household. Seventeen-year-old Tiny helped out with housecleaning and child care jobs, leaving Mary to help Ida run the house and tend to the family. With winter coming on, Josiah would be lucky to get jobs that weren't too strenuous for his physical condition. An early fall storm which dumped more than three feet of snow didn't help to make the prospects bright.

Josiah Herwick, much like a cat, always seemed to land feet first, and this time was no exception. Soon after he was able to again work full time, a contract was let for an extension of the Lower Cactus Valley Ditch by the Silt Light, Power, and Water Company, and Josiah was the successful bidder. Taking Guy and Oren with him, he hastened to the Antlers area with all the equipment and set up a winter camp. He intended to work straight through, unless the weather became too bad for man or beast.

Christmas of 1908 ended on a positive note. The Herwick family had suffered much anguish, fear, and sorrow, but a corner had been turned and everything was going well.

Early that morning, Ida sat with a cup of coffee in front of a blazing fire, waiting for the children to come bounding into the parlor for their Christmas treats. She thought of the many past holidays, and counted them off one by one, much as a devout Catholic would have said her rosary. Thirty-two of them—thirty-three counting the year she and Josiah met. Some seemed amazingly sharp in her memory, while others were quite dim and almost forgotten. The most poignant were of the all-too-few holidays with

Mother Herwick, and the unforgettable Christmas dinner on Battlement Mesa with Josiah's sister, Sarah, and her family. She recalled the holidays of abject poverty, such as the one at the State Bridge, and the more affluent ones, the fun-filled ones, the sad ones. The memories came flooding through Ida's mind, rushing on to be replaced by other images. The people she'd loved, the people she'd lost, the people she had to bid farewell. She couldn't tell whether the tears, meandering down her face, were from joy or sorrow, but she did know they were filled with so much love.

Wiping her eyes, Ida heard Joe yelling to Susan, "Get up sister, get up. Let's go see what Santa Claus left in our stockings."

∞ On April 26, 1909, the southern portion of the Holy Cross Forest Reserve was established as the Sopris National Forest.

∞ The first motion picture made in the Rocky Mountains was filmed on Muddy Creek in the vicinity of Marble, Colorado. The film was called "The Big Bear Hunt" and featured a bear whose collar could be seen.

∞ Joseph Bellis arrived in Grand Valley, Colorado and started his promotion of the prospective oil shale industry.

∞ The Shoshone Dam and Generating Plant was completed in the Glenwood Canyon of the Grand River by the Central Colorado Power Company. Costing $2.7 million, it was estimated to be able to supply all of the company's electrical needs as of 1905.

∞ The "Free Silver Shaft" on Smuggler Mountain at Aspen, Colorado, was drained of water by the sophisticated use of deep sea divers in their bulky suits. After the divers had repaired the pumps, they trained some Aspen men to also dive in the event of pump failure.

∞ While many Glenwood Springs residents were enjoying the "Apple Pie Day" activities in Rifle on October 3, 1909, the Citizens Bank of Glenwood Springs was robbed of $10,000. The two bandits were chased by a quickly formed posse but eluded the officers. The discarded money containers were later found above the cemetery on Jasper Mountain.

JULY, 1909 GLENWOOD SPRINGS, COLORADO

Members of the Herwick family were having a very busy year, and Ida sometimes felt as if she was standing in the middle of a tornado while everyone whirled around her. Josiah, Guy, and Oren had completed the Lower Cactus Valley Ditch Extension and signed it over to the Power Company in March. Josiah then began to work on another ditch for the Cactus Valley District Ditch Company. He figured he should be able to keep busy for at least a year on his ditch construction. He and the boys were living at Divide Creek, and Ida saw them infrequently, usually just long enough to bring their dirty clothes home and re-provision the bachelor quarters.

Fred was spending most of his energies on real estate deals in the Silt Township. There seemed to be no end to potential buyers, and he had been able to make a decent living. Fred's periodic visits to his mother were always filled with optimistic enthusiasm, but Ida thought she could detect some strain in his voice when he discussed the gay party life with his wife. He did admit that Madeline wasn't very content in the small hamlet of Silt. She much preferred the excitement of the larger towns and used her newspaper job as an excuse to frequently stay overnight with her friend in Glenwood Springs. Fred was quick to make excuses for his worldly spouse. Too quick, perhaps, Ida thought.

Norman and Birdie, and Wid and Jenny had moved to Aspen where Norman was stationed with the Forest Service, and Wid was working at ranches and sawmills. Some Aspen residents still struggled to eke out a living in the various mines, but much of the land was now being used for agriculture and logging. Foresters were required to help manage the grazing and timber sales within the newly established National Forests.

For her last year of school, Tiny had moved to Aspen to be with Birdie's family. Ida keenly felt her daughter's absence, but it was time that she grew her own wings. She was particularly adept at mathematics and had enrolled in the six weeks summer session for student teachers in Leadville. She hoped to come home and find a job in one of the rural schools, if she passed the examination and was able to get her rural teaching certificate. Ida felt such pride when she thought about her daughter. This was the first of her children who had been able to graduate from school. Mother Herwick would be so proud of Tiny. Of all of Ida's children, Tiny had the personality most like Susannah's.

After Tiny left, Ida tried to spend extra time with her fifteen-year-old daughter, Mary. She missed her older sister dreadfully. To complicate matters, Mary's trips to Silt to take piano lessons from Aunt Madeline had dwindled to almost nothing, in large part due to Madeline's excuses of being so busy. Ida had tried to keep Mary busy with household chores and church activities, but the poor dear girl moped around much of the day.

Ida remember not so long ago when there was always something to be done around the house. No one had to try to be busy. But now with only four children at home, she actually had time on her hands even though the rest of her family never seemed to light for very long. The problem was that after thirty plus years of being a wife and mother, what does a woman do with free time? For the first time in Ida's life, she felt something akin to boredom. Although the peace and quiet were a welcome blessing, there was also a sense of being in a vacuum. She observed other ladies who enjoyed clubs and organizations so much, but that didn't seem to suit her. Ida was truly terrified of meeting new people. She had never had trouble talking with close friends, but she just couldn't make herself go out and try to fit in with the women in these various social organizations. She rationalized her stand-offishness by telling herself that she looked forward to the peace and solitude after raising a house full of children. Maybe when little Joe started school in two more years, she would try harder to fit in.

Ida didn't want Mary to follow in her footsteps though. There was no reason she should be tied to the house, taking care of the younger children and handling all the chores, when Ida had plenty of time to tend to them herself. Mary needed to get out and begin experiencing a bit of life on her own. Providence seemed to be answering Ida's prayers for Mary, as well as for herself, when she heard about a family down the street who needed someone to care for the house and two children while the mother was convalescing from a serious illness. Ida urged Mary to apply for the job, and she was promptly hired for the remainder of the summer. She no longer had time to worry about being bored, and it also took care of some of Ida's spare time, because she took over Mary's household chores. She was quite content to let the other women gossip in their club meetings while she stayed home and took care of her own little realm.

CHRISTMAS DAY, 1909   GLENWOOD SPRINGS, COLORADO

The noise level and general confusion unnerved Ida, and she wryly reminded herself that a few months before, the quiet seemed deafening. The entire family was again home for the holiday, and the house threatened to pop at its seams from all the bodies crammed within its walls. Josiah, Guy, and Oren had arrived from Divide Creek. Birdie and Norman, and Wid and Jenny spent precious money on railroad fare from Aspen to Glenwood Springs. Fred, the last family member, had arrived on Christmas Eve without Madeline, and by the look on his face, the family knew something terrible had happened. His eyes were wide and watery, and he was clearly having trouble controlling his voice. "I might as well get this over. I've got some bad news, and it'll probably shock you. I guess I'm still in shock myself. Madeline has left me. She says she can't stand living in a rude town like Silt any longer, and she plans to go back to Salt Lake City as soon as possible. I can't say I'm totally surprised, because she's been complaining about living down in Silt ever since we were married. Maddy... Madeline...isn't one to lead a quiet life, and I guess she just couldn't take it any more."

His words fell onto a stunned silence. No one moved for what seemed an eternity, and then his sisters ran to draw Fred into an embrace. The men stood mute, helpless to show the emotions pulling at their insides. Josiah harumped deep down in his throat, a sign that he was deeply disturbed. Ida turned and walked aimlessly to the back of the house. She couldn't put into words the depth of her shame and sorrow. How could she have been so fooled by that woman? "Serves me right," she thought. "Fred's marriage was a real prideful thing for me. I was so proud that my son could catch such a charming woman. I even stood up with them less than two years ago."

Birdie's prophetic words replayed in Ida's mind. Indeed, what had the woman seen in Fred Herwick? How could Madeline do this to him and his family?

Fred later found his mother in her bedroom, sitting silently in the old rocking chair.

"I'm so sorry, Ma. I knew this would throw you for a loop. For what it's worth, Maddy really did love you. She told me many times she admired how you'd kept a home for all of us. It just wasn't her way. She'd never had a proper home, and the only thing she knew was the life she'd grown accustomed to." Fred hung his head. It was hard for him to say the rest. "You need to know all of it, Ma. This wasn't Maddy's first marriage. She told me she'd run away from her first husband because he treated her so mean. She said she'd gotten a divorce in San Francisco. I believed her, and we both agreed that no one needed to know about this because it had nothing to do with us. I'm sorry I didn't say anything, Ma, but I knew you'd think poorly of her, and I really wanted everyone to love her as much as I do."

Ida felt that her blood pumping through a heart racing with anger. "You mean to tell me that you married a divorced woman, and you deliberately lied to me and your family? I can't believe you'd do such a thing, son. It's obvious that...that...woman must have cast a spell over you. How could she have fooled us all so much? We took her into our family and we loved her, and this is the thanks we get! It's going to take me some time to accept this. I know you are in pain right now, and you should be. A marriage started with deceit is doomed from the beginning. I just can't believe that you'd bring such a person into our family. I'm disappointed in you, son."

Needless to say, Fred's news cast a pall over the remainder of the Christmas holiday. Ida's love and admiration, which she had willing given to Madeline, suffered a severe wound. She couldn't imagine how she could have been fooled by such deceit, and it was many weeks before she could finally forgive her son for his part in the divorce cover-up.

Part of her believed that no self-respecting, God-fearing woman would ever divorce her husband, let alone turn around and marry another man. But, another, smaller, voice argued that maybe there were circumstances that warranted such behavior. The bottom line was that Madeline Herwick had stolen her son's heart, not to mention the affection of the other family members, and then just abandoned everyone because of her selfish needs. There was nothing in Ida's life experience that could convince her to forgive Fred's soon to be ex-wife. Decent women simply didn't leave their husbands. She told her family that, as far as she was concerned, Madeline Herwick had never existed, and she didn't want to hear the woman's name mentioned in her house ever again. And so it was.

∽ During 1910, the Federal Government announced plans for a transcontinental highway. The towns of western Colorado lobbied for the road to be designated through their area. Glenwood Springs and Grand Junction, the two largest towns, were particularly active in the campaign.

∽ Haley's Comet was observed in Glenwood Springs. Tours to the observatory on Lookout Mountain occurred every night.

∽ A state-wide storm raged through in February, 1910. Colorado Midland trains were snowbound in both directions from Buena Vista. Passengers remained in the trains while as many as 100 men shoveled out the drifts which had even stopped the rotary plows.

∽ Between the years 1910 and 1920, prospectors filed on 30,000 oil shale claims on four million acres. Over 250 companies were incorporated to sell stock, and 150 Corporations sought to develop oil shale.

∽ In 1910, a man named Billy Griffith went berserk in the town of New Castle, killing two people and wounding another before he was cornered and committed suicide.

∽ The Cardiff coke ovens were shut down in 1910 when the demand for coke declined. This spelled the beginning of Cardiff's demise, the final knell sounding when the Colorado Midland Railroad ceased operations in 1918.

MAY, 1910 GLENWOOD SPRINGS, COLORADO

Business was booming in the Silt area, and Ida had been swept along by the combined energies of both her husband and son. Josiah was still working on ditch extensions in Cactus Valley, while Fred was busy buying and selling property in Silt. Thinking to also make money on the property deals, Josiah had invested some of his profits in town lots, putting them in Ida's name to keep the two businesses separate. It was all very confusing to her, but she trusted her husband and son. Still there was the slightest hint of a doubt every time she was asked to sign all the legal papers. "I know Josiah and Fred wouldn't do anything shady, and I'm sure that everything is on the up and up. It's just that I never know what's going on, or what I'm supposed to be buying or selling. I wish they could find another way of doing business without my name having to be used. Half the time I feel like I'm on the edge of a cliff, not knowing if the rocks are going to roll out from underneath my feet. It's good to see Fred so busy he doesn't have time to think about that woman. I must admit the money is welcome, but I just wish I could be left out of it."

Her wish seemed to come true when Josiah started talking about the opportunities on down the river toward Grand Valley. He'd made a good profit on the Cactus Valley project and was looking around for construction contracts in which he could utilize the steam tractors, plows, fresnos, and other equipment he'd acquired throughout the past few years. The perfect solution seemed to be the Havermeyer Canal project which was starting up west of Rifle.

The Wilcox Canal Company, first formed in 1893, had finally succeeded in attracting the financial backing of Arthur Havemeyer of the American Sugar Company. The eastern investor envisioned fields of sugar beets growing on the eight thousand acres located north of the Grand River, between Rifle and Grand Valley. He even made plans for a sugar refinery at Grand Valley. Josiah's friend, Theodore Von Rosenburg, was the engineer on the project, and Josiah was sure he could find a place for him. "I think this is a good chance for me to get the tractor and equipment paid off, and then we'll be doin' real good, Mother. You always said you'd like to move back to Battlement Mesa. Maybe it's time we start thinking about it. I hear tell that they've built a bridge over the river to Morrisana and Battlement Mesa. We won't know the old place. There's a couple hundred families living down there now."

Ida's first response was to speak against the proposal. She'd been in this house for five years, the longest she could recall being in the same place, and the thought of being uprooted again was not pleasant. "I don't know, Josiah. I'd really like to stay here for the children. They have their friends and are doing well in school. I hate to move again. Can't we just keep on the way we've been doing?"

"Well, I'll be working about forty miles away, and I wouldn't be able to come home each week. Besides, I've been bachin' for a long time, and it'd be nice to have you down there so I could get home every night. I'm not a young man, you know."

After several more conversations, a plan of action was devised. Josiah would go down to see if he could get on with the canal project. If he went to work, he'd then look around for a place for the family. In the meantime, Ida and the four children would stay in Glenwood Springs until they could be certain that the work would last long enough to warrant moving. Ida felt as if she'd received a reprieve, albeit a short one, and she started to plan her summer activities in case she'd be moving before winter.

Tiny was home for the summer and helped her mother put up all the fruits and vegetables as they ripened in the garden. She teased Ida about the prodigious amounts being preserved, and wondered if there was going to be a famine next year. While Ida accepted the good-natured joking, she seemed to be powerless to do otherwise. Once again her survival mechanism had been triggered by Josiah's urge to move. She still remembered the terribly lean years when she barely had enough food for her children. Now when she was confronted with change, she always made sure there would be sufficient food. It didn't matter that they would only be going fifty miles downriver. You could never tell what was around the next corner.

One early summer evening, Ida and the children were sitting on the front porch when Fred drove up with a guest. "Hey there, Ma, I've got someone I want you to meet. This is Miss Ware–Irene Ware. Her Pa let me kidnap her for some dinner in Glenwood Springs, but we've got to hurry so I can get her home early. Otherwise, I'll be looking down a shotgun barrel!"

Ida looked at the dark-eyed girl, and she felt a tightening somewhere in the vicinity of her heart. Dear Lord, didn't that young man learn anything from his last experience? She still vividly felt the shame and betrayal of the infamous Madeline, and she couldn't understand how Fred could be so eager to get involved again. "Welcome, Miss Ware. Come up and sit with us for a few minutes."

A thin young slip of a girl, Irene Ware had a beautiful smile which seemed to invite others to smile back. Crinkly laugh lines framed her eyes, which looked at you with sincere interest. But there was also a faint restraint in her manner, deferential, polite, waiting. Ida liked that. This girl knew how to behave, unlike that "other one" who invaded people's lives with her take over ways. "Come sit down and tell me about yourself."

Ida learned that Irene still lived with her parents in Peach Valley, just west of New Castle, and that she was twenty-three years old. She did some part-time substitute teaching around the area but hadn't yet gotten her own school. The young lady answered all Ida's questions with a guileless manner and chatted easily with Tiny and Mary about things that were of interest to girls their age. She seemed at ease with everyone, but it was obvious that her interest centered upon Fred. No matter the topic of conversation, Irene's eyes were never long away from his figure, looking for approval, seeking his attention. She was obviously enamored by the tall, handsome fellow, and his returning glances left no doubt about his feelings.

In the coming days, Ida wavered between her doubts regarding the young woman, and an intuitive feeling that Irene Ware was not another Madeline. Ida wanted badly to believe that her son had found a nice, morally fit girl, who would make him a good wife. On the other hand, she was afraid to trust. Madeline Herwick had left a residue of suspicion which was difficult to get past. That all became a mute point when Fred announced in early August that he and Irene had set the wedding date. "I know you think it's too soon to get married, Ma, and you could be right. But I really believe that Irene is the girl for me. I love her so much, and I think she loves me. She understands what my life is, and she won't run back to a big city when things get rough. Irene's one of us, and she'll be a good wife. I hope you'll give us your blessings, and come to our wedding. But, Ma, one way or the other, I'm gonna marry that girl."

On August 26, 1910, the New Castle *Garfield County Democrat* ran the following article:

HERWICK-WARE

At the home of Mr. and Mrs. H.V. Ware, in Peach valley, occurred the marriage of their daughter Irene to Fred J. Herwick of Silt, on Wednesday afternoon. Rev. Mr. Trompen officiating.

The bride is one of the county's popular teachers and the groom a promising business man of Silt.

The happy couple left on Number 16 for Denver and Cheyenne. They will be at home at Silt after October 1st. The Democrat *echoes the wish of their friends for a long and happy life.*

"It was a lovely little wedding," Ida conceded as she read the article. "I hope and pray they will be good for each other."

At the approach of fall, final plans for Ida's move to Grand Valley were made. The children had started school in Glenwood Springs but knew they would be leaving in the next few months as soon as Josiah made arrangements for some property. In mid-September, he traveled home and told Ida that he'd found some land on the lower part of Battlement Mesa, right next to the Grand River. He needed $750.00 for the down payment. He had come home to re-mortgage Ida's house at 10th and Palmer. He assured her that they could pay back the money as soon as the property was sold in the next few months.

Before Ida and her family left Glenwood Springs, there was one more thing she had to do. Loading up the youngest children one Monday morning, she boarded the Midland train for Aspen to see her newest grandson, Lorain Herwick, born on September 23rd to Wid and Jenny. She didn't know when she'd again be seeing her children and grandchildren, what with living so far down the valley, so she stayed for a few days. The fall weather had been cool and rainy, but the sun had finally come out. The quaking aspen trees, high on the surrounding mountains, had already lost their leaves. The trees at the lower elevations were still a golden blaze of color on the hillsides, mingling with the reds of the scrub oakbrush. A warm haziness was in the air, with just a touch of the cold weather yet to come.

Ida savored the scenery from her seat on the train and remembered, with some amusement, how frightened she had been of the mountains when she first arrived in this country. Now it would be difficult to imagine living anywhere else. Their majestic beauty had become a vital part of her, and it was very easy to feel a spiritual connection with the Creator whenever she gazed upon the snow-covered peaks. How could anyone not be happy, living in such a world of beauty?

Ida found the members of her Aspen family in various states of financial security and contentment. Birdie lacked little in the way of material things, but she was obviously discontented with her life, as was her husband, Norman. "I doubt if those two will ever find happiness with each other," Ida sorrowfully mused. "They are both too obstinate to ever give in to the other. I guess they'd rather be right than happy."

Wid and Jenny Herwick, on the other hand, were very contented with each other and their married life, but they were poor as church mice. Making a living in Aspen was not an easy thing to do, unless you had a steady job like Norman Ashlock. Wid worked all the time, but the wages were low, and it seemed to take every penny to stay current on their grocery bill and rent. Stanley, their first born, seemed a little sickly and Ida wondered if he'd gotten enough nourishment from his mama before she'd weaned him before his brother's birth. Looking into the newborn eyes of baby Lorain, Ida believed she could see the same expressions on his face as she had on his father's when Wid was also a wee babe. He seemed to be a contented baby, and his mother clearly loved her children very much. "Wid did a good thing by marrying the little Scottish girl," Ida thought.

TUESDAY NOVEMBER 15, 1910   GLENWOOD SPRINGS, COLORADO
Ida silently looked around the bare room and then swiftly shut the door before she could burst into tears. This house had been home to her family for five years, and it was like saying good-bye to an old friend. She lingered on the front porch, her favorite place to be in the summertime, and plucked a bronze mum from the bush adjacent to the steep steps leading to the sidewalk. The household furnishings had been packed and freighted to the railroad cars which would transport them and the milk cow to their new home. Ida knew of nothing sadder than an empty house waiting for the next batch of humans to imprint their lives upon it.

"C 'mon, Mother, we've got to get on the road or we're gonna be traveling in the dark tonight. If this weather holds, we might be able to make it clear to Grand Valley by night fall, but we sure as hell won't if you don't get a move on!" Josiah scolded.

Ida silenced him with a withering look and slowly made her way down the steep steps. "You've been hurrying me from one place to another for thirty-four years, Josiah Herwick, and you can damned well let me take my time this morning!"

The children and their father were too shocked to answer. "Mother said a cuss word," whispered Joe to his sister Susan.

"Hush it up," Susan replied. The children intuitively knew that their Mother was dealing with some very powerful feelings, and they weren't about to call her attention to themselves.

The sun shone brightly but without any warmth. Steam was pouring from the nostrils of the draft horses, who were stamping their huge hooves in anticipation of the impending trip. Tiny and Mary had gone to Silt a few days earlier with Fred and Irene. They would be soon going down to Grand Valley on the train. That left Al, Susan, and Joe to be tucked into the back end of the wagon. Josiah had arranged dry hay in the bed, and Ida wrapped the children in their warm coats and then bundled thick quilts around them. By the time they were settled in under the covers, about all that could be seen was the occasional tip of a nose as they came up for another breath of air.

The horses started off at a fast clip over the Grand River Bridge and on to the main road leading down the valley towards New Castle. The little buckskin Indian pony, named "Colorow" was tethered behind the wagon. The horse was old as the hills–over twenty years–but there was no debate as to whether the faithful old animal should accompany the family to their new home. He'd been bought from his namesake, the infamous Indian Chief, Colorow, when Wid was about ten years old, and he'd been ridden by everyone of the Herwick children. He was not happy about being led, much preferring his own freedom, but Josiah said he'd settle down once they got a few miles down the road.

Although well traveled, the road still remained a rather primitive track. The advent of better transportation routes would not be forthcoming for another ten or twelve years after automobiles were firmly ensconced in western Colorado. By the time they'd traveled the nineteen miles to Silt, the Herwick family was more than ready to dismount at Fred and Irene's house.

Irene had anticipated their arrival and prepared a steaming dinner for everyone. Ida was grateful for the warm respite. She could see that the younger children had worked up a very good appetite.

All too soon everyone was bundled back in the wagon, and the horses started off on the final twenty-one miles of their trip. The weather wasn't warming up. In fact it looked gray and cold in the western sky. They had been traveling for most of the afternoon when the first snow flakes fell on their faces.

The snow was slowly covering the barren adobe hills along the roadway, and Ida frequently glanced back to see how the children were faring. Her hands had long ago lost their feeling, and her feet felt like solid blocks of ice. She could see that Josiah was also feeling the cold. His bare hands on the reins were a gray-blue color, and she feared he would soon have frost bite. "I wish you'd put your gloves on," she beseeched her husband. "Your fingers are getting pretty white, and you're going to end up with frost bite."

"It's too damned hard to feel the reins when you've got gloves on," he grumbled, but Ida noticed he did pull on the leather gloves.

"He must really be cold," she thought.

"The Dave Metherd place is several miles down the road," Josiah said. "They seem like decent sort of folks, and I imagine they'd put us up for the night, Mother. Then we can go on tomorrow morning. What do you say? I imagine the younguns would welcome a warm fire. How about you?"

Ida numbly nodded approval. By the time they pulled in front of the large two-story log house, the snow flakes were getting thicker, and the light and warmth coming from the windows had never seemed more welcome. Dave and Hattie Metherd both came out into the storm to welcome the chilled travelers. Hattie drew Ida and the children into the warm house, while Dave and Josiah took care of the stock. The animals, especially old Colorow, had seen a long day, and they soon settled down to snug warmth and feed offered in the old log barn. The human travelers were no less appreciative of the warm hospitality offered to them.

---

ow *The Balzac Bridge over the Grand River at Rulison Siding was completed in 1911. The Seventh Day Adventists formed an industrious colony on the south side of the river.*

ow *A stucco addition was added to the Grand Valley School, first built in 1890. The new addition was used for the first high school in the area. This building served the community until 1937 when it was torn down to make way for the construction of the present brick structure.*

ow *The town of Marble, Colorado was a lively little place in 1911. The payroll at the marble quarry varied from 700 to 850 men. Twenty-four buildings housed grocery and drygoods, newspapers, schools, barbershops, poolhalls and saloons.*

SATURDAY, SEPTEMBER 9, 1911   BATTLEMENT MESA, COLORADO

"Joe Herwick, leave that dog alone and get in this wagon, or we're gonna leave you behind."

Young Joe reluctantly left his canine pal and hopped over the tail gate to squat down in the back of the buggy as his father flicked the reins and the team started up the steep hill from their riverside property. Tina and Mary were sitting upright and proper, careful not to wrinkle their starched white dresses or mash the big bow sashes. Nine-year-old Susan sat quietly by her mother, content for the moment that her pesky, younger brother was in the back of the buggy and couldn't reach her bows or braids.

The Herwicks were on their way into town for "Grand Valley Day," a much awaited event. It was somewhat like a county fair where people brought in their choicest produce to be judged, with ribbons being awarded for the best of the crop. A baseball game was scheduled in the afternoon, featuring the star players of Grand Valley who were challenging some of the best athletes from Glenwood Springs. Early that morning, Ida had sent little Joe over to the Werhonig place, just a half mile west on the river, to see if Mrs. Werhonig would like to go into town for the festivities. Ida's heart went out to the German lady whose son, Rudy, had drowned earlier in the summer. Ida was especially sensitive to the pain of losing a child, and she had tried to cheer Margaret in every way possible. "It would do her good to get off the ranch for a few hours. I doubt you'll be able to convince her to come, Joe, but try your best. Tell her I'd take it as a special favor if she'd accompany us today."

When Joe returned he was shaking his head from side to side. "No, Ma. She says 'Danke,' but she has too many chores to do today."

Ida shook her head in dismay. Margaret Werhonig seemed to be in perpetual motion. Ida wondered if she even slept. She was the only person Ida ever knew who actually kept her hands busy knitting while herding her little flock of sheep. "Well, we tried," she said with some resignation.

As the team of horses reached the top of the lane and pulled onto the main Battlement Mesa road, other horses, pulling various conveyances, were heading in the direction of Grand Valley. The Herwicks waved to their friends and neighbors. The horses, sensing the excitement of the day, started down Studt Hill at a fast clip, picking up speed until Josiah was forced to rein them in to a fast trot. They passed the big house that Charles Studt was building on his property. It would be completed by fall, and Ida spent a brief moment of envy wondering what it would be like to live in such a grand place. She then frowned, recalling that she and Mrs. Studt had gotten off to a less than favorable beginning.

The Studts were Seventh Day Adventists whose Sabbath was celebrated from sundown Friday night to sundown Saturday night. Several months after they arrived, Mrs. Studt and Ida happened to be in the Doll Brothers' store at the same time. Ida's face burned with indignation, but also a little pleasure, as she recalled their conversation.

Mrs. Studt said that it made her very sad when she saw Ida going to town with her butter and eggs each Saturday, while the Studt family was observing their Sabbath. Ida, taken back, had replied that she certainly could understand Mrs. Studt's sadness, because she, too, felt the same way when she drove to church on Sunday and saw Mrs. Studt hanging out her wash! Since then the two ladies had kept a respectable distance from each other, but Ida knew that someday the misunderstanding would have to be healed. It was the neighborly thing to do.

Ida's other relationships had been more affable. The ranching community was made up of fifty or so families scattered throughout the three land benches called Battlement Mesa. There were other women Ida's age, who offered her a whole-hearted welcome. Some of the families had been there when Ida last lived on Battlement and she happily renewed their acquaintance, not without a pang at the thought of dear, dear Sarah Huntley who had made her life so happy for those few short months.

Ida, Josiah, and their family arrived on Front Street just as members of the Grand Valley Band were striking up their first march and getting into formation for the parade down the street. The men, looking very impressive in their new blue uniforms, strutted smartly to the beat of the music. The parade offered the usual assortment. Then the Grand Valley baseball team came walking down the street, amid roars and cheers. Every once in a while one of the men would veer into the crowd to plant a kiss on the cheek of some elderly woman, who would giggle like a young girl.

Ida glanced at her daughters and intercepted the gaze between Tiny and young John Duplice, one of the ball players. There was definitely something going on between those two, despite Tiny's protests to the contrary. It wasn't that Ida had anything against John. She had known his grandfather and parents since they had all lived in the Red Cliff area before the Duplice family moved west and eventually ended up on Battlement Mesa in 1896. They were hard working, God-fearing people, who were trying to make a living off of their Battlement Mesa ranch, just like the Herwicks.

At twenty-two years of age, John Duplice was an outgoing, likable, rather brash young man. His gift of gab reminded Ida of her son, Fred, who could also talk your leg off if you'd let him. Ida could see how twenty-year-old Tiny might be attracted to John. Ida, too, had been attracted to a bold young man at one time. She only hoped that John Duplice was as serious about Tiny. Ida did not want her daughter hurt by some young buck who liked to play with a girl's heart. She sensed that the relationship had recently undergone a change. Tiny no longer displayed the demure, girlish flirtiness that she had, heretofore, shown toward John and other potential suitors. In its place was a knowing, mature look, which said that she had found her man.

Ida had seen that look earlier, just a few days before, when John had brought them a hindquarter from a deer he'd been lucky enough to track down and kill. Even though it was illegal to hunt deer and elk, the local ranchers weren't terribly deterred by the moratorium. "Farmer's season" was always open for those who were able to find one of the scarce animals. Sometimes it would take all week to find fresh tracks, and when you did you'd better stay with them until the game was found. Ida considered John's gift to be tantamount to bribing his girlfriend's mother. But neither one said a word about his intentions.

After the parade, Ida strolled along the street visiting with other folks from all around the area. The town of Grand Valley was a hub of commerce for four distinct farming communities: Parachute Creek, Wallace Creek, Morrisiania Mesa, and Battlement Mesa. Occasionally people from Rulison, to the east, would also travel to Grand Valley to do some shopping. This was one of the few days of the year when everyone had an opportunity to visit with folks from the other ranching communities. If you lived on Battlement Mesa and a friend lived up Parachute Creek, fifteen miles away, you didn't get the opportunity to see each other very often. Even folks in the same ranching community often went for long periods without visiting, especially during the summer months when everyone was busy getting their crops in.

Belle Duplice and Cecilia O'Toole waved to Ida and waited to include her in their stroll over to the bandstand for the concert, which was just starting. After the concert there would be a prize fight between one of the local boxing heroes and an out-of-town contender. After lunch, the baseball game would attract everyone who wasn't napping under the big cottonwood trees after a picnic lunch. Ida and her friends planned to saunter through Doll Brothers and the drug store, relishing the rare time to inspect all the new items brought in for this special day.

As evening drew near, the older girls sought out Ida and begged her to let them stay in town with some of their chums so they could all go to the evening dance. Ida frowned at the thought of Tiny and Mary going to a dance. Her church clearly condemned dancing, drinking, and card playing. She had never danced, and she had raised her children to respect those same beliefs. However, she was forced to admit that times were changing, and public dances were seen as a normal recreation in this part of Colorado. The Battlement Mesa School House had frequent dances on Saturday nights with whole families attending. When it came time for the little children to go to bed, they would be bundled up in some old blankets and placed along the walls of the dance floor. The local musicians would play until two o'clock in the morning, occasionally continuing until dawn after the hat had been passed to pay for their extra time. Then the families would pack everyone in the buggies and wagons to hurry home in time for the morning milking.

Ida knew the girls would be well chaperoned by their friends' parents so she found it difficult to turn down the request. She knew that by giving in to the girls, she'd have to live with her guilt for letting them go, but if she made them go home with her and miss the dance then she'd have to listen to their sighs for a week, not to mention the guilt for making them miss out on their fun. Any way she looked at it, she was going to lose.

"You girls know how I feel about dancing. Go ask your father. If he says yes, then I guess you can go."

Tiny and Mary soon came back with an affirmative answer from their father, which Ida had predicted. If you don't want to make a decision, let someone else do it! Josiah's approval allowed everyone to win.

*T*he fall had been busy with the harvest, then winter preparations. The brisk mornings seemed to be a harbinger of cold days to come. Josiah and Al hurried to get the last of the hay cut and the grain in before an early snow could ruin the crop. Ida, Tiny and Mary had been equally busy with canning, preserving, and storing away the winter's food. The house seemed remarkably quiet during the day while Susan and Little Joe were in school. It was refreshing to not hear Susan's squealing while being subjected to another of her brother's devilments. After all these years, the house was finally quiet and still. Ida didn't know if she'd ever get used to it.

Around the first of November, however, Ida sensed some intrigue going on. She couldn't put her finger on it, and when she questioned Tiny and Mary, they were noncommittal. But the feeling persisted, especially when Ida would happen upon the girls and they'd interrupt their conversation abruptly. Although Ida couldn't do anything about her suspicions, she wasn't able to shake the thought that she was being kept in the dark about something.

Thursday morning, November 16, 1911, dawned dark and cloudy with some promise of storm before the day was out. Ida was up at her usual time of five-thirty a.m. stoking up the kitchen fire and putting the coffee on to boil before Josiah came back in from milking.

Arousing Susan and Joe out of their warm beds, she then looked into Tiny and Mary's room to wake them, as well. Looking toward the bed, Ida could detect only one lump under the covers. Curious, she stepped forward to take a better look. Shaking Mary awake, she said, "Mary, wake up. Your sister's gone, and you're going to tell me where she is, young lady!"

Looking into her mother's angry eyes caused Mary to awaken very quickly. She averted her eyes. "Tiny left you a note, Mother. I promised her I wouldn't say anything until they had a chance to get up the road, but she's been gone for several hours, so I guess it's okay. She told you all about it in her letter, but I'll tell you what I know. She and John have run off to Glenwood Springs to get married. Remember last Sunday when John came down to take Tiny for a ride? Well, I guess they decided then they were gonna run away. Tiny wouldn't say why, but I think it's rather romantic."

Ida sank to the bed and opened the sheet of paper her daughter had given her. There was nothing in it that Mary hadn't already told her, except that Tiny said they expected to be back to Battlement Mesa in several days, and she hoped that Ida and Josiah would understand.

"Understand! What's there to understand? My daughter has seen fit to run off and get married without giving her parents the respect of telling them. She's certainly old enough. That's not the problem. I'm just hurt that she felt she couldn't confide in me. I thought we had a good understanding, she and I. Maybe she thought I'd object to John, but that's not true. If he's good enough for her, he's good enough for me. I can't understand why she'd take off like that. It would've been nice for her to be married here, with her family around. Maybe that's the problem. Maybe she didn't want us at her wedding, but I don't know why she'd feel that way. Oh dear, I've got to tell her father. I wonder how he'll take the news?"

By the time the new Mr. and Mrs. John Duplice returned home to Battlement Mesa, the worst of the furor had died down, and Ida was able to greet her daughter in a civil, if aloof manner. The young couple was planning to move into a small place on some land adjacent to his parents. John would farm part of the acreage and continue to hire out to other ranchers in order to make a living. He was an enterprising young man who would always find a way to put food on the table, Ida and Josiah realized that their daughter could have done much worse.

Christmas, 1911, was a quiet affair—or as quiet as Little Joe would allow it to be. It was too far for Birdie's family and Wid's family to make the trip from Aspen. Guy and Oren couldn't get away from their stock feeding jobs on Mr. Acorn's ranch at Antlers, and Fred and Irene were spending the day with her parents in Peach Valley. The dinner table looked positively empty, compared to previous years. Josiah, Ida, Mary, Al, Susan, and Little Joe were joined by John and Tiny for Christmas dinner. Later in the afternoon, Bill Duplice, John's older brother came to visit, and Ida saw familiar signs of yet another relationship forming–indeed, if it had not already formed.

Bill Duplice, twenty-eight years old, was ten years older than Mary Herwick and quite the opposite of his brother John. Where John was outgoing and brash, Bill was quiet and more passive. He was working for Anthony and Mary Ische who owned property southwest of the Duplice place. Although Bill was still living with his parents, Mr. and Mrs. Ische had offered a small house on their property to him. They could not afford to pay a very good salary and hoped the free housing would convince him to stay on as their hired hand. They both teased him about getting married before he got any "longer in the tooth."

Ida could see that he was clearly enamored by her daughter. His gaze seldom left Mary as she flitted around, doing busy work, remaining aloof from him, yet sending obvious signals that she knew he was observing every move she made. Her coy behavior was new and left no doubt in Ida's mind about her intentions. Mary was ready for married life, and it looked like she had found her future husband. The fact that Bill Duplice was not putting up any resistance made it all the more probable. When John and Tiny suggested that Bill and Mary accompany them on an afternoon buggy ride, Ida thought, "Hmmm, I wonder how long it will be until there's another marriage in our family?"

That event came sooner than even Ida expected. Just a week later on New Year's Eve, Mary had gone with John, Tiny, and Bill to a social at the schoolhouse. The next evening Bill appeared at the Herwick doorstep looking very nervous, but determined. Mary linked her arm in his and faced her parents. "Mother, Father, Bill has asked me to marry him, and I've said yes. We're planning to go to Glenwood Springs a week from this coming Saturday to get the license and we'll probably be married up there. I'm eighteen so I don't have to have your permission, but we'd like your blessings. Do we have them?"

"Well, I don't know, daughter. How many more Herwicks do you think will end up marrying a Duplice boy?" asked Josiah.

"Quit teasing us, Father! But there is one more brother left in case Susan needs a husband in a few years."

"What do you think about all of this Mother?" Josiah said, turning to Ida. "It looks like Miss Mary has her mind made up. I guess the supper table will be shy one more plate. Do you think you can take care of my daughter, young man?"

Ida at last joined in the discussion about Bill and Mary's future. Where would they live? How would they make a living? She knew it was useless to argue against the marriage, not that she'd do such a thing, when her daughter had made her mind up to do it. Mary was a strong person who knew what she wanted.

Later Ida and Josiah were talking about their headstrong daughters. "Come to think about it, all of our daughters seem to have that same fault or virtue, whichever you'd care to call it. Even Susan wastes no time in expressing her beliefs and she's not even ten yet. My mother would turn over in her grave if she could see how these girls act. In Ma's day women simply didn't have opinions, let alone voice them. Lord, the world is changing, and I'm not sure it's for the best."

"Well, Mother, they get their strength from you and I think you should be proud of them."

"Oh, I am proud of them, but I'm not sure they got their strength, as you call it, from me." It was evident that Josiah would never see that part of her that wanted to stand up and be noticed. So much of her life had been spent suppressing thoughts and feelings that she just couldn't bring herself to put before him.

At the moment, however, Ida couldn't put into words the feelings that bubbled around inside, prickling her with their intensity. She knew that it was natural to feel somewhat lost and alone when one's children started leaving the nest. She certainly wasn't alone as a woman struggling with old ways versus new. Strong women are, historically, surprised and mystified by the strengths of their own daughters. But this was the year 1911, and the world was not ready for personal introspections of this sort. Men and women were too busy keeping body and soul together to spend precious time trying to figure out how they felt. Leave that to the rich and idle who could afford that type of extravagance. So Ida simply accepted the news from her daughter, gave her blessing, and pushed the uncertain feelings down a little deeper.

~ *The winter of 1911-12 was very cold and snowy. On March 12, 1912, it started snowing and finally quit on April 20, 1912. The Grand River was completely frozen.*

~ *The luxury liner "Titanic" sank April 14, 1912, taking 1,513 people with her to the watery depths. One of the survivors was Margaret (Mollie) Brown of Leadville mining fame.*

~ *The Havermeyer Canal was dedicated on May 4, 1912, amid much pomp and ceremony, although the day was very cold and miserable. One month to the day after the dedication the high waters of the Grand River took out the headgate, thus spelling the end of a dream for the sugar beet industry at Grand Valley.*

~ *The Elks Lodge of Aspen, Colorado, and citizens of Pitkin County started a movement to get a few head of elk transported from Wyoming. They hoped to build up the elk population which had been almost completely obliterated by the greed of the mining camp hunters during the previous thirty-five years.*

~ *From 1912 to 1915, the town of Thomasville on the Frying Pan River was the site of a construction camp for workers building the Colorado Power Company's transmission line to Denver.*

~ *On September 13, 1912, the motorman, brakeman, and two passengers were killed on a runaway train coming down Mill Mountain from the quarry at Marble, Colorado.*

~ *The Wheeler Opera House in Aspen was the scene of two fires in two weeks. Arson was suspected.*

~ *While in Milwaukee campaigning for the presidency, Theodore Roosevelt was shot in the chest. The bullet penetrated the papers containing his speech and glasses case before embedding in his chest. Despite the wound, he insisted on giving his scheduled speech before receiving medical attention.*

MARCH, 1912 BATTLEMENT MESA, COLORADO

Josiah came stamping in the kitchen door, a swirl of snow blowing about him like a mini whirlwind. "It's colder than a witch's...ah...heart out there," he exclaimed. "I thought we'd put all this crappy weather behind us when we left the high country. I damned near froze clear through today. Give me something warm to thaw my bones out. I envy Wes. Him and his family's pullin' up stakes and movin' to Oregon. Shouldn't be so cold out there. Seems like it gets more bitter every year, or maybe it just bothers me more."

"Susan, pour your father a cup of coffee. Let me take a look at those ears. What about your fingers and toes?" Ida bustled about examining her

husband's extremities for the white tell-tale signs of frostbite. "Little Joe, go
get your father a dry pair of stockings. I don't think the snow's let up all day.
Al made sure the stock were all okay before he came in, didn't you, son? I
hope we can get up to Rifle to see Wes and Rena before they leave for Portland. I wonder how Rena will make it through."

Josiah was one of the many men with horses and equipment who were
battling the weather in order to get the Havermeyer Canal finished before
spring—if indeed there would be a spring this year. In spite of frigid tem-
peratures and storms, the project which started three years ago was actually
progressing according to plans. The hope was that water could be turned in
for the spring planting of the arid land north of the Grand River. Everyone
remarked that it would be a grand sight to see all of the bare 'dobe land
covered with green crops, specifically sugar beets.

Josiah had acquired some of the contracts for the headgates on the extension ditches, a skill he'd not yet developed. But he quickly learned because a man had to be resourceful in order to keep the contracts continuing.
Running concrete in this weather was a real challenge, but he and his crew
seemed to be doing all right. Josiah privately looked ahead to getting future
contracts for some of the concrete bridge abutments which would be needed
in this part of the country. These new-fangled automobiles couldn't ford the
streams and rivers like a horse. They'd have to build better bridges and roads
if they expected to use the machines in western Colorado. Everyone was in
a hurry to get where they were going these days.

At age fifty-eight, Josiah was finding it more difficult to do the work of
men half his age. He'd never admit to it, but he spent a lot of time thinking
about the day when he'd no longer be able to make a living with his hands.
This was a fearful specter for a man who had, all his life, been able to keep
one step ahead of "the wolf" by his brawn and brains. If there were private
moments in which he assessed his past less-than-successful ventures, it was
not apparent. But his tired-looking face and slouching body showed graphic
proof of his fatigue.

"I talked to James Doyle today. He sure is fired up about the future of
oil shale in this country. He's applied for patents all over the area, and is
thinking about building a better trail up Cottonwood Gulch. He said for
me to look him up when I get done with the canal. I've been thinking that
it wouldn't be a bad idea to apply for some patents myself. If Doyle and Joe
Bellis are right, this place will be booming in the next few years."

Ida sighed as she listened to her husband's conversation. It sounded like another pipe dream, which Josiah always seemed to find so attractive. "I wish there was just one time he'd find something that actually paid off," Ida thought to herself. "Josiah's always been a hard worker, but his worst fault is that he still thinks that every scheme will make him rich. I wonder what would have happened if we'd stayed put on that first place at Edwards. George Townsend started out with not much more than we did, and he ended up doing very well with his ranch. I've got to admit that we haven't ever starved, but there's been some mighty lean times. I feel bad when I see Josiah looking so tired, like tonight. He's getting on, and I wonder how we're going to live in a few more years. I doubt that Josiah's put anything away for our old age. It seems there's always some place for our money to go. It makes me tired just thinking about it." Ida put down the mending she was working on and rubbed her eyes. Whenever confronted about the financial challenges in their life, Ida could always revert back to a mindless state of being, where she left the economics to Josiah and concentrated on the mundane, everyday problem of her family life. "I've got to have faith that God will provide for us in our old age," she said. But it sounded more like a plea than a statement of assurance.

Josiah wasn't the only one getting older. Ida also felt her age on days when it seemed she'd never get done with all the ranch chores. With Josiah gone from dawn to dark, and Al hired out on other ranches, Ida, Susan, and Little Joe were left with the bulk of the work. The winter had been hard on the stock, who required more feed than normal. Every day Ida hitched up the old team to the hay wagon and drove them to the field next to the Grand River while Joe and Susan threw hay off the back end for the few head of cattle which were feeding there. The worst times were when they had to break through the thick layers of ice so the cattle could water at the small slough adjacent to the main river. With the weather so frigid, she had to take the axe and pry bar down to the water hole every day, where she'd chop and poke until there was sufficient water for the animals. No matter how careful, she always came away soaked and thoroughly chilled to the bone.

One morning, Ida bundled up to her nose and entered the corral to herd the milk cows into the barn. There, laying dead on the ground, was the faithful old horse, Colorow. He had been roaming over the mesa since coming with the family from Glenwood Springs. Gates hadn't been invented that could keep the plucky little "line-back" buckskin from escaping his confinement. He had soon became a common sight at all of the Battle-

ment Mesa ranches, and people were accustomed to his comings and goings. They all knew the story of his first owner, Colorow, and treated the
horse somewhat like a celebrity.

The Herwick family often discussed their horse during the cold miserable days of the winter and worried how he was faring, but then he'd return
home for a day or two for some oats before heading out again on his continuing adventures. Josiah and Ida knew his days were numbered and tried
to prepare Susan and Joe for his impending departure from this world.
However, his sudden demise profoundly affected everyone, adults and children alike. For the adults, the horse represented a time, two decades ago,
when life seemed so different. Then, western Colorado was still wild and
rugged, unlike the present civilized living they all enjoyed. In those days,
the Indian Chief, Colorow, would pop up out of the blue, leading his string
of ponies, followed by his three or four wives and sub chiefs. Any pioneer
woman, upon his appearance, would start baking biscuits, for which Colorow
had a particular passion. It became a matter of pride to see how many
biscuits he could eat at one sitting.

The frozen ground was too hard to be dug in the miserably cold weather,
so the horse's body was dragged over to the edge of the field until the spring
thaw. Everyone grieved at the thought of their long-term pet and mascot
laying out there, cold and stiff, never more to roam the hills he loved so
much.

If the work was hard, it felt good to have both Tiny and Mary located
near her on Battlement Mesa. Both girls were settled in their households,
and Tiny was getting big with her first child, which was due in May or June.
They couldn't visit more than once a week or so, but it was a comfort to
know that some of the children lived within a few miles of her.

The residents of Battlement Mesa were a tight knit group brought together by their common goal of eking a living out of the fertile but rocky
soil. The big rock schoolhouse, built in 1897, and enlarged in 1907, was the
heart of their community. Children were schooled, funerals held, sewing
and Bible study groups started, and water district meetings scheduled. Dances
and potlucks provided periodic entertainment. All combined to lend color
to the substance of ranch life on Battlement Mesa. No one was rich, although there may have been several families who possessed a few more as-
sets. But you knew that everyone was there to help, if help was needed. It
was a comforting thought.

Ida had managed to make some friends and became part of a circle of women all close to her own age. They occasionally got together at each other's homes to visit while their hands flew through knitting, crocheting, and tatting. Ida enjoyed these afternoon events and, for once, did not feel shy around these women. What a blessing!

Spring was finally coming—fitfully, sporadically. One day the sun would shine with great promise, and the next day it would again be hidden under ominous black clouds. The shoots of green in the fields came slowly so the animals still had to be fed. The last stack of hay and Ida seemed to be running a race to see who would give out first!

One Sunday in April, Josiah, Ida, Susan, and Little Joe bundled themselves up to the eyeballs to drive to Rifle to say good-bye to Wes and Rena and their family. The doctor had recommended a move to a lower elevation because of Rena's health, and they had settled on Portland, Oregon, where Rena had some relatives. Rena, and the children would be departing on the train in another week, leaving Wes, son Clarence, and brother Owen to close the sale of the south Rifle property. The three men would be following in the next month or so.

It was a sad day for all of the Herwicks. Although distance had separated the two families many times, they always knew that the others were available, come the need. The day was spent in recollections of the "good ol' days" when they first came to Colorado, and the years the two families had lived close by on the Roaring Fork River. Ida and Rena spent time in the kitchen, seasoning the food with an occasional tear, followed by renewed promises to correspond on a regular basis. The men, finding it more difficult to speak of their pain, discussed horses and crops, and all the other things that men talk about instead of talking about their feelings.

Chances were, they'd never see each other again. It was true that people were starting to travel all over the country on railway vacations, but the Herwicks weren't those type of people. It would just never occur to them to go on a prolonged holiday. They were all in their fifties and knew they were starting into their declining years. When good-byes were said in mid-afternoon, despite protests to the contrary, everyone knew this was really a final farewell. It felt like the Herwick family had disintegrated before their eyes. For Ida it was just one more person to say good-bye to, so why did it still continue to hurt? The ride home was very silent, each person lost in their own thoughts of the relatives who would soon be just part of their memories.

The calendar said May, but spring seemed to have missed its entrance cue. Hundreds of people were gathered at Webster Hill to dedicate the Havermeyer Canal. The day was miserably cold, and everyone was huddled in their warm wraps. The mountains glistened with their heavy burden of winter snow. The already high muddy waters of the Grand River would be a raging monster when warm weather finally arrived. Ida thought she might never again warm up and could hardly wait to return to the ranch. She tried to surreptitiously wiggle her toes to get the circulation going.

Josiah would be going to the banquet at the W.O.W. Hall that evening to hear his old friend Theodore Von Rosenburg deliver the keynote address, but she would be content to stay at home, near her fire. Let others go who enjoyed that sort of thing more than she did. Ida always felt guilty when she turned down Josiah's invitation to attend these gatherings because his social life was so important to him. But the years had not helped her to become any more adept at making small talk in large groups. While Josiah flitted from one group to another, joking, laughing loudly, shaking hands, being very sociable, Ida was struggling to do more than just smile and nod her head. No matter how much she primed herself beforehand, it seemed that her brain took flight at the door. She was aware that people must consider her quite stupid or else very uppity. What a wonderful gift to be able to tell everyone what was in her mind. But that had never happened and she'd finally resigned herself to the fact that it never would. So, she made excuses whenever possible, staying away from these public events unless there were a goodly number of friends there who accepted her for what she was.

*B*y the end of May, the weather had finally warmed up some and one morning Ida was busy setting the last of the tomato plants in her garden when she heard, before she saw, a rider galloping down the steep road to their house. Spying her in the garden patch, the rider veered off his course and came to an abrupt halt within a few feet of her. "You've got to come," shouted a very excited John Duplice. "It's Tiny. She's having pains, and I'm gonna get Doc Miller. Mary's with her, but she's asking for you. Will you go be with her?"

John wheeled the horse around not waiting for an answer and raced back up the hill road, while Ida ran toward the barn to get a horse saddled. She traveled the few miles quickly and arrived at the Duplice place within thirty minutes to find her daughter in labor. There was no doubt that a baby would be born before the end of the day.

Hours later, Ida gently cradled a new grand-daughter, named Esther, in her arms while she rested from the hours of assisting this birth. She tenderly smiled at the downy-headed baby, recalling the pale fuzz on her own babies' heads. "There's something magic about a baby," she whispered. "No matter how sad, no matter how tired, the very act of rocking an infant causes one to settle down and relax. God made them tiny to fit just right in the crook of your arm. It's amazing how little, but how perfect they are. Hello little girl. You're very strong. Just look how you hold onto my finger. I wish I could stop the world, and just sit here and rock you for the rest of my life. I'd like that."

A few weeks after little Esther arrived, Ida received a letter from Aspen informing her that she had another wee grandchild. Ruby Herwick had been born to Wid and Jenny on June 11 and was doing well. Ida was sorry that her family was settled so far apart from each other. It would be wonderful to have them all together so the babies could grow up around each other, but it wasn't to be. Birdie and Wid's families seemed to prefer the Aspen area, although it was difficult to make a living up there these days.

The eventual arrival of warm, spring weather was not the blessing it might have been for the residents of Battlement Mesa. When the high country snow started melting, the Grand River did become a raging beast just as Ida predicted. It swept everything away in its mighty current, including the new headgate of the Wilcox Canal. The debris tumbled and swirled in the rushing water taking the dream of a new Eden with it.

When Josiah arrived home that night, the person-to-person news network had already covered Battlement Mesa with the disastrous report.

"What in the world will happen now?" Ida asked her husband.

"God only knows. The Havermeyers went up to look over the damage, and they've sent for Von Rosenburg to give them an engineering estimate. I doubt that anything can be salvaged of the headgate. What a damned shame. All those people who've sunk their money into land. Now they won't be able to get water to it. Yessir, it's a damned shame."

Community leaders were searching for other kinds of commerce which would put their little town on the map and bring money to everyone's pockets, since the promise of irrigation water had, at least for the time being, been swept away. The advent of the automobile and the constantly increasing demand for oil and gas seemed to be a divine solution. The federal government, concerned about a future shortage of fuel, started listening to the reports coming out of western Colorado of potential oil shale production, and sent the U.S. Geological Service to survey the area to determine the extent and value of the deposits.

This was fodder for the constant fires of ambition stirring within Josiah Herwick. He sensed a great opportunity to get in on the ground floor of this newest enterprise.

"Mother, I think it's time the boys and I get some claims staked out for ourselves. If this thing really goes to town we might be sittin' pretty. I think I'm gonna have a talk with those mining district boys, and maybe go to Glenwood Springs to see what's already been claimed, and what's still up for grabs."

"Whatever you think, Josiah," Ida replied. She didn't set too much store in this newest craze, but she knew that her husband wouldn't be content until he got a piece of the action. "You know, I was thinking the other day, while you're home for a while I might take the train up to see Birdie and Wid's families in Aspen. I don't want to take Joe and Susan out of school, but Tiny and Mary are close by and they'll help out for a few days. Would you mind too much? I'd like to see the new baby. I might get off and visit with Fred and Irene on the way back. It's been some time since we last heard from them."

"Go ahead. We'll get along here." Josiah had his mind on staking claims and probably didn't even realize what he'd just agreed to.

When Ida returned from her short holiday, she told her husband that their son was following in his footsteps. "Do you remember the time you thought about running for sheriff of Eagle County? What year was that— 1899? Well, guess what! Fred is running for Garfield County Sheriff on the Progressive Ticket! He seems to be having a wonderful time riding around the country, and getting votes. I declare, Josiah, he really is your son. He loves to be wherever people are. And, Irene is right in there with him. That girl loves him so much. He's a very lucky man." Ida wouldn't mention the first Mrs. Fred Herwick, but Josiah knew she was thinking about that other woman and thanking God that Fred had found Irene.

"Doesn't that beat all! My son running on the Progressive Ticket! In order to vote for him I'll have to do something I've never done in my life, and that's scratch my ticket. I've never voted for anyone but a Republican, and now my own son is gonna ruin my record!"

No one ever knew whether Josiah did, indeed, vote for his son, but it really didn't matter in the final November election count. Fred was badly beaten, over five to one, by the Republican incumbent. Even the Democatic candidate outdistanced Fred by four to one. To add insult to Josiah's injury, Woodrow Wilson, the democratic candidate was elected President of the United States. Not only did his son lose the sheriff's race, but now the country would have to put up with "The Damned Democrats."

∾ The destruction of Colorado's game herds finally forced officials to enact hunting laws. There was a moratorium on deer hunting until 1918. The suspension for elk, mountain sheep, and antelope lasted to 1924. Thus began the "farmer's season" in which game was poached by the local residents. Game wardens and furtive hunters played cat and mouse for many years after the enactment of these laws. Every native family probably had at least one favorite story about how the warden was out-smarted.

∾ May 16, 1913 - The DeBeque Bank's vault was blown up, but the robbers were scared off before they got to the strongbox which contained $10,000.

∾ July 18, 1913 - Nineteen autos with the Indiana Automobile Manufacturers' Association traveled through Garfield County on their Pacific Coast tour. A road west of Grand Valley had been built on the north side of the Grand River, although the state engineer had plans for the road to be built on the south side. The local towns were anxious to get designated as part of the coast to coast highway.

∾ August 1, 1913- The U.S. Geological Service sent out a research team to conduct field tests on local oil shale samples. They erected a small retort in the DeBeque area which processed 100-pound batches. Woodruff and Day estimated that Colorado's shale could produce from 16 to 61 gallons of oil per ton.

∾ December 16, 1913 - At 10:20 am the Vulcan Mine at New Castle exploded, killing thirty-seven men. This dangerous mine was eventually closed forever.

MARCH 3, 1913   BATTLEMENT MESA, COLORADO

The sound of a loud wail broke the silence of the room. Bill Duplice nervously moved about the kitchen and looked toward the bedroom door as his mother-in-law entered, carrying a small blanket-wrapped bundle. "You've got a beautiful baby daughter," Ida said as she pulled back the blanket to show him the tiny dark haired infant making sucking noises with her mouth. "Would you like to hold her?"

Bill gingerly took the child. He was not accustomed to being around small children and babies. It was apparent that the thought of holding the squirming infant was intimidating at best. "How's Mary? Is she all right?" he asked, never taking his eyes off of his charge.

"She's fine," Ida replied. "She had a difficult time, but everything's okay. Dr. Miller is just finishing up. You'll be able to see her in a few minutes. Would you like me to take the baby so I can get her cleaned up?"

Bill readily relinquished the child to her grandmother. He mumbled something about tending to a chore and bolted for the outside door. Ida suspected he needed time to be alone with the emotions evoked in him by this momentous event. A man's firstborn usually created some strong feelings which he found difficult to express. Bill would likely be back in a little while, ready to assume his new role as a father.

As Ida washed the perfectly formed little body, she thought back to all the birthings she'd gone through. Each one of the fourteen deliveries stood out in her mind, some painful, some pleasant, but each one distinct. "The act of bearing a child is so unique," she mused. "It's almost like the personality of the child is determined by the birth process. Or perhaps it's vice versa. No matter, it seems that each baby makes an imprint by how they come into the world. Some come in kicking and yelling, others are born without a whimper. I wonder if they know what's in store for them? Seven grandchildren now with Henry almost a young man, at fifteen. They grow up so fast. It doesn't seem possible that my own Joe will be eight this coming June. It makes me tired just thinking about it all." She wrapped the baby in a soft towel and cuddled her close.

Spring was trying to arrive earlier this year, perhaps making up for its tardiness last year. It had been bitter cold, but now the sun was warming the earth more every day. Green shoots were beginning to appear in the fields, and the roads were drying out so a person could get to town without having to stop and clean the mud from the spokes of the buggy wheels.

Josiah was becoming more intrigued by the promise of an oil shale empire but, if his head was in the clouds, he had thus far kept his feet on the ground. He and his steam tractor, or teams of horses, were kept busy building ditches, clearing farmland, or building roads.

The Havermeyer interests raised a small amount of capital and hired Josiah and ten or fifteen other men to attempt repairing the canal headgate which had been washed out the previous spring. After several weeks of steady work, the engineer finally decided the project would be too costly because almost nothing of the original gate could be salvaged. He recommended no further financial expenditures until there was enough money earmarked for reconstruction of the entire project. By that time the Havermeyer interests were focused elsewhere, with the brothers reluctant to sink any more funds into the jinxed venture. To compound the problem, area residents, assuming the project was forever doomed, started pilfering all the material they could carry away from the twenty-seven mile canal. Redwood from parts of flumes, gate valves, and other sundry items started appearing in other valley projects. Before long all that was left of the infamous Wilcox Canal was a twenty-seven mile slash at the base of the Bookcliffs.

AUGUST 19, 1913   GRAND VALLEY, COLORADO

Ida and the children had just finished their milking and other chores when Josiah rode into the dooryard. "Hey, Pa," Joe yelled. "Is it true that the whole town's burned down?"

"No, son, but a lot of it has. All of the block with the European Hotel and the Post Office is gone. There wasn't anything we could do to save any of the buildings. It had too good a headstart."

Josiah wearily climbed down from the saddle, giving the reins over to Joe and accompanied his wife and daughter to the house. The hot August wind still carried bits and pieces of ashes across the Grand River into the yard.

The night of the fire, Ida had been awakened by the odor of smoke in the air. Long fearful of fires, she had risen from the bed to see if she could determine from where the smoke was coming. Stepping outside, she spied flames leaping into the air across the river. Great puffs of smoke were billowing above the flames, and it looked like the entire town might be on fire. Rushing inside she shook her husband awake. "Josiah, wake up! It looks like the whole town might be on fire. Get up and see."

In less than ten minutes Josiah was dressed, saddled up, and racing toward town. At the top of the hill he met other men on horseback and in buggies also hurrying to the scene of the inferno. The smoke was so thick that they couldn't make out how much of the town was on fire, so no one knew what they were riding into. Throughout the day, wives and mothers stood watch from Battlement Mesa, peering into the distance to see what progress, if any, was being made in quelling the raging fire.

By the end of the day most of the firefighters agreed they could safely leave the burning remains of the entire block between Parachute and Hallett

Avenues. Owners were slowly walking among the ruins of the buildings trying to locate any items of value which hadn't been completely destroyed. Stories of the day-long struggle were retold, including the bravery of Helen Sipprelle who dashed into the burning Post Office to retrieve the first class mail before it could be consumed by the flames.

"I don't know how much of the block will be rebuilt," Josiah told his family. "I talked to Martin Streit, who not only lost his house but also the European Hotel. He doesn't know whether or not he can afford to build again. Of course they'll find another building for the Post Office, but it's doubtful that the store or warehouse will be rebuilt. It's a damned shame."

Ida agreed that it certainly was a "damned" shame. All her life she had lived in fear of the dreaded flames which carried away so many people and their possessions. She had drilled into her children the importance of safety with both the stove and kerosene lamps.

"Does anyone know how the fire got started?" she asked her husband.

"Na, there's no real way to tell. Everything's too badly burned. That warehouse of C.D. Smith's was full of chemicals, but no one seems to know whether any of them were combustible. I doubt that they'll ever figure it out."

Ida said a thanksgiving prayer for her family's well being, at the same time she was offering up prayers for the stricken.

CHRISTMAS DAY, 1913   BATTLEMENT MESA, COLORADO

The gray clouds covered the sun and it felt barely above freezing. Ida shivered in her warm shawl as she stood on the porch, spending a few precious moments of quiet before going back in to dish up the holiday meal.

The house was once again full of family, even though not everyone could come. Fred, Irene, Guy, and Oren had traveled from Silt and Antlers to join the Duplice families at Ida's well-provisioned holiday table. Little eighteen-month-old Esther was enjoying the attention of all her elders, while baby Olive was content to sit on her mama's lap watching all the noise and confusion from her safe perch. Ida felt very old when she remembered all the past Christmases when her own babies had been toddlers.

"Has it really been twenty-five years since I held Guy on my lap for our first Christmas dinner here on the mesa with Sarah and her family? Now he's a grown man," Ida sighed. "My, time does fly."

It was good to see her three sons because visits had been infrequent since Ida and Josiah moved down valley. It was also sad because this would be the last time she'd see Fred and Irene who would be leaving for Pocatello, Idaho soon after January first.

The projected success in selling land in the Silt area had not materialized for Fred. He had managed to eke out a living on the few deals he made, but it was clear that he would never get rich out of the venture. He had been seriously looking for other options when he discovered that the properties of one of Silt's promoters were to be sold at a public trustee sale in January. This would spell disaster for the real estate venture. Fred had to admit that the town's growth would come steadily but slowly as a result of the growing farm community and not because of any grand plan to develop residential property.

During the course of his real estate business, Fred had become acquainted with numerous other land promoters who also were developing areas outside of the state. One of these acquaintances had made Fred a job offer in Pocatello. The area, located near the Blackfoot Indian Reservation, had been a railroad center since the 1890s. Federal irrigation projects were turning the desert land into productive farm acreage. This new agricultural opportunity was causing Pocatello to be the hub of commerce for a vast surrounding area. Fred's friend was developing some new residential districts in the growing city, and he invited Fred to come be one of his real estate salesmen.

It was a good opportunity for the young man to get started again, but Ida's heart broke at the thought of how far away he would be. Until now she had enjoyed the thought that her children were all within a day's travel. That would be changing with Fred's departure. Part of her was happy for her son, but part was grief-stricken.

"But, I'll never see you again, if you move so far away."

"Now, Ma, that's not true. All you have to do is hop on the train, and you'll be at our doorstep in less than two days. It'd be good for you to take a trip and see some new country. Why don't we plan on you coming up next summer? We'll be settled in by then, and ready to have company. Isn't that right, Irene?"

Irene quickly re-enforced her husband's invitation. "That would be wonderful, Mother Herwick. Please do come. By then we'll be homesick, and your dear face will be so welcome."

Ida looked at her daughter-in-law and thought how lucky Fred was to have found such a sweet girl. Irene was so in love with her husband that she'd go to the ends of the earth with him, if he asked. This move would be difficult for her. She'd never been away from her doting parents, and Ida knew the first few months would be a period of harsh separation for Irene.

"Well, we'll just have to wait and see what happens," Ida replied. "It's hard telling what might be goin' on next summer."

Later when Ida entered the dining room, she overheard a piece of conversation: "Guy, I thought you were gonna tell the folks your news," laughed Oren, as he egged on his brother.

"What news are you talking about?" Ida looked at Guy's face which was turning beet red.

"Nothing, Ma. Oren's just being funny," replied her son. "He thinks I'm real serious about a girl, and he won't let me alone. Just you wait, brother, until you start courtin' someone. I'm not gonna let you have a minute's peace!"

"Suppose you tell me about this girl, Guy. What's her name and where's she from?"

Shooting a dark look at his brother, Guy answered Ida's questions. "Her name's Laura Brenton. She's Bob Brenton's daughter, from Rifle. I've only seen her a couple of times, when we went to a dance down there, but she seems real nice, Ma. I've been thinking that maybe I'd go pay her a call, but it's nothing serious, you know. I just think she looks like a nice girl." Oren hooted at this last remark, and hurried from the room before his mother could issue a reprimand.

Ida stifled a smile and thought that her son was probably more serious than he realized. She'd never seen him act this way before, and that must mean Miss Brenton was important to him. Time would tell. Guy had always been a rather serious fellow, and once he found the right girl, he'd know what to do. Oren would certainly miss him, though. The two boys, so close in age, had been like twins. Where one went the other usually went, too. They'd been at Antlers for over three years, and Ida wondered what would happen to Oren if Guy did get serious and marry.

As the family crowded around the dinner table that afternoon, Ida spent a few moments to offer up thanks for her healthy and moderately successful family, and to ask for continued blessings for all those near and far. "We thank Thee, Lord, for the bounty you have given us this past year. We ask your blessings on all our family. Be with Fred and Irene as they move to their new home in Idaho. Be with Birdie and Wid's families today and everyday. And, God, please be with all the unfortunate and grieving families who lost loved ones in the Vulcan explosion. Grant them peace and understanding, Lord. Amen.

∾   By the end of January, 1914, the DeBeque area could boast of one big producing oil well. Other oil companies were being formed to start field work. The high grade oil was worth $2.85 a barrel.

∾   The U. S. Federal Income tax was started. The rate was set at 1% for single persons with an income of more than $3,000, and for married persons with an income of more than $4,000. A surtax, ranging from 1 to 6% was imposed on people earning more than $20,000.

∾   The Yule Marble Company received the contract for the marble to be used for the Lincoln Memorial. The contract specified that the stone was to be completed within two years.

∾   On April 7, 1914, the town of Grand Valley voted that the saloons must go. Poolhalls would now take the place of saloons.

∾   In November, the town of Rifle also went "dry."

∾   During May, 1914, six thousand seedlings were set out in the White River National Forest to check the erosion caused by the indiscriminate logging practices of the previous century.

∾   Gold was discovered at Dr. Raymond Morelock's claim on Upper Mamm Creek in August, 1914. This set off a minor gold rush. The Rifle paper reported that one hundred men were staking out claims in the area.

∾   A rainstorm of mammoth proportions hit Rifle Creek on October 9, 1914. Almost 2.5 inches of rain fell in thirty hours. Parts of Rifle were flooded along the low-lying banks of Rifle Creek.

SEPTEMBER, 1914   BATTLEMENT MESA, COLORADO

The afternoon sun slanted in the north window of Ida's kitchen. The ray of light, displaying particles of dust, fell upon rows of jars recently filled from the bounty of the garden. Tiny and Mary had joined her in the food processing tasks which made the tedious job of scalding, peeling, cutting, and boiling go much faster. It was almost like old times in the Eagle River country when the girls were younger and they worked side by side to put away the winter's food supply. By early afternoon they were done, both Tiny and Mary leaving for their own homes, taking a share of the preserved bounty to be stored in their cellars for tasty wintertime meals.

Ida was waiting for Susan and Joe to get home from school so they could help her move the week's worth of filled jars to the dug-out cellar near the back door. She sat down at the kitchen table with a cup of hot tea to admire her handiwork. It was always wonderful to survey the fruits and vegetables in their sparkling clean jars..Ida thought they looked jewel-like with the sun's shaft of light hitting them. "I guess that's the only jewels I'll ever have," Ida wryly laughed to herself.

The open kitchen door brought in sights and smells of the warm autumn afternoon. Ida wished she could put into words the feelings she had on a day like this. The air was warm and carried scents of all the over ripe produce of the ranch, not an unpleasant odor, but rather one that signaled completion of another cycle. There was a fine golden haze caused by all the disturbed pollen and dust, which seemed to color everything with a shimmer. Bright summer colors were now becoming muted. The willows and cottonwood trees along the river were starting to turn color. They would eventually stand in glorious golden tribute to the past summer. Ida knew if she looked south from her front door she would see the vibrant reds of the oak brush blending with the shimmering yellows of the Aspen trees at the base of Battlement Peak. There wasn't a prettier sight to be seen. She sat quietly, enjoying the feeling of being immersed in the liquid autumn afternoon. She wondered how anyone could be sad while experiencing such a day. Some people said the fall season was depressing because it heralded the chilly, dark days of winter. Ida had never thought them depressing. To her they symbolized a season of completion and fulfillment, a time to enjoy all the rewards of a long and busy summer. She remembered the past three months and heaved a sigh of contentment.

Thus far, this year had been a good one for the Herwick family. Maybe it was her advancing age. She was now fifty-three . Or maybe it was just the satisfaction of feeling truly settled in. Whatever the case, Ida was as happy as she could ever remember being. Josiah had plenty of construction jobs to keep a decent amount of money coming into the household. Ida had two grown daughters and their families nearby. Susan and Joe were at an age where they were more help to her than she to them. Al had taken over most of the outside stock chores, leaving her with only the usual household duties. Compared to most of her life, it seemed that she had practically nothing to do!

She enjoyed hitching up the team to the light buggy and going into town on Saturday with her butter and eggs to exchange for food staples. It was the one leisurely activity she allowed herself. Strolling through Doll Brothers' store she could look to her heart's content, running her hands over all the beautiful bolts of cloth and handling the newest shipment of kitchen gadgets.

Other ladies would come and go, stopping to chat with each other in the store. These brief moments were often the only opportunity busy wives and mothers had to socialize. They talked about their children, exchanged recipes and shared tried and true home medical treatments. The ranch wives relished these interludes and looked forward to the weekly ritual.

After looking over all the finery, Ida would sigh and turn to the business at hand, which was buying the essentials her ranch couldn't produce. Coffee, sugar, tea, flour and syrup were some of the weekly staples, costing more than the small amount of her butter and egg revenue. Occasionally Ida would long to spend her hard-earned money on some sort of extravagant piece of material or lace, with which to dress up her usual somber attire. But years of thrift were ingrained deeper than her emerging vanity. At the last moment the items would be returned to the shelf in favor of some sensible yarn or thread or buttons. Occasionally she'd give in to Susan's pleas for some new ribbon or lace, excusing the added expense. Susan was becoming a young lady, and it was natural that she'd want nice things like the other girls. It was much easier for Ida to buy for others than for herself.

Whenever the weather permitted, Ida also enjoyed riding into town for church on Sunday mornings. The organ playing and the choir singing her favorite songs brought a sense of serene fulfillment to her. The Ladies Aid Society did a good job of keeping the church tidy and clean, and Ida felt guilty that she wasn't able to do as much society work as the town ladies seemed to do. She had tried to be more social, accepting luncheon invitations whenever she could. She worked hard to fit in with the other church ladies, but as usual, Ida's innate shyness was an obstacle she had to conquer on every occasion. By the time Ida could think of an interesting comment to add to the conversation, the women had moved to another topic, and she was left to frantically think of something else to say. It was easier to fade into the background and listen, but after a time people forgot she was there, and she was apt to be left out of future activities. Socializing was the most demanding ordeal she faced.

Because Ida felt so socially inept, she would have been very surprised but equally pleased to know that her closest friends and acquaintances saw her in a far different light. She was always ready to go anywhere at any time to help a neighbor in need. This might be for a day, or for several. She always managed to be there for them. She shared her considerable childbirth experiences with fearful expectant mothers. She soothed and taught new mothers who were terrified of the tiny one left in their care. Ida could be sure to be at the death watch of her elderly and ill friends and would prepare their bodies for the final farewell. Her good works were of a physical nature and stood by themselves. Her quiet voice and hand on a hot brow were guaranteed to bring comfort to those in need, but all of this was hidden from her personal scrutiny on the fine fall day.

Fred and Irene had been in Idaho for almost a year, and Ida missed them terribly. However Oren would soon be rejoining their circle. He was leaving his ranch job at Antlers after the crops were in and would be coming down valley to work with his father. Josiah needed a younger man to help him with the heavier tasks, and Oren seemed ready made for the job.

"I think he's lonesome since his brother went and got married," Ida had told his sisters earlier in the day. "It'll be good for him to be back for a while. He's too thin. Maybe some home cooking will put meat on his bones. I never saw anyone with a more touchy belly. Everything seems to upset him."

Oren was twenty-five, and Ida thought it was time he find a wife and settle down. Guy and Laura had gotten married in May and Oren seemed a bit lost. Ida hoped that having him home for a while would make him think about the good things of family life and want that for himself. She thought about her other sons and daughters and was thankful that they had done well in their marriages, with the possible exception of Birdie, who was still a concern.

The periodic letters from Aspen didn't contain any disquieting news, rather it was what Birdie didn't say that bothered Ida most. Birdie seldom ever referred to her husband, Norman, and then only in passing. Her letters certainly did not contain news typical of a happy family unit. In her last letter Birdie had mentioned that she was considering taking a job cooking at one of several local mines when Ruth got out of school next spring. Henry, now over sixteen, would soon be ready to take on a man's job and would probably stay with his father. To Ida this news certainly boded no good for her daughter's family. There wasn't a day she didn't offer prayers for their well-being.

Lately whenever the Herwick family got together, the topic of oil shale always seem to come up. The Parachute Mining District was organized in the spring of 1890 and had filed on a number of claims located around the forks area of Parachute Creek. The men hired by the federal government had published their findings on the first shale survey, done in 1913. They estimated that western shale deposits could produce sixteen to sixty-one gallons of oil per ton. This was good enough for many of the would-be-prospectors who were positive that their claims would be a ticket to untold riches.

Josiah, never one to pass up an opportunity, had been doing a lot of talking to the mining pioneers, specifically Jimmy Doyle, who was involved in almost every mining deal in the area. Doyle had been excited by the 1913 report and tried to ignite more interest in filing on as many claims as possible in the area.

"I was talking to Jimmy," Josiah told his family. "It seems a person can't file on more than a twenty acre claim, although any number of claims can be filed in each mining district. Jimmy says the best way to do this is for up to eight family members to each file a claim, one right next to the other. Then the claims can be put together in one holding of 160 acres. It's kind of stupid, if you ask me. Those same eight people can hold as much as 1,280 acres in the district, but I guess they are tryin' to keep one person from monopolizing the whole she-bang. That shouldn't be any problem for us, should it? We've got plenty of people to file on the claims, and then after the patents are granted, one can buy out all the others. It takes five years to prove up on the claim, and we'll have to do $100.00 assessment work on each claim each year. But, hell, that shouldn't be a problem. We'll just go camp out for a few weeks, move some dirt around and file the improvements in the Clerk and Recorder's Office. Shouldn't be a problem at all."

Josiah's children, although accustomed to his "Boomer" schemes, went along with their father's future plans. It would take some time to look over the claim possibilities, and to find out which had already been staked and which was still open . It didn't sound like this would be a big financial investment, and who knew—maybe this scheme would be the one that'd pay off. In the meantime they all had to scramble to make a living, and that didn't leave them a lot of time to engage in idle dreams about what might be.

∾ On December 10, 1915, the Hotel Colorado and Hot Springs went into receivership. *The stockholders were mostly English citizens and unwilling to invest any more money in the venture.*

∾ *The marble for the Lincoln Memorial was cut and shipped in late 1915.*

∾ *It snowed four feet between Christmas and New Year's Day, 1916 at Grand Valley, Colorado. It continued snowing every day throughout January, 1916.*

SUNDAY, AUGUST 8, 1915   BATTLEMENT MESA, COLORADO

Josiah's voice boomed outside John and Tiny's door. "Hey there. Where's everyone? I understand I've got a new grand-daughter, and, by damn, I'm here to see her."

"Shhhhh," warned Ida. "If you wake that baby up Tiny will never speak to you again."

Ducking his head through the low doorway, Josiah made his way to his daughter's bedside. "Hey there, daughter. I'm sorry I haven't gotten up to see you sooner, but I've been busy from dawn to dark this past week. No rest for the wicked, as they say. How are you feeling? Where's that little mite I've been hearing about?"

"I'm doing fine, Pa, and so far the baby's holding her own. She really is tiny. It's a little scary, but she eats often, and seems to be gaining in strength. Say a prayer that she stays that way. Go see her in the kitchen."

Ida led her husband out of the bedroom into the adjacent kitchen. There, on the oven door of the wood cook stove, was the baby in a small padded box. Leaning down, Josiah opened the covers to reveal the most minute child he had ever seen. Little Winifred could easily fit onto her grandfather's open palm with room left over. It seemed impossible that such a tiny creature could maintain life, but maintaining she was. The oven door had become an early edition of what would one day be called an incubator. The goal was to keep the infant as warm as possible, and this seemed the best way to do it. The only time she was allowed to leave her cocoon was for diaper changing and frequent feedings.

"Seven days old, and you're still smaller than a mouse," her grandfather exclaimed. "But I understand you're starting to use your voice, and that's encouraging, although you sound more like a new-born kitten mewing. Never mind, pretty soon you'll be chasing your older sister around."

Mary joined her father and mother in visiting the miracle baby. She and John had helped Tiny deliver this premature child who no one really believed would survive. When Doctor Miller arrived hours after the birth to find the tiny infant blue, but breathing, he recommended that they keep her as warm as possible and feed her every hour for as long as she was able. Premature babies do not have the strength to suck long enough to get adequate nourishment, so she had to be fed almost continuously if she was going to survive. It was a frightening task which faced Tiny and her diminutive off-spring. Prayers were regularly offered for the child's well being while the family watched in awe. Gradually she started putting on weight and began to act like a full term baby should act. Everyone gave thanks for the miracle of little Winifred.

The summer of 1915 was the coolest in forty years, but it was also a dry one. Very little rain fell and forest fires broke out in the Battlement Mesa Forest. A particularly bad one blazed on Holmes Mesa. Much of Battlement Mesa was showing the signs of drought. Most of the irrigation water had dried up in early August, with the exception of the Huntley Ditch, which had second rights. Ida was grateful for Conner Spring, on their property, which gave forth wonderful, pure clear water the year around. It provided water for both the family and barnyard stock, and even irrigated the good-sized garden plot. The hay fields would produce a thin third cutting, but Ida's vegetable and flower gardens flourished.

As fall arrived, the ladies of Battlement Mesa found more time for church and social activities. Nels Good, one of the first school board members, was a lay minister who had been asked to conduct Sunday services at the Battlement Mesa Schoolhouse so churchgoers wouldn't have the make the three to five mile trip into Grand Valley, especially in the spring months when the mud was axle deep.

One Sunday in October, Ida, Susan, and Joe arrived at the schoolhouse to see people in small groups talking and gesturing about something. Tying their horse to the hitching rail, Ida stepped over to see what was causing all the excitement. Clara Mahaffey, Belle Gardner, and Adelia Underwood were in the nearest group. Clara reached out and took Ida's arm, her voice heavy with emotion. "Good morning, Ida. Did you hear about Harrison Kerlee? He and five others escaped the county jail Friday night. The sheriff says that somebody smuggled a file into the jail. One of the prisoners was caught in South Canon, but there's been no sign of Harrison. I doubt they ever find him. That young man'll know where to hide out in the mountains. I wonder if any of his family had anything to do with this?"

Upon hearing the news, Ida felt an overwhelming sadness for the Kerlee family. It had been difficult for them to go on with their lives when Harrision was arrested last May for murder. Some people had been downright mean and hateful to the rest of the family, as if the murder had been their fault. Ida's heart especially went out to the children, who had been shunned by their playmates who called them names and jeered that their brother was a murderer. The close-knit ranching community had suffered from the tragedy, too, but gradually the taunts and insults had diminished. Now with this latest news, Ida feared it would all start again. She mentally vowed to visit the Kerlee home that afternoon to see if she could offer any support.

Ida had trouble listening to Mr. Good's sermon. "Why are people so cruel," Ida silently wondered. "It's a sad commentary that most folks want to believe the worst in situations like this. We're all sitting here listening to the word of God and I wonder how many will remember the message after we go home. How many will take the time to visit Jess and Lizzie to assure them they still have friends. Don't we all do the very best we can to raise our children? Dear Lord, what would I do if it was one of my children? I'd want to die." Ida sat on the hard bench letting her imagination run away until she was brought back to reality by the congregation's standing to sing the final hymn. She shivered as if throwing off the fears for her family that always seemed to be operating just under the surface. "Protect us all," she prayed.

Ida had always tried to live her life according to the word of God, and several weeks after the jail break, she pondered her previous sad commentary about the less-than-spiritual behavior of some of her neighbors. Was there something more she could do to promote a deeper sense of brotherly love? She had joined Mildred Parker, Tiny and Mary in teaching Sunday School, but there was little time during the short Sunday morning sessions to instill any great amount of spirituality into young minds. She finally mentioned her concerns to them and they started discussing the possibility of having a day-long Bible school, where they would be able to focus more on the concept of spiritual love. They could present stories from the Bible which reflected those values, and maybe Mr. Good would talk to the children about the need to love their neighbor. The more the women discussed this plan, the more excited they became. They wanted to turn their mutual frustration into something positive.

The Saturday before Thanksgiving was chosen, and notices were sent out to all the area families, regardless of whether they regularly attended the Battlement School Services. This would be a non-denominational event. They especially wanted to get the Kerlee children there and enlisted the help of Susan who was a close chum of Bess Kerlee. Maybe she could encourage Bess to come and bring her brothers and sisters.

The day dawned cool but clear, with promise of mid-day warmth. Mr. Good joined the ladies during the morning class, where he preached a short sermon about the life of Jesus, intended to impress the young people. A long hymn singing period followed the recess, which had worked off some of the youthful enthusiasm of kids like Joe Herwick, who couldn't stay still for more than five minutes.

Everyone had brought a dish of food to be shared at the noon potluck meal. After lunch, a local photographer dropped by to take a picture of the thirty-four assembled women and children. This was a big event. There were few occasions where photographers were available, especially in rural farming communities, and everyone was properly impressed by this rather momentous occasion. The afternoon ended with quiet turns of reading Bible stories which reflected a spirit of love and forgiveness. Ida couldn't say whether any child had been inspired by a spiritual awakening, but she knew in her own small way she had contributed to something more positive than gossiping about her friends and neighbors.

∾ The Spring Gulch Mine near Glenwood Springs was abandoned in 1916 when Colorado Fuel and Iron suspended operations in Pitkin and Garfield counties. This forced many miners out of work and caused more people to take up small farm and ranch operations in order to eke out a living.

∾ On May 30, 1916, the Rio Grande train derailed two miles west of Grand Valley. Seven people were hurt in the accident, including engineer Fahrmeyer who was pinned under the boiler and badly scalded from the steam.

∾ Top yearly wages for railroad workers were: Engineers, $2,195; Conductors, $1,878; Foreman, $1,317; Brakeman, $967.

∾ The Colorado Yule Marble Company went into receivership. The quarry remained closed until April, 1922.

∾ On November 24, 1916, the Harvey Gap Mine caught on fire underground. It was shut down until the fire was extinguished on December 22, 1916.

∾ The Naval Oil Shale Reserves were created November 16, 1916, when President Woodrow Wilson withdrew 45,444 acres of oil shale land in western Colorado for the exploration, research, and development of the resources.

FEBRUARY, 1916   BATTLEMENT MESA, COLORADO

It was past dark when Josiah rode into the barnyard. Unsaddling his horse, he rubbed it down before giving it a ration of grain. The cold weather was hard on animals, and he wanted to be sure his favorite saddle horse stayed in good condition. Looking around the barn and yard he could see that Joe had fed the stock and had gotten them bedded down for the night. The warm animal smells, mixed with hay and manure, weren't unpleasant and he lingered a moment or two in quiet reflection before braving the cold air outside.

Opening the barn door, Josiah breathed in the sub-zero atmosphere and walked through the deep snow, which crunched sharply under his footsteps. It had started snowing between Christmas Day and New Year's and had laid down four feet of the fluffy stuff in one week. The storms continued almost every day in January until the Valley of the Grand River was completely covered in a mantle of white. Work had virtually come to a standstill, except for keeping the livestock alive and chopping wood to feed the voracious appetites of the cook and heating stoves. School children packed along hay in gunny sacks to feed their horses while they were in class to keep the animals well fed. No one ventured too far away from their house if they could help it.

Smells of the supper cooking hit Josiah's nostrils as he came through the door. Ida, Susan and Joe were assembled around the kitchen table, the children doing school work, and Ida working on the seemingly endless pile of mending. The doors to the parlor and bedrooms had been closed to conserve heat, which meant that everyone would be jumping into an icy cold bed that night.

"It looks like we've finally heard from our Idaho son and daughter-in-law," Josiah said as he threw a packet of mail on the table. On the top of the bundle was a letter postmarked from Pocatello. "Open it up, Mother, and let's hear what they have to say. Maybe the baby has come."

Ida eagerly tore open the envelope with her fingers, careful not to tear the enclosed sheets of paper, and started to read aloud:

Dear Mother and Father Herwick & Family,

This note is to tell you that you now have a grand-son in Idaho. Daniel Dean Herwick was born February 2nd and he is doing fine. He is a husky little fellow and I think he will be a big man like his father.

I am still abed, but will be able to get up in a few more days. Fred is doing well in the real estate business and stays very busy. He is quite proud of his first-born son, although I think he will be more comfortable with Daniel when the baby grows some.

I hope this finds you all well. Our weather has been very cold and snowy. I presume yours is the same. I look forward to spring, as I also look forward to your letters which give me news of home. We miss you and pray that all is well. We are still awaiting your long promised visit, Mother Herwick. If you come see us you may rock your grand-son to your heart's content.

Affectionately,
Irene, Fred, and Baby Daniel

Ida smoothed the pages and returned them to the envelope.

"Well, Ma, what about it? Are you goin' to Idaho?" Joe eagerly looked to her for a reply. "It would be great to go to Idaho. Can I go with you?"

"Not so fast young man. In the first place, I wouldn't think about going while the weather's so unsettled. Your father needs us here to tend the stock.

Besides, it'll cost too much. We've got better uses for our money, although it would be nice to see the children I'm afraid we'll just have to wait and see what the future brings."

"Ah, Ma, that's what you always say. Just wait and see—criminetly! I'll be old and gone before you go see Fred!"

"Well, then, I guess you'd be able to buy your own railroad ticket," Ida laughingly replied. "If you spent more time on your school work and less time on day dreams about taking trips and becoming a bronc buster you'd be a smarter boy. Let's get back to those arithmetic problems. Susan, how are you coming along with that spelling list?"

Gazing at her daughter, Ida wondered where Susan had gotten her looks. She really didn't resemble either Ida or Josiah's side of the family. Always a quiet child, Susan had been a good student since starting school. She loved reading and could always be found with her nose in a book when she should be doing chores. Sometimes Ida forgot she was around because Susan never seemed to make any racket, which was a blessing considering that her younger brother, Joe, made enough for both. Most of her school chums were older and had already gone into Grand Valley to attend high school. Susan's present close friend was Bess Kerlee who was some months younger. Ida frowned a little when she thought about Susan being such a follower. She didn't take an active role in any decision making and seemed quite content to go along with any activity someone else suggested. Ida was accustomed to her older daughters, all three of whom had very distinct values and ideas about life. This young girl didn't seem to be cut from the same fabric.

"There's another letter here," Josiah said as he riffled through the remainder of the mail. "It's from Aspen. Must be from Birdie."

Ida took the envelope and sighed as she pulled the thin sheets from their cover. For some reason she was reluctant to hear how her daughter was. There seemed to be so much tension in her marriage that Ida always expected the worst news possible. No matter how much Ida wished otherwise, the fact remained that Birdie and Norman's marriage continued to be a rocky one. Ida feared someday the latest letter would tell her news that she never wanted to hear.

Ida slowly glanced through the lines, while everyone waited for her to read aloud, as she usually did. Instead, she laid the sheets on the table and walked into the icy cold bedroom, shutting the door behind her. Josiah, not knowing what to say or do, cleared his throat and reached across the table to retrieve the pieces of paper. Putting on his reading glasses, he searched for the portion that caused Ida such distress. Then he very deliberately placed the letter back in its envelope. Going to the cook stove he lifted one of the iron lids and consigned the letter to a fiery death. Susan and Joe looked quizzically at their father, knowing better than to ask what the trouble was.

"Your sister says that she is separating from Norman this coming May." Josiah silently walked toward the cold, dark bedroom to comfort Ida, leaving Joe and Susan to ponder this latest calamity to hit their family.

SEPTEMBER, 1916   BATTLEMENT MESA, COLORADO

Ida walked along the river, enjoying the quiet solitude of flowing water, golden leaves starting to fall from the majestic cottonwood trees, and smells which only occur in the autumn months. "Another year come and gone. They seem to go so fast anymore. There are days I feel every one of my fifty-five years, but then there are times I can hardly believe I'm this old. It seems there's a young girl inside of me that has become imprisoned in this tired old body, and screams to get out."

A sharp, grinding pain in Ida's gut caused her to catch her breath and find a log to sit on until the brief spasm was over. "I must have eaten something that didn't agree with me," she thought. "I'll bet it was the spareribs and sauerkraut I had last night. I never seem to get enough. Must be all that good German blood in my veins."

It would be just her and the children for supper tonight. Josiah, Guy, Laura, Mary, and Oren had gone prospecting for the oil shale claims which had been in the planning for some time. Josiah had made a trip to Glenwood Springs to see which areas were still available. On this trip they would be going up the Doyle trail which went through the rim at the head of Cottonwood Gulch northeast of Grand Valley. Looking across the valley, Ida could see the faint outline of the trail snaking its way up the barren slopes of the Roan Cliffs. It seemed that every able-bodied man was out in the hills right now trying to get his name on one of the placer claims. Area weekly newspapers were full of written hype about the unlimited potential of this newest commerce. The oil shale fever was clearly in full swing.

There was talk that President Wilson would be withdrawing a large chunk of land from the patent process to create a naval oil shale reserve, and it was imperative that the claims be filed before the proclamation was issued. As soon as the last cutting of hay was in, the Herwick men (and women) packed out to the mountain to mark their spot.

Ida was surprised by her children's reaction to the oil shale venture. She thought they'd all be pessimistic after the many years of Josiah's boom and bust schemes, but they, too were fired up with enthusiasm. Mary had even convinced Josiah to let her accompany him and her brothers. Wid wrote to tell his father that he wanted in on the claim filing, and he would come down from Aspen next year to help with the assessment work. Guy and Oren seemed only too anxious to go along on the expedition. Ida compared the family's eagerness and optimism to that of the Leadville gold miners almost forty years ago. It seemed that everyone believed they were going to get something for nothing.

Two of the daughters, however, had not been as optimistic. Birdie had written to say that she wanted no part of the venture. She believed it was a wild goose chase, and she'd rather bet on a more sure thing. Tiny also declined. She was quite content to be a wife and mother and had no wish to disrupt her life by going "prospecting." She offered to take care of Olive while Mary was on the mountain and wished everyone the best, but she wouldn't be going with them.

"I guess I really can't complain too much," Ida scolded herself. "It isn't as though we've ever been truly deprived because of Josiah's ideas. He doesn't drink and gamble like some other men do. He's been a hard worker and a faithful husband. I really shouldn't begrudge him these occasional "flings." It's just that I don't understand why he wants to do these things. If he had put all that energy into something more stable, we'd be a whole lot richer today. What is there in some people's mind that cause them to always look for the rainbow?" She shook her head in wonderment. "I wish I knew."

The Herwick prospecting team had come home by the first of October full of high spirits from their adventure. Five claims had been located and staked. Some excavation work had been done to prove that the claims were being worked, and then the group rode down so Josiah could go to Glenwood Springs to file their claims at the courthouse.

When Josiah arrived home three days later, he silently handed Ida the filing papers. "Take a look at these, Mother," he said.

Ida glanced through the many paragraphs of legal descriptions. "Oyler...you've called them the Oyler Claims?"

"Yeh. We talked it over and decided that they should be named in your honor. You've kept this family together for a long time, and we thought it would be nice if you had something named after you. I know we don't tell you very often, but you're important to all of us."

Ida turned her head to blink back the tears which threatened to escape her eyes. She could get through just about any kind of crisis without crying, but let someone do something nice for her and she couldn't hold back. "Tha... that's thoughtful of you Josiah," she said, her voice quivering. "I doubt that I deserve such credit, but thank you for honoring my family. There are times that I forget I wasn't always a Herwick. This will be a good reminder for me." Going to him she took his face between her hands and planted a gentle kiss upon his lips. "You're a good husband."

- Wildlife conservationists claimed that the elk and deer herds were multiplying because of the elimination of hunting seasons until 1918. By the end of 1916, officials estimated there were 690 elk and 1,000 deer in the Battlement Mesa Forest Reserve.

- Buffalo Bill Cody died in Denver, Colorado, on January 10, 1917. He was buried at Lookout Mountain near Denver, a decision that has been hotly disputed by the State of Wyoming since the internment.

- The U.S. declared war on Germany on April 6, 1917. The first United States Division, under the command of General Pershing, arrived in France and engaged in the first action by June, 1917.

- Oil shale exploration and development were in full swing. Retorts were being built and equipment shipped in for several area companies. The Congressional Record of September 29, 1917, suspended oil shale assessment work for 1917-1918 because of the labor shortage due to the War.

- In November, 1917, the federal government began rationing sugar because of the war effort. Each person was limited to 3 pounds per month. Although not being rationed, flour was also in short supply. It was recommended that all flour not used within the month be returned for redistribution. Five Battlement Mesa ranchers shipped a railroad carload of honey from their local hives.

SUNDAY, APRIL 8, 1917   BATTLEMENT MESA, COLORADO

The usual Sunday morning camaraderie of the Battlement Mesa churchgoers was marred by sad faces, tear-filled eyes, and anxious sounding voices as the congregates filed into the schoolhouse. Some of the people could still remember the devastation of the Civil War, and they shuddered at the thought of the inevitable slaughter that was to come.

Unrestricted German submarine warfare had finally caused President Wilson to declare war on the European central powers of Germany, Austria-Hungary, and Turkey. The declaration had come last Friday, April 6, and there had been little else discussed since then. The news didn't come as a great surprise to most people who had known it was just a matter of time until the United States joined the Allied forces of France, Britain, and Russia. Many young men, chomping at the bit to take part in the war-induced excitement, had already enlisted in the Allied military service, especially those who were pilots yearning to take part in the newly established Air Force units.

While young men hurried to sign up for military service, their mothers cried tears of anguish at the thought that their sons would soon be sailing across the Atlantic Ocean to face the dreaded enemy. There was talk that military conscription would commence immediately, and many women hoped for some minor physical impairment which would keep their sons from active service.

It was rumored that men from the age of twenty-one through thirty would have to register, and this possibility struck particular fear in Ida's heart. Guy, Oren, and Al would fall into that age bracket, and the thought of her three sons engaging in warfare was more than she could endure. Her fervent prayers that morning carried petitions for the continued well being of the Herwick men in the coming months.

Josiah had returned from Glenwood Springs yesterday on the morning train with all the news of that town's wartime excitement. Even her husband seemed strangely exhilarated by the specter of war, and Ida felt a revulsion deep down inside. How could anyone think this was a good thing?

Josiah had gone to Glenwood Springs to register the latest of the oil shale claims. The ten Herwick Claims were located at the head of Wheeler Gulch on Parachute Creek. Once again the Herwick children comprised the group which filed on the 160 acres. Snow was melting on the south slopes of the mountains, and they would soon be able to get to the claims to start the assessment work. The surrounding claims would be filed by Jimmy

Doyle, who was acting for a Denver syndicate. Josiah was extremely confidant that these claims would prove to be valuable in the event of an outright sale, or exchange for better pieces of property. He hoped to get into some of the bigger money deals which seemed to be floating so freely these days.

Ida knew that Josiah desperately wanted this to be the "big one." He had been considering his own mortality since his brother died last winter. He had been deeply touched by his death. Eight years older than Josiah, Frederick had stayed on with the railroad in Ossawatomie, Kansas and had done reasonably well. "My God, it's been almost forty years since I last saw my brother," he said to Ida. "It doesn't seem like it's been that long until I remember that I'm sixty-three. You're married to an old man, my dear. I had hoped to be better off financially by now, but I think these oil shale claims are gonna pay off for us. The way the war is going, we've got to have more oil deposits, and this seems like a sure thing. Yessir, I think this time we've got a winner."

As Ida silently listened to her husband, she wanted to confront him with the fact that they would already have some financial stability if he had stayed at one thing long enough. Frederick's years with the railroad had paid off for him. His wife and daughters had been well taken care of. None of the "Boomer" mentality for him. Why was Josiah so different? But she didn't tell her husband her secret thoughts. He was getting older, and she didn't want to accentuate his thinly veiled anxiety about the future. He had enough on his mind without adding to it.

If Josiah had his own private fears for the future, so did Ida, but hers were of a more personal nature. The pain in her lower abdomen, which had come on so suddenly last fall, was a source of continuing concern for her. Like an elusive sprite, it would suddenly strike, clenching Ida's gut into a vise-like cramp, then darting away, to return once again when she least expected it. She had become beset with anticipation of the next occurrence, only to find it absent for several days. Just as she convinced herself that the problem had passed, the rhythm of pain would start all over again.

Ida had successfully kept her problem from her loved ones until May when most of the Herwick family had gone up to Cottonwood to do assessment work on the Oyler Claims, leaving Ida and Joe at home. The pain had come on suddenly one afternoon, in greater intensity than ever before. When Joe arrived home from school, he found his mother curled into a tight ball on the bed, beads of sweat dotting her forehead, her breath coming in ragged puffs. "Ma, what's the matter?" Joe anxiously sat down beside her, fear evident in his voice. "Can I help you? Can I get you something?"

The spasm relaxed its hold on Ida, allowing her to take a deep breath. "I'm okay now, son. I must have eaten something that didn't agree with me. I'll be all right, but you might make me a cup of peppermint tea. Maybe that'll settle my stomach. Then you go ahead and do the chores for me, okay?"

"Sure, Ma, don't worry 'bout the chores. But, are you sure you don't want me to go get Tiny?"

"No, Joe, your sister's got her hands full without worrying about me. I'll be fine, I promise."

After Joe had brought her the tea and went to do the chores, Ida laid back on the pillow and tried to relax. This was the most severe pain she'd felt thus far, and it left her visibly shaken. She was beginning to realize that this was no ordinary stomach distress, but what could it be? The pain finally subsided, leaving a nagging, cramping sensation in the backside of her lower abdomen.

She simply couldn't be sick! It was up to Joe and Ida to keep the ranch running while Josiah and the rest of the family were on the mountain. Tiny, with two small children and another on the way, was not in any position to come down and help out, although she would, if asked. "No," Ida, decided, "I've got to get rid of this pain once and for all. I guess I'd better go see Dr. Miller. Maybe he can give me some medicine for whatever ails me."

The Herwick oil shale entrepreneurs returned from their assessment trip full of good spirits brought on by plenty of fresh air and sunshine. In addition to the assessment work, there had been time to hunt and enjoy the outdoor life. The trip had been especially exciting for Susan who had never been on this type of camping excursion. To heighten the excitement, a female bear had been shot and her cub captured. Susan, always an animal lover, had fed and nurtured the tiny bear and made it her pet while at Cottonwood, but had been forced to give it up to one of the construction workers when they broke camp and started for home.

Ida, having sworn Joe to secrecy, was feeling much better since her visit to Dr. Miller, who had assured her it was probably a little bit of intestinal trouble, not uncommon for women her age. He'd poked and prodded her abdomen, but nothing seemed to be amiss, so he gave her a pain killer to help with the cramping pains, and some paregoric for the occasional diarrhea. Since starting the medication Ida had felt much more relaxed and pain free. "I should have gone to Doc a long time ago," she scolded herself.

The Selective Service Act of World War I was passed in May. Guy and Oren joined other Grand Valley boys who traveled to Glenwood Springs to get signed up. Al would be signing up in Wyoming where he was working in the oil fields. The local Troop "M" of the First Cavalry was being billeted at the Denver Fairgrounds and anticipated being called for Mexican border duty by July 18. Several local boys were among the first of the recruits to be called.

Throughout the summer, Ida waited with trepidation for news of her sons' call to military service. Each week she would utter a guilty prayer of thanksgiving when their numbers weren't picked. Al, knowing how she worried, wrote weekly from the Wyoming oil fields to tell her that his number had not been called. She often wondered how it must be for the mothers of those young men who had been picked, and she vowed to visit them more frequently to offer what little support she could give.

In July, another little girl baby was born to Tiny and John. Dorothy was a robust baby, compared to her tiny sister, Winifred, born two years before. As the family gathered around her, a silent thanks went heavenward for the blessing of this healthy child after the scare they'd had with Winifred. Amidst the joy of a baby's birth, Ida watched Laura's look of wistfulness as she gazed at the infant. Married three years, Guy and Laura still had no baby, and Ida knew this was a sad fact for her son and daughter-in-law. In a family who seemed to be very fertile, it must be hard to wait for a child. Ida silently asked for blessings on the two.

Josiah came home one evening in early September, waving a paper, with a smile on his face. "I was talking to Jimmy Doyle today and he tells me they have incorporated the other claims in Wheeler Gulch and formed the March Oil Shale Company. Don't ask me why, because neither one of the officers is named March. Anyway, Jimmy says that he thinks the company is very interested in buying up our claims. I knew we had some winners! Jimmy said we should get some of the quit claims deeds done right away, so he can be ready when the company approaches him again. You and the rest of the family will need to quit claim to me. Then I quit claim half of the claims to Jimmy, then we sell to March Oil. Jimmy wasn't sure what the price will be, but he's goin' for top dollar, probably about $1,000 a claim. Dammit, Mother, I knew these claims would pay off!"

"That's fine, Josiah," Ida said, in a tired voice. Looking at his wife, Josiah realized that her skin was a pasty color. She looked sick.

"What's the matter, Mother? Aren't you feeling good?"

"No, I think I must have eaten something that didn't agree with me. I've had gut cramps all day, and I'm sick to my stomach. I think I'll try a cup of peppermint tea and go to bed. Susan is getting supper on the table."

"You probably just need a good night's sleep," Josiah replied. "You go take care of yourself. Everything will be just fine. Take some of that medicine Doc Miller gave you. It will help you to relax."

The next morning Ida woke feeling more refreshed than she had in some days. "I guess I just needed the extra rest," she told her family. "I can't be sick right now. I got all those tomatoes to put up before they get too ripe. And there's that bushel of windfall apples to be made into applesauce. There's just too much to do for me to be sick!"

But the coming days brought little relief. Ida was finding it increasingly difficult to eat without having pain in her abdomen. One morning she was shocked to realize that her clothes were hanging on her. She had lost a lot of weight. The medicine Doc Miller had given her helped for a little while, but she was having to take it more often and in greater doses. When she ran out, she decided she should probably go to see him once more.

Fred Miller was the perfect prototype of a country doctor. Coming to Grand Valley in 1905, he had embedded himself into the life of close to every citizen of the community. He had worked tirelessly, almost killing himself in the process, when epidemics hit his patients. He was there for birthings and deaths, and everything in between. It was hard to find a family who couldn't tell some story about how "Doc" Miller had pulled a loved one through some sort of medical crisis. More importantly, he was a friend to the people he served, knowing each intimate detail of their life, spiritual as well as physical.

When Ida walked into Dr. Miller's office one afternoon in early October, he was dismayed by her appearance. Never a fat woman, Ida, nonetheless, had always had sufficient flesh to make her body sturdy-looking. Now her clothes hung from a spare frame that was beginning to look too thin. Her hair and skin had a dry, brittle look that usually portended a major illness. She had clearly declined in physical health since last May.

Calling his wife, Margaret, to prepare Ida for an examination, Dr. Miller silently prepared himself for a less than positive diagnosis. This time the exam was more thorough. Each inch of Ida's abdomen was palpated for signs of an underlying growth. When he touched her right side, his fingers moved more slowly, searching and probing for some tell-tale sign of what he suspected. Yes, there it was! His expert fingers noticed a minute enlargement of the intestinal wall, a sign that something could be growing in that section. His probing also caused Ida more discomfort. He watched her face screw up in a silent scrunch of pain as he manipulated the flesh beneath his fingers. His eyes met those of his wife across the exam table, and he gave her a barely discernible shake of his head. There was definitely something amiss. Ida sat across the big desk from the doctor, her gut still tender from the extensive exam. She watched his face as he fumbled with some papers on his desk and wondered why he seemed so hesitant to talk. Her anxiety rose, and she waited with bated breath for his words.

"Ida, I think I've found the cause of your distress, but I can't be sure. It appears there is some sort of growth in your intestinal tract, specifically your colon, which is the last six feet or so. I can't be positive about it, but I'm sure enough that I'd like for you to get a second opinion. I'd suggest that you see Dr. LeRossignol in Rifle. He's actually more of a surgeon than I am, and I think we should hear his opinion. Sometimes these growths are benign, and you just have to change your eating habits. But let's see what Doctor LeRossignol thinks. In the meantime, I'm going to give you some more paregoric, which will help the bowels to relax. And I want you to stay on a soft diet, but eat lots of food. You need to gain some weight, or you'll be down sick from malnourishment."

Ida sat in silence. She didn't know what to say. Something growing in her? It couldn't be. Doc must be mistaken. He continued to talk. She could see his mouth moving, but she couldn't hear what he was saying. All she could hear in her head was the word "growth." She'd known women who'd been afflicted with "growths"–dreaded things that swelled up in your belly until it looked like you were nine months pregnant. Most of the poor things finally died from them. But, surely, that's not the kind she had. Maybe it was a better kind. Maybe Dr. LeRossignol knew what to do for it. Maybe he had some kind of medicine that would help.

Her mind was still whirling as she stepped into the buggy and flicked the reins over her horse's back. One second she was choking on the panic, and the next minute she was saying it wasn't so. It was all a big mistake. She'd go see Dr. LeRossignol like Dr. Miller suggested. In the meantime she had to keep the fear down. What would she tell her family? It was embarrassing to talk about something so personal, especially in that part of her body. How would she explain it? Her face grew hot just thinking about what she'd need to explain. Her first response was to say nothing until she went to see Dr.

LeRossignol, but she'd need Josiah to take her to Rifle in the car. Besides he'd never believe any story about her needing to go to Rifle by herself. That's something she'd never done, and it was a little late to start being independent.

Ida chose their bedtime as the time she approached her husband with the news. She wanted to tell him before she shared it with the children. She owed him that. "Josiah, I need to tell you something."

"Yah..." Josiah answered sleepily. "What is it, Mother?"

"I went to see Doc Miller today." She could sense a sudden tenseness in his body.

"And, what did he say?" His voice sounded less sleepy, more alert.

"He thinks I've got a growth in my gut. Actually it's in my colon which is the lower part of the bowel." Her words came tumbling out in an attempt to get it over with.

Josiah turned over to face her and reclined on the pillow. "What does he say can be done?" His voice was steady and restrained, like someone holding back for fear of speaking out of turn. "Does he have any medicine that will help?"

"No, he wants me to see Dr. LeRossignol. He thinks maybe we should have another opinion. Doc didn't say what could be done. He just gave me more of the medicine and told me to eat soft food, 'cause I'm gettin too thin."

"Well, I'll call Dr. LeRossignol's office tomorrow when I go to town. If he's available, maybe we'll go see him day after tomorrow. No sense putting it off, hmmm?"

Josiah's voice was solicitous but non-committal. There was no outward sign that he was more concerned than ever. Ida couldn't say why, but she felt let-down. What had she expected? Did she think her husband would reflect her own rising panic? Had she expected him to take her in his arms and soothe her fears? She couldn't say, but she did feel the emptiness within. He had treated the news so matter-of-fact. She might as well tell him she had the sniffles. Curling up in a ball she lay beside her husband, fighting against the demons of the future.

Josiah's giant body stretched out in the majority of the bed. He willed himself to relax. He couldn't let her know of the fear infusing every inch of him. The man and woman, who had shared the same bed for forty-one years, lay side by side so lost in their own thoughts that they couldn't breach the incredible distance created by fear of what the future held.

∾ The burgeoning Oil Shale Industry continued to dominate much of Grand Valley's economy during 1918. The February issue of the National Geographic Magazine contained an article about the new development.

∾ In July, 1918, Ward Underwood of Battlement Mesa was the first hometown casualty of World War I.

∾ The Colorado Midland Railroad ceased operations, by Government order, on August 5, 1918, leaving the entire railway business to the Denver & Rio Grande Western. The final Midland train went through the Busk-Ivanhoe Tunnel in 1918. The tunnel was then sold and renamed the "Carleton Tunnel." Auto traffic went through the tunnel for more than a decade.

∾ By October, 1918, the Spanish Influenza was on the increase. There were 12,004 new cases in Army camps. Bert Tomlin died in one of the training camps. Grand Valley had one case. Dr. Morelock of Rifle was the District Health Officer. The newspapers were publishing warnings about the need for universal health precautions against the deadly disease.

∾ The Allies signed the Armistice with Austria-Hungary on November 13, 1918. Armistice Day was declared to be November 11th.

SATURDAY, MAY 4, 1918   BATTLEMENT MESA, COLORADO

Ida slowly moved amongst the piles of household goods stacked in and outside the farmhouse. Susan had packed the last of the kitchen utensils, used for the morning meal, and was carrying another laden box to the dooryard. By this evening the Herwick family should be completely moved into their new home in Grand Valley.

Ida lovingly took her last look at the house as she moved from room to room. It had been her home for eight years, and she would miss the spaciousness. The newly built residence in town was smaller, and Ida knew she would have to rid herself of certain furnishings she had accumulated through the years. She had given away some of the less favorite things to Guy and Laura and Tiny and John, but she clung to much more than the new little house could accommodate. Finally, in desperation, she had packed everything, vowing to eliminate as she unpacked in her new home, and praying for the strength to get her through the exertion of the uprooting.

The early morning air was unusually crisp, and Ida hugged a heavy sweater closer around her thin body. She shivered and hurried into a spot of bright sunlight where her family was busy loading the furnishings into a heavy wagon for the three-mile trip into town. Guy and Laura, along with

Tiny and Mary's families, had arrived early to assist in the move, and Ida was deeply grateful for their help. She knew that her fading energy would not be sufficient to do much more than the most basic of tasks. She watched as the family members scurried around, and she remembered her own vitality during the move from Glenwood Springs in 1910. Now she felt like a frail, old woman.

The past eight months had been an incredible roller-coaster of emotions. First came the anticipation of a medical cure for her condition, followed by the disappointment of another doctor telling her there was nothing he could do. A period of profound depression would occur, to be lessened by the news of another specialist who might know the magic cure.

Ida had been examined by the Rifle and Glenwood Springs physicians who had sent her to Grand Junction for consultations. These surgeons and specialists shook their heads and recommended some Denver doctors who might have more experience with colon cancer. Ida was scheduled to see several of these city doctors sometime in June. In the meantime, all that could be done was to give her enough pain killers to take the edge off of the frequent, gut-wrenching spasms. Her body had wasted away several dress sizes, and it was a daily chore to get enough food down to sustain her body. It seemed that the monster eating away at her insides was feeding upon every morsel without giving her nourishment. Ida could see the look of concern and disbelief on the faces of her friends and family.

Glancing at her husband, Ida saw that Josiah was also showing the strain of her illness. He seldom talked about her physical struggles, but there were times she glimpsed a variety of emotions in his eyes; love, concern, fear, anger, sadness. She knew it was a difficult time for her man, who had relied on her for much of his emotional sustenance. He had always seemed to be the strong, outgoing one of the pair, but they both secretly knew that she had been the strength behind his strength. Ida wondered what would happen to him if there was no cure for her condition. Who would look after him and Susan and Joe? She shook her head, as if to shake off the morbid feelings of the moment. She couldn't allow herself to focus on what might be when there was so much to be done in the here and now.

"Susan, grab that broom and mop and get started on the bedroom floors. We don't want Mae and George Kerlee to move into a dirty house. Hurry up, now. The wagon will soon be back for the final load, and we'd better be ready to go into town with it."

THANKSGIVING DAY, NOVEMBER 28, 1918
GRAND VALLEY, COLORADO

The mid-day sun streamed into the south-facing living room windows and fell upon the table laden with food which was perched in the middle of the living room. All the other furniture had been pushed to the walls to make room for the table and chairs surrounding it. The wonderful aroma of holiday food preparation wafted in from the open door of the kitchen, making the children's mouths water in anticipation.

Guy and Laura, and Bill, Mary, and Olive arrived early in one buggy, followed by John, Tiny, Esther, Winnie, and Dorothy in a second wagon. The day was crisp and clear, just above freezing. The horses belched forth great gusts of steam in the morning air as they were reined in and halted in front of the house. The children, all with red noses and cheeks, were handed down to hands waiting to pack them inside to the warmth. The men set about unhitching the harnesses and preparing the horses for the day-long visit.

Laura, Mary, and Tiny had invaded the kitchen to start the final meal preparations. They firmly seated Ida on a kitchen chair to supervise the tasks, knowing that she lacked the energy to prepare a meal for herself, let alone fourteen people. It was a new experience for her to observe rather than do, but she had to accept the fact that her life was no longer the same, thanks to this unwanted guest in her belly.

The summer had been spent in another round of medical appointments, all to no avail. The doctors in Denver had clearly explained that they could remove the growth, but they would have to remove the colon, which she couldn't live without. They reported that there seemed to be no medicine which would eliminate the growth entirely but recommended a variety of bowel cleansers to keep the intestinal tract as open as possible. She had been placed on a liquid diet of cream, butter, and eggs to help her get more nourishment, and she was sick to death of the rich eggnogs which had to be forced down her throat frequently each day. But her weight had stabilized for several weeks, so this news was encouraging.

In late September she had made the trip to see Fred, Irene, and Daniel in Pocatello, Idaho. They had prevailed upon her to come see a specialist in that city, who was reputedly having some success in treating intestinal problems. Although Ida was anxious to see her two-year-old grandson and his parents, she was most reluctant to subject herself to another physical exam. How could she explain the degradation she felt each time she was forced to submit to another unfamiliar man probing the most delicate parts of her body? She yearned to say no to the new physician but stopped herself by the thought that maybe this person would hold the key to her recovery. Unfortunately, that wasn't the case. This medical person couldn't give Ida any new reassurances. She came home, weak, tired, discouraged, and prepared to face the fact that she wasn't going to get well.

As the family squeezed their bodies into the cramped dining space, Ida was almost overcome by the realization that this might be the last Thanksgiving she would spend with her family. She looked around the table at each individual, memorizing this moment in time for future, eternal recollections. Years from now would her grandchildren remember her and this day? What would happen to them as they grew up? How many more children would she never know? Ida was coming face to face with the grim specter of future years and future holidays of which she would not be a part. Her secret musings were lost in the noise and hubbub of the family conversations, but they marked the beginning of Ida's letting go of fifty-seven years of living.

Blessings can often be found in the midst of pain. Poking through Ida's sad preparation for her departure was profound thanks for everyday things. The Armistice, on November 11, brought sincere and intense thanks to her Creator for preserving her sons during the war.

She had visited Adelia Underwood several times after the news of Ward Underwood's death became known. Ida had no difficulty in sharing Mrs. Underwood's pain. Although the Herwick boys had been spared from the war, Ida keenly remembered the barren graves in Eagle County, and her heart went out to this mother who was suffering such sorrow. She searched for comforting words to share.

The second blessing was that, because of her illness, her sister, Ella Wright was coming to stay with Ida for a while. Ida could hardly believe it! She had not seen her little sister for over forty years and she was excited about becoming reacquainted with her. They had corresponded over the years, and exchanged information about their respective families, but that wasn't like visiting in person. For the first time, since Grant, Ida would be able to reach out and touch a blood kin. The anticipation brought temporary energy to her.

Ella had married Mr. Wright and had moved to Decatur, Michigan where they had raised three sons; Jonas, Hubert, and Clarence. Ella decided there would never be a better time to come for a visit. The boys were grown, and she had no one to look after. Although Ida had not specifically talked about the seriousness of her "condition," Ella sensed that there was much her sister wasn't telling her.

Ella stepped off the train, just a block from the Herwick home, to a sea of unfamiliar faces. In the foreground stood a very tall, large, white-haired man with a diminutive woman standing beside him, which she took to be her sister and brother-in-law. Surrounding them was a cluster of men, women, and children who were apparently with the couple. Ella walked closer to the thin lady, and in the space of a second, looked into the same dark eyes and saw her own reflection. The two women silently entered each other's arms, and stood mutely trying to bridge forty-five years. Tears inched down their faces unheeded, as the family stood by as silent observers. Finally, the embrace was broken and Ida presented her sister to her family.

Life settled into a routine with Ella to manage the household. Susan had made an attempt to do the household chores, but she was much more interested in her chums than the efficient operation of a home. Now long neglected chores were getting done, although Ella lacked the diligence that Ida had always shown regarding housekeeping. It was comforting to have another woman, especially her sister, to visit with, to confide in. Ella's arrival seemed to act as an elixir for Ida, who spent several pain-free weeks before the gut wrenching began again.

Ella was a younger physical version of Ida, although her features were somewhat softer. Ida's strong chin had been slightly blurred in Ella, although their noses and facial shape was remarkably alike. Ida's loss of weight made her features stand out in sharp contrast, whereas Ella was better padded. In personality, the sisters were somewhat different. While Ida had always been content to stand back, Ella was more outgoing. When company called, Ella could be relied upon to actively participate in any conversation. She told amusing stories which entertained Ida and helped to keep her mind from the daily discomfort and anxiety.

The household lost some of its gloom while the occupants tried, for a short time that fall and winter, to believe that Ida was getting better. Her family had stopped trying to find new doctors who may or may not have a cure, and Ida was relieved about that. She relied on visits from both Dr. Miller and Dr. LeRossignol, who gave her compassionate support without trying to confuse her with optimistic predictions. Slowly, slowly she came to accept that her days were numbered, and she silently prepared for that time.

Christmas was a quiet affair, with only Ella, Susan, and Joe to share the dinner with Josiah and Ida. The two Duplice families were celebrating in their own homes, and the Guy Herwicks had gone to Rifle to Laura's family. Oren wrote that he was so busy building houses in Lusk, Wyoming, that it would be impossible for him to take time off from work. As for Al, he had written to tell his parents that he'd met a woman by the name of Nell Grove, who had a small son, four years old. He seemed very serious about making this woman his wife and becoming a father to her child. He sent his regrets that they would not be able to make the trip from Laramie. Although both Oren and Al knew of their mother's illness, neither suspected its extent or severity.

The holiday seemed so quiet, after years of noisy family feasts. Ida wondered if the family had made excuses because they thought it would tire her too much. Maybe they were just uncomfortable around her, now that she was ill. She acknowledged that people certainly dealt with illness in a myriad of ways. Take Josiah—he continued to be concerned and available when Ida requested his presence, but otherwise, he behaved as if nothing was wrong.

Josiah had become a land commissioner for the federal government, so part of his time was spent with people who were proving up on their home-steads. He continued to be an active participant in oil shale development and had started dabbling in real estate, while still doing some construction work. He had been visibly relieved when Ella had arrived to take charge of the household. The only inkling Ida had of his present emotional state was an occasional reaching out for her hand in the middle of the night. They would both drop off to sleep, her small thin hand encompassed in his gigan-tic paw. Come morning, it was business as usual.

∾ Work was completed on the Grand River Bridge, joining Battlement Mesa and Morrisania Mesa to Grand Valley. The old wooden bridge, erected in 1890, had been built too near the water. During the spring run-off months, the floor of the old bridge had usually been submerged.

∾ On January 6, 1919, Theodore Roosevelt died at his home in Oyster Bay, New York. His death marked the end of a pioneering era for western Colorado.

∾ Oil shale development continued to flourish in the Roan Cliffs area. The Mount Logan investors reported that their plant was now ready to begin production.

∾ The "Manassa Mauler", Jack Dempsey won the world heavyweight boxing title against Jess Willard on July 4, 1919. The Colorado native started his boxing career in mining camps throughout the state. In the early 1900's he had been housed in the Grand Valley jail one stormy night because he had no place to sleep.

∾ The fall and winter of 1919-20 was extremely cold and snowy. One couple walked over the top of fences on their way to the family Thanksgiving dinner on Battlement Mesa. It was the only time in 39 years that the mail carrier, Bob Green, could not deliver all the mail along his rural route in one day.

MARCH 1, 1919   GRAND VALLEY, COLORADO

Ida's eyes tried to focus through the drug-induced haze. The weak winter sun, barely risen, broke over Morrisania Mesa and shone into her southeast bedroom window. She could hear subdued voices in the kitchen as the fire was stoked up and preparations began for breakfast. Ida nestled further down into the quilts. Josiah would soon be building up the fire in the living room stove, which would eventually send its warmth into the adjoining bedroom, but right now her expelled breath was little puffs of white vapor. The temperature must have fallen drastically overnight.

Her mind wandered in a combination of sleep and sedation. Little vignettes of the past three months flitted through her mind, like children scampering to and fro. It had become increasingly difficult to concentrate on specifics. The level of pain killing medication had been increased to the extent that Ida was often unable to collect her thoughts for more than a short time. She sensed that she had entered into another dimension created by the drugs but was primarily grateful for the respite of relief from the ever present gnawing in her belly. The worst times were just before another dosage was due.

Ida ran her hands over her body lying under the heavy warmth of the bedding. She could feel little fat under the chamois-like skin. The monster within had devoured most of the nourishment from her being, leaving only skin stretched over protruding bones. It had been a few days since she viewed herself in a mirror, and she dreamily wondered if she was now too small to see. She smiled at the absurdity of that thought but, indeed, it sometimes felt as if she was disappearing piece by piece each day. Her body and mind were gradually removing her from an earthly existence.

Reverend Mallory came to the house every day or so to pray with Ida. They had known each other for almost twenty-five years, and his presence was a great comfort to her, although he continued to be most dogmatic in his spiritual beliefs. Ida had thoroughly examined her own convictions during the past two years, and she couldn't always agree with the good Reverend, but she knew that deep down he was sincerely concerned about her both before and after death. She chuckled a little to think how intimidated she used to be around men of God. It was as if the disease had also stripped away her fear of people, places, and things. Perhaps it was because persons looking to the ultimate experience of death realized that everything else took second place. If you can face that, you can face anything, Ida suspected.

Was that Tiny's voice in the kitchen? No...no, it was Ella, rousing Susan and Joe for their breakfast. "Let's remember. When were Tiny and Mary last here? It must have been last weekend. I recall overhearing Tiny tell Mary that Ella wasn't keeping me clean enough. They thought I was asleep, but I wasn't. What difference does it make whether I bathe today or not? I don't do anything but sleep and eat a little bit. Tiny has better things to do than worry about me. She's getting so big. I can't remember when the baby is due. I think it's the end of the month. Is this March? I wonder if it will come before I leave?"

Ida opened her eyes to see someone peeking around the open door. Seeing she was awake, Joe came into the room. "Mornin', Ma. How you feelin' this mornin?"

Ida looked at her gangly young son, thirteen going-on-fourteen. His long arms and legs poked out of his rangy body. A strand of hair always seemed to escape the comb and end up draped across his forehead. Ida longed to reach out and smooth it back, but she knew this would be an unwelcome gesture to the young man. Her baby–the last of fourteen. Was she ready to leave him? Did he still need her?

"I'm feeling pretty good, son. Now that it's getting warmer in here, maybe I'll sit up for a little bit. Would you put your father's pillows behind me? And I think it's about time for my medicine. Maybe you could bring me a glass of water."

Susan next popped her head into the room. Ida looked at her daughter and marveled at the way nature puts people together from parts of their parents. Susan seemed to resemble none of the other children, yet her features were definitely part of Ida and Josiah. She had the prominent Herwick nose which, in her rather thin face, seemed even more conspicuous. Her eyes, much like Joe's when they were younger, seemed more close-set than her siblings. And she had not been endowed with the full, curving lips of her sisters. Hers were similar to her mother's but turned down at the sides, as if finding nothing to be amused about. Not a tall girl, she appeared more so because of her thinness, accentuated by mouse-colored hair which was usually pulled severely back into braids.

"I fear that Susan will not have an easy life," Ida mused. "There's something about her. She's so fragile but she covers it up with indifference and an uncaring attitude. I've watched her with small animals and children, and I know she feels deeply about things but not many people see that side of her. All they observe is the homely gawkishness, the sharpness, the lack of humor. She's almost seventeen, and she'll be on her own before long. Somehow I worry more about her than the rest."

Josiah, full of breakfast, came to say good-bye before leaving for the day. As they talked about the common ordinary daily events, Ida could see that her illness had also had an effect on her husband. Josiah would be sixty-five years old, come October, and she could see new wrinkle lines on his face. His white hair was now quite thin on top of his head, and his heavy muscled body ran more to fat. Ida could see the confusion in his eyes when anything was mentioned about the ailment. Josiah would much prefer to ignore the signs of her gradual weakening and generally offered silent response to any conversation about it. But Ida also could see signs of his deep abiding love for her. It was just that he didn't know how to handle a situation which he could not throw his strength and authority against. It was frustrating to sit helplessly by and watch something take place over which he had no control. So Ida played the game by chatting about inconsequential things that brought no heavy emotional response from either of them. She'd have to hope that he knew, deep down inside, how she felt about him, their married life, and her hopes for his and the children's future. It was time to let go of her need to orchestrate outcomes for her family.

MARCH 8, 1919 GRAND VALLEY, COLORADO

The voices and faces swirled around. Some would bring images of her child-hood along the Missouri River. Then another vignette would take her to the early years on the Eagle River, when she and Mother Herwick struggled to help their menfolk carve a home out of the newly-settled land. Mental pictures of the children came to mind—both living and dead. Every blessed, precious face moved into view, warming her with their presence. Her Pa stood smiling in the background. "Oh, how wonderful to see you, Pa! It's been so long, and you're looking fine. Who's that with you? Why it's young Paul–my blessed boy–and you're all well. I'm glad you've at last met your grandpa. None of the other children ever knew him."

Rousing momentarily Ida heard subdued voices in the living room. It was the middle of the night—or at least she thought it was. What were people doing here at this hour?

Oh, yes, now she remembered. Some of the children had come for a visit, but she couldn't remember who. It didn't matter, because she was so busy visiting with all her departed family members who seemed to be with her right now.

The pain was gone. She felt very warm and comfortable. It was so good after all the torment of the past months. Opening her eyes, Ida saw figures around her bed—Josiah, flanked by some of the children, but she couldn't see their faces. She heard someone crying, and she longed to go comfort them, but she couldn't seem to move. No matter, the crying had stopped. She struggled to focus on the people around her bed.

In the corner, a dazzling bright light was forming. As it grew bigger it began to take shape. Ida peered into the brilliance and could see two figures emerging. Mother Herwick and Ida's own Ma stepped to the bedside and smiled down upon her. Mother Herwick carried the baby Helen in her arms, now fat and happy. Oh, Ida wanted to hold her darling baby whom she hadn't been able to nourish. Ida reached for the child only to find her hands in those of her mother's. They gently urged her to rise and come. She felt herself being lifted from the bed and walking with the women. They approached a tunnel-like opening through which the dazzling white light shone forth. She could see other people standing just beyond–Grant, Pa, Paul, baby Collins and the poor little crippled babe who now seemed the picture of health. "Why, they all turned out to greet me!"

Ida joyously stepped through, anxious for the reunion.

EPILOGUE

MONDAY, MARCH 10, 1919   BATTLEMENT MESA CEMETERY

The six, tall, stalwart sons lifted up the plain coffin from the hearse and marched in silence to the edge of the grave. The large, slightly bent husband followed the men, accompanied by three weeping daughters and their families. Last came young Susan and Ella Wright, clinging to each other's hands.

The day was clear and cold. Puffs of breath sputtered from Reverend Mallory's mouth as he offered the final prayer and invited the assemblage to join him in the Lord's Prayer.

> *Our Father which art in heaven*
> *Hallowed be thy name.*

"Take care of her Lord....she certainly took good care of me and the children all these years."

> *Thy kingdom come, thy will be done,*
> *On earth as it is in heaven.*

"I'll try to be the person I know you want me to be, Mother. I feel so lost right now."

> *Give us this day our daily bread.*
> *And forgive us our trespasses as we forgive*
> *those who trespass against us.*

"Forgive me for any pain I ever brought you, Ma. I know you always worried about my headstrong ways."

> *And lead us not into temptation, but deliver us from evil.*

"There wasn't an evil bone in her body, but that damned preacher talks like she was the worst sinner in the world. Blast him to hell!!"

> *For thine is the kingdom, the power, and the glory,*
> *for ever and ever,*
> *Amen*

"Good bye, dear friend and loved one. What will we do without you?"

APR 1 5 2002